ROOTS
OF SOUL

ROOTS OF SOUL

THE PSYCHOLOGY OF BLACK EXPRESSIVENESS

An unprecedented and intensive examination
of black folk expressions in the enrichment of life

*Alfred B. Pasteur, Ph.D., and
Ivory L. Toldson, Ed.D.*

ANCHOR PRESS/DOUBLEDAY, Garden City, New York
1982

Grateful acknowledgment is made for the following:

Excerpts from the book *Muntu* by Janheinz Jahn. Copyright © 1961 by Faber and Faber. Reprinted by permission of Grove Press, Inc.

Reprinted with permission of Macmillan Publishing Co., Inc., an excerpt from *Healthy Personality* (Fourth Edition) by Sidney M. Jourard and Ted Landsman. Copyright © Macmillan Publishing Co., Inc. 1980.

An excerpt from the book *The Crises of the Negro Intellectual* by Harold Cruse. Copyright © 1967. Reprinted by permission of William Morrow & Company.

Excerpts from the book *Things Fall Apart* by Chinua Achebe. Copyright © by Chinua Achebe. Reprinted by permission of William Heinemann Ltd.

Excerpts reprinted with permission of Macmillan Publishing Co., Inc., from the book *For Colored Girls Who Have Considered Suicide/When the Rainbow Is Enuf* by Ntozake Shange. Copyright © 1975, 1976, 1977 by Ntozake Shange.

Excerpts from *The River Niger* by Joseph A. Walker. Copyright © 1973 by Joseph A. Walker. Reprinted by permission of Hill and Wang, a division of Farrar, Straus and Giroux, Inc.

An excerpt from the book *Pigments* by Leon Damas. Copyright © 1962 by Leon Damas. Reprinted by permission of Présence Africaine.

This hardcover edition is the first publication of *Roots of Soul*
Anchor Press edition: 1982

Library of Congress Cataloging in Publication Data

Pasteur, Alfred B.
Roots of soul.

Includes index.
1. Afro-Americans—Psychology. 2. Afro-American arts. I. Toldson, Ivory L. II. Title. E185.625.P373   155.8′4′96   AACR2

ISBN: 0-385-15880-7
Library of Congress Catalog Card Number 80-3004

A special dedication is due to our parents who had the wisdom to help us grow and become "ordinary" black people. Accordingly, we further dedicate this book to James Haynes, Angela Adjoa, Nicholy Azena, and Ivory Achebe Toldson; to Lincoln, Reginald, Roderick, and Renard Pasteur; and to all young blacks everywhere, that they may understand and appreciate themselves and their rich heritage.

ACKNOWLEDGMENTS

We are deeply grateful to our many friends and relatives who have shown understanding and given support in this effort which exceeded ten years. We are particularly indebted to Hurtis Bell, Dr. Donald H. Smith, and Dr. Charles H. Smith for their belief in these ideas and our efforts to advance them.

More practically, we are grateful to our graduate students at Southern University and Hunter College for their research assistance. The clerical tasks were never ending, and had it not been for many diligent and thoughtful persons the numerous deadlines could never have been met. We take this opportunity to thank them all. However, special mention must be made of two: Belvin Givens and Deborah Bolden who served untiringly and well.

Finally, we express our appreciation to the Doubleday Senior Editor, Marie Brown, who recognized that the ideas in this work deserved to be shared with the reading public, and to others at Doubleday who have greatly assisted us.

CONTENTS

ROOTS
OF SOUL

PART I

THE BASIS OF BLACK EXPRESSIVENESS

1

ON HAVIN BEEN
TO THE MOUNTAINTOP

Introduction: Affirmation
of Black Culture

And for every thing they took away, we came up
with something new. . . . We sang some new songs,
and danced us some new dances. . . . See, you can
put a hurting on the body, but you can't touch the
soul.

Al Young[1]

It was the hottest January day we had ever seen, though not unusual in Lagos, Nigeria. In the sprawling African metropolis
nearly the size of Chicago, we roamed about lightly clad, sweat-
ing profusely, marveling at the striking likenesses of the native
African peoples to black Americans, black West Indians, and
black Brazilians already familiar to us. We found ourselves quite
indistinguishable from the Africans in the huge crowds that
packed the streets; in fact, one of us was frequently mistaken for a
native Nigerian in marketplaces, shops, and government offices. It
made us feel easy within ourselves, not being conspicuous.

We stopped, delighted, to watch an officer gustily directing
traffic with rhythmic gyrations of arms and legs that gave him the
appearance of a dancing conductor: he seemed to orchestrate, in
perfect rhythm, the flow of onrushing music. At an intersection of
one-way streets, he stopped the traffic coming in one direction
with a periodic, artful extension of one leg, while he moved it forward in the other direction with alternate, looping swings of his
arms. The motion started with one arm reaching down, crouching
his body, then sweeping through the air, lifting the body, only to
bend again with the downward reach of the other arm. His limbs
vibrated and zigzagged, pulling the cars forward by the rhythm
of whirling arms, mooting the force of engines that ordinarily
propelled them.

Rhythm is the thread that runs through the fabric of black culture; it is therefore at the base of black expressive behavior, evident in the music, dance, poetry, drama, oratory, folklore, sculpture, and other expressive forms of the black community. These
gangly, invisible threads that we call rhythm are the "Roots of
Soul." Do blacks have a natural rhythm? The question is inherent
in the purpose of this book.

Our primary purpose is to present new explanations regarding
the nature and characteristics of black expressiveness. We define
"black expressiveness" as the readiness or predisposition to express
oneself in a manner characterized by vital emotionalism, spontaneity, and rhythm. Often these traits act in combination with one
or more other essential characteristics; naturalistic attitudes, style,
creativity with the spoken word, and relaxed physical movement
(all to be discussed later). These interact to produce human be-

havior that when expressed or perceived registers images, sounds, aromas, and feelings of beauty to the senses. It is the intensity, duration, frequency, and utilitarian features of the behavior, resembling those of traditional African people, which make it unique.

As psychologists, we have organized our thinking on this subject into a psychological theory, relating it to the genesis of popular culture in our society and to the quest for living happily in our modern world. Using information about culture, brain geography, and a genetic substance called melanin, this book highlights rhythm as the basis of soul, of black expressiveness, and of popular culture in America and in the Western world. It introduces a theory offering a view on the whole of humanity and human behavior that is shaped by the black/African experience as seen through the ways, customs, and expressive arts of black/African people. For that reason, excerpts from artistic works are used throughout this book. We document the conceptions advanced not with numerical or statistical data but with appropriate artistic renditions, more particularly those in the black folk tradition. Black folk expressions and literary commentary on these expressions become the bases for explaining the source from which they come—the soul.

There is a dual secondary purpose, to which we have already gestured, beyond explanations of the theory. It is related to contemporary aspects of popular culture, and underscores the fact that the popular culture enjoyed by all, music, dance, drama, and so forth, come in large measure from ordinary blacks who are more in tune with the rhythmic pulse of the soul. In carrying forth the intentions of this book, we show the almost total dependence of the present forms of popular entertainment upon black expressiveness. What is the history of the stand-up comedian in this country? The first comics on stage in this country performed in blackface. If the media (radio and television) were to refrain from the use of music whose origins were black-based, to what would most Westerners listen? If black athletes vanished, would baseball, basketball, football, boxing, and track sports in the Western world maintain their vitality and style? While addressing questions like these, the book relates the theory to the mental health aspects of society as a whole. Western society, particularly in America, is gripped by tension, strain, frustration, and other stresses that significantly lower the quality of life. It is the rhythmic force that gives momentum to black expressiveness, we argue, that provides relief from the stresses of Western life. Blacks have given America and the West a cherishable facet of their African heritage—soul—a medium for the attainment of increased happiness.

In search of answers about the vitality of the black soul and its transforming impact on Western style, we have toiled long unraveling its secrets. It represents nearly a decade of striving. We arrived on the Eastern seaboard, fresh with doctorate degrees in counseling psychology, as professors in a degree-granting program in counseling psychology. We were met by a group of white students who were aware of our appointment and almost immediately made a request: "Please bring us some better methods of working with disadvantaged black students." It did not take us long to learn that the students' request had been shaped by some devastating social calamities. Our university was located less than half a mile from the second most drug-saturated community in the country. The local school district, almost 70 percent black, suffered the highest dropout rate in the nation. The rates of unemployment, crime, and teenage pregnancies were high. The students who approached us had become aware that in order to work in these environments they would need a kind of training not provided in their program of preparation.

Of course, we were stunned because our training had been the same as that of the other professors in the department. However, as we explored and pondered the request, we had to admit that our experiences had been different from the others—we are both products of the rural South with ordinary black backgrounds, which gave us at least a point of departure.

With our life histories before us, we reasoned several things. This urban community which appears, to the untrained eye, to be pathological had its roots in a cruel slavery, oppression, and continued poverty. In spite of the myriad afflictions, blacks had survived in these United States. How? (An entire chapter, "We Ain't Misbehavin—It's How We Got Ovuh," treats this point at length.) We extended our reasoning to suggest that the methods of servicing the needs of ordinary black people are at odds with their expressive styles, and further, that every culture has its own methods of attending to griefs of the soul. We learned that the key to understanding the method utilized by ordinary black people in managing stress often resides in an appreciation of their dependence upon music, movement (dance and athletics), the spoken word (poetry, preaching, "rappin"), styling (the way one expresses his individuality or differentness), and profiling (articulating one's difference, usually through movement or showing off) to express the strivings of the soul. This interesting phenomenon became graphically clear early in our search, when we were conducting group sessions with some black students experiencing academic difficulty.

Sarah was one participant. She was a nineteen-year-old student who had been at the university for two years; however, she lacked sufficient credit to enjoy sophomore status. She had come from a broken home in a black ghetto and brought to the college environment limited academic facility, typical for a graduate from her community school. Bright and talented musically, Sarah majored in music and experienced little difficulty in her music-related courses. However, in the college-prescribed courses outside the music department, she was failing. This distressed her greatly, because for many reasons she was eager to succeed at this prestigious university.

Sarah was one of a few black students in any of her classes, and when her inability to achieve was discovered by her white peers, they offered her assistance. But even with the assistance she was unable to catch up and keep up in this fast-paced environment. She became utterly frustrated and had moments of disillusionment. To our surprise, throughout the recital of her predicament she repeatedly remarked, "but I had a good time." Eventually the group learned that she meant by "a good time" dancing and relaxing to music, playing the piano for the entertainment of friends, telling jokes (keeping others and herself laughing), exchanging gossipy tidbits about the lives of peers, playing cards, "hanging out" in the student union, heavy dating, in short a life of merriment and "partying," apparently an escape from the duress placed upon her by her anxiety about failing.

During our discussion of Sarah's case, we found that her coping mechanisms were also used by most of those present in the group. The key became apparent. Had Sarah not had at her disposal the propensity to seek relief from her mental weariness through the use of black expressive forms, she might very well have suffered a severe emotional malady.

Sarah's case history depicts a longstanding use of expressive forms in the black community, universally, to deal with suffering. Considering the heritage of cruelty and oppression, most blacks in this country would probably have gone crazy without the expressive medium provided by the church on Sundays, places of relaxation on Friday and Saturday nights, and other expressive outlets in black culture.

After we formulated a basic theoretical beginning, we zealously observed black popular culture as expressed through musical recordings, street conversations, dances, drama, poetry recitals, church services, funeral processions, festivals, parades, parties and social minglings, athletic events, concerts, barrooms and juke houses (popular reference in rural South), in effect the entirety of black folk culture. Then we thoroughly examined black expressions in literature as recorded by black artists and literary critics.

It is doubtful that this book could be presented had it not been for the persistent reminder from black artists that black expressiveness is a real and deducible phenomenon. Had it not been for them, particularly black writers, this work would be without much of the artistically supportive data it contains.

As important as black artists are, having recorded and reflected black expression, most important is the viable source of their materials—ordinary black people. "Ordinary" black people is a term used throughout this work. Occasionally it is interchanged with "common," "average," or sometimes "typical" black people. We use the terms synonymously to describe people who have retained noticeable behavioral characteristics of the African heritage. Many do not recognize that certain aspects of their behavior are African-based. Most often, blacks exhibiting these behaviors are unacculturated and exist on the edge or outside the mainstream of Western or European culture. Sometimes middle-class blacks portray these same African tendencies exclusively. Some choose, particularly those in business and the professions, to reserve the expression of these tendencies for certain social occasions. However, where black expressions are exhibited in the diaspora (outside of Africa) the artists have been able to capture and record with great accuracy the inherent beauty of these expressions.

The writers go way back. Equiano, the first African in America to write his autobiography, asserted that we (Africans) were almost a nation of artists, naming particularly musicians, dancers, and poets. Since Equiano, black writers of poetry, prose, and drama have proclaimed that blacks have a special appetite for artistic innovation, that they possess untold artistic creative power, that they place very high value on emotionally or spiritually motivated behavior, that they use art functionally, and that blacks, therefore, provide the Western world with creative aesthetic momentum. Perhaps more important, black writers have known and written that black survival, at least in the West, has been predicated on these attributes.

Most black writers do not claim, however, that black people are unique in their affinity for creative expression. They suggest, rather, that the major cultural groups of the world have developed characteristic modes of intellectual, affective, and psychomotor expression that are clearly recognizable and clearly different from those of other major cultural groups. Moreover, they suggest that black people react to the environment in rather creative ways. That is, common blacks seem to perceive the environment and respond to it with musical notes (spirituals, jazz, blues, gospel, reggae, samba), movement (dance and athletics), and lines (graphic arts and sculpture) more often than whites or acculturated blacks who are more dependent on printed words and numbers in their search for consonance with the world.

After observing black expressions firsthand and perusing the major literary works, we were able to formulate a research study to validate our premises, one of which was the essential similarity of the expressive behavior of ordinary black people everywhere.

Our research travels took us to the major cities in the United States where there are large numbers of blacks. We also visited the West Indian islands of Barbados, Trinidad, Jamaica, Puerto Rico, and Haiti. In South America, we journeyed to Rio de Janeiro and Bahia in Brazil. The highlight of the travels took us to Lagos and Benin states in Nigeria.

In Lagos we visited the Second World Festival of Black and African Art and Culture (FESTAC), which brought together the largest congregation of black people ever to assemble in any one place at any one time. The participants came from sixty-five nations of the world, representing a kaleidoscope of art and culture stemming from a common cultural source—Africa.

The Festival featured various forms of dance, music, drama, films, graphic arts and crafts, literature, and colloquia. The categories of dance included ritual, ceremonial, masquerade, birth, child naming, marriage, initiation, chieftaincy, acrobatic, vocational (e.g., hunters, farmers), traditional Afro-American, Caribbean, Australian, and contemporary dance theater. Similar to the dance events, the remaining arts exhibited and the colloquia were presented by categories of usage.

Through looking, listening, feeling, and reading, all broadened and enriched through traveling, we identified the five aspects of black expressiveness addressed in Part II of this book: depth of feeling, naturalistic attitudes, stylistic renderings, poetic and prosaic vernacular, and expressive movement. Each aspect, constituting a separate chapter, is treated independently of the others. This may give the appearance that they are separate and distinct entities. On the contrary, they overlay each other and act in combination to produce wonderful expressions of the soul.

The first aspect, depth of feeling, discusses the utility of feelings or emotions in black expressiveness, most particularly in musical form. Spirituals and gospels, blues, and jazz all are presented as expressive media that abundantly utilize feelings in their derivation and expression. Feelings cover the whole range of black behavior, in their expressive forms, in their folkways, customs, and personal relationships. It is in their relationships with others that feelings are most discernible, when not considering those evident in different forms of music.

For example, those who are unfamiliar with this special propensity of ordinary black people are forever perturbed by the noise levels when ordinary blacks assemble in groups. When we served as psychological advisers to an elementary school in a predominantly black urban school district, we were asked immediately about the amount of noise the children made in the lunchroom while eating, and while passing from class to class. One of the first meetings with the staff was to explain that this is not unusual behavior among ordinary black youngsters or adults. We helped them to understand that the children in their charge felt deeply and expressed their feelings openly and without reserve when the opportunity was available.

Shortly after this discussion with the staff of the school, we accompanied a busload of the parents of these pupils to a dramatic production in a nearby city. We were not long on our way before all competing sounds, including the roar of the bus motor and the sounds of passing vehicles, were muted by laughter, joke telling, sounds of transistor radios and tape recorders, and "signifying" by the parents in quest of relaxation and enjoyment. Their quest seems to be characteristic. Ordinary blacks, generally, mix relaxation and enjoyment with most things that they do. Therefore, the children of these parents, in the halls or the lunchroom of their school, structured an environment which permitted relaxation and enjoyment through the expression of their feelings with one another.

Naturalistic attitudes, the second aspect, flow from a free acceptance of nature and self, which permits the acceptance of others. These attitudes are evident in the acceptance of the common human drives (including those that sustain life and express sensuality), and in such simple manners as relaxed posture, uninhibited walk, nonpretentious voice tone in conversation, and the ability to be comfortable with the natural scents of the human body. We are suggesting that bodily scents that we in the Western world cover with sweet, artificial odors, such as perfumes and deodorants, are accepted as natural consequences of being human by ordinary blacks.

The third aspect involves stylistic renderings. "Style" is the way in which one puts one's personality on display. Although it is perhaps most readily discernible through dress and costume, there is an infinite variety of ways of expressing individuality. The way or ways one chooses to express his differentness is his style. It is possible to make the same step that everyone else might make, on the same foot, to the same beat, and yet do it differently. The desire to do it differently is widespread in the black-folk community. Therefore, style is an expressive feature that sets that community apart from Western culture.

The fourth aspect is poetic and prosaic vernacular. The language spoken in the ordinary black community is rarely understood and appreciated outside the community. The chapter entitled "Jive Talkin" thoroughly explores this aspect.

The fifth aspect of black expressiveness is expressive movement. Ordinary black people are action-oriented. Recall our earlier description of the traffic director at the beginning of this introduction. His movements typify this propensity of ordinary blacks to harmonize the senses through motion.

The book, at this point, moves to the final section, and highlights the uniqueness of the work. Similar books have been written on black expressiveness but have been either anthologies, compilations of isolated aspects of black expressiveness, or single volumes discussing one aspect, e.g., language, music, dance, or religion. This volume strives for holistic coverage of the subject, including a description of black expressiveness, identification of its source, and, most distinguishingly, formulation of a theoretical position with practical provisions for helping blacks and others attend to their mental health needs. The third section of the book, an appendix, represents this latter emphasis.

In our therapeutic and educational work with groups and individuals, we use popular forms of black contemporary expression (music, drama, dance, graphic arts, poetry, folklore, fashion, sermons, stories) to help them improve their chances of living happily in our modern world. The appendix is intended to be a guide to self-directed searches for enhanced self-fulfillment. We have recorded some of the more successful experiences and offer them as suggestions for readers from among the general populace. The suggestions in the appendix provide a practical path leading from the theoretical base.

This book will raise many questions that have only speculative answers. In fact, it is our intent to raise questions and offer tentative answers that are in the process of becoming. In other words, our offering, through this work, has not been constrained by what is acceptable, rather, in many instances, it has dared to present now what is certain to gain acceptability. In this sense, it is cast in the spirit of the innovative artist-scientist who is content to precede the popularity of his ideas.

2

HOW COME BLACKS ACT THE WAY THEY DO?

A Factor of Hemispheric Confluence and Melanin Quantity

You'll find that root-Black people seem to be very much in touch with their intuitions and emotions. Now I'm not saying that you go through the world not thinking or analyzing, but the European way of doing things gets us so bogged down in analysis that we dull the edge of our instincts.

You see, I feel that the instinctive mind is far more logical than the analytic mind. When we go into mysticism what we are really doing is expanding the mind so that it accommodates even greater logical possibilities.

Joseph Walker[1]

On a misty Sunday night in Baton Rouge, Louisiana, a jammed roomful of people indulge the preliminary acts, awaiting the star attraction, B. B. King. As the evening advanced in maturity, their wait was made more tiresome by thoughts of the nearness of Monday morning. But suddenly the near-stuporous audience was electrified: the blues released from "Lucille" (the name B. B. has given his guitar) ignited collective seizure. The audience went mad with "blues delirium." By the time delirious ecstasy waned to controlled enjoyment, restoring analytical powers to the happy audience, amazement swept through the crowd. The bass player was asleep on his feet, apparently narcotized by soaring jubilance. Amazement turned to suspense. All eyes were upon the bassman. His plucks responded with crisp preciseness to "Lucille." Was his musical aptitude during a slumber state the result of the left or right side of the brain or both? Were there cultural factors involved? And, we dare ask, might there have been genetic factors involved? Providing answers to these questions is the work of a growing number of scholars. To understand their answers, it must be recalled that the expressive nature of blacks in the Western world, illustrated by the capacity of the sleeping bass player, derives from African reality.

The black/African mind is one that appears not to be burdened by a massive unconscious area. Modern psychology, spurred by the thinking of Sigmund Freud, generally compartmentalizes human awareness into three areas: conscious, preconscious, and unconscious. The unconscious contains censored thought hidden from awareness. These exiled thoughts are imprisoned by repressive defenses: denial, repression, rationalization, intellectualization, and others. The black/African mind appears not to be so affected because of the propensity to use song, dance, oratory, painting, sculpture, etc., to expel urging impulses that ordinarily become the content of the unconscious in the Western-oriented mind. The diminution of these defenses seems to give free rein to the rhythm impulse, which acts as an inner source of excitation. Inner excitation seeks expression, we believe, by compelling the mind to creatively manage the simultaneous emission of urging impulses.

Repressive defenses prevent stimulating emissions from fully entering awareness. The mind is relieved of teasing excitation but at the cost of being less creative. A repressed mind has fewer vital stimuli to manage, and is therefore artistically restricted. Recent brain research suggests that the unconscious capacity of the mind resides in the right side of the brain.

We can argue, then, that the readiness of the black mind to comprehend and express reality in aesthetic forms, giving credence to its artistic nature, is the result of fluid contact with the area of consciousness that is responsible for our experience of imaginative-imagistic sensations and impulse signals, the right side of the brain. Easy contact with this side of the brain is denied Westerners, who, forever seeking to be in control (of themselves and others), reduce their awareness of sensuous impulses by introducing into the mind repressive defenses. The split brain theory (left and right sides) or hemispheric specialization offers a convincing explanation regarding expressive differences between blacks and whites.

What some scholars are saying, including those at the Institute for the Study of Human Knowledge and at the Langley-Porter Neuropsychiatric Institute of the University of California at San Francisco, is that consciousness is a factor of the role that each side of the brain plays in determining human awareness. Their contentions further suggest that role specialization, and therefore human consciousness, is susceptible to differentiation in humans as a factor of cultural predilections.[2]

Robert Ornstein, in his book *The Psychology of Consciousness*, insists that Easterners and Westerners operate on different modes of consciousness.[3] Stated with less technicality, blacks, particularly the unacculturated, and whites operate on different systems of thought. They see and come to understand the world somewhat differently, and therefore their expressive behavior and value systems present sharp contrasts. Lilyan Kesteloot is more descriptive:

> Just as whites are indelibly marked in their way of thinking, feeling, or expressing themselves by Western European civilization, whose key values are Reason (for the mind), Technique (for work), Christianity (for reli-

gion), Nature (for art), and Individualism (in the social
life), black people are formed by their culture, of which
we already know the principal traits: Solidarity, born of
the cohesion of the primitive clan; Rhythm and Symbol-
ism in artistic and religious manifestations; Participation in the cosmic forces, "special reasoning processes,"
which, although neither prelogical nor alogical, do not
necessarily follow the Western mind or its syllogisms.

. . . Whatever their social status and the overlay of
Western influence, as long as they have remained in a
sufficiently large group, they retain more or less intact
the traits of specifically Negro African psychology,
which gives their culture an easily recognizable flavor:
in music, the special rhythm of jazz, for example, in poetry, a style which transforms any foreign language it
uses according to its own particular cadence and sensibility.[4]

The contrast seems to reflect differences in the uses of the left
and right hemispheres of the brain.

At the Institute for the Study of Human Knowledge and the
Langley-Porter Neuropsychiatric Institute, the integration of two
approaches to knowing is being promoted, those used by modern
science, which involve predominantly the left hemisphere of the
brain, and those of traditional Eastern cultures, involving predominantly the right hemisphere of the brain.

The left hemisphere approaches tasks in a logical manner, examining, comparing, and contrasting. Information is taken into it
bit by bit, processed in a straight-line, logical fashion, and it carries on verbal and mathematical reasoning. It is the site of
speech. Breaking things down into parts to the point of specificity
is its function. The left hemisphere, then, makes decisions and
renders solutions that are based on a single chain of sequential
links. It is responsive to material reality.

The right hemisphere perceives images in holistic gestalts.
Thinking abstractly, it processes information in a spatial and intuitive way. It uses nonverbal modes of communication involving

images of the visual, tactile, kinesthetic, and auditory processes. Though it comprehends and uses words, they are more pictorial representations, or "word-pictures." It is responsive to spiritual reality. Further, the right hemisphere seems to be the seat of our creative and artistic capacities, and our appreciation of form and music. "All artistic structure," Ehrenzweig notes, "is essentially 'polyphonic'; it evolves not in a single line of thought, but in several superimposed strands at once. Hence creativity requires a diffuse, scattered kind of attention that contradicts our normal logical habits of thinking."[5] The simultaneity of the right brain system is at work in Ehrenzweig's point.

The right hemisphere is an underused thinking system of Western man. Characterized by spontaneous, spiritual, and ecstatic experiences, it demands immediate release of energy through action, and expressive discharge in the direction of total freedom in both the feeling and movement domains. This side of the brain does not think through the mental manipulation of facts. Its decisions are instantaneous. We could say that it thinks without thinking. It fuses everything together. The simultaneity of rhythmic feelings and impulses peculiar to this hemisphere threatens the need of the Western mind to remain in control. Gilbert Rose holds that this brain system, the seat of passion and emotive forces, is the object of repression in the Western mind.[6] Westerners, therefore, develop a dominance and reliance on left hemisphere functions.

The dominant side, for Western man, "separates, discriminates, details, and focuses," no doubt as protection against feared overstimulation by the right consciousness system and the consequential loss of control.[7] The left brain system, Gilbert Rose contends, advances "reason and logic," aiming to establish security feelings in the face of the ambiguities of the right brain system. Therefore, immediate action is neutralized into thought, and release is postponed for another time and place. The chief characteristics of the left brain system are thought, discrimination, and separateness, leading toward control.[8]

The obsession with regard to control fosters a neurotic affliction. It ensues as a factor of massive repressive structures inserted in the mind to ward off the free, spirited energy of the right brain system. The result is a personality style characterized by a need for rules and regulations, exactness, procedure, and other devices of control. Too, it is a style that is sensually bank-rupt.

Persons of nonassimilated black ethnicity appear to have available a very functional right hemisphere, in which feeling and movement are primary to the organization of that brain system. In comparison to the West, the cultural, expressive forms of black society far more frequently draw upon the awareness system of the right side of the brain, and more frequently involve the right hemisphere of the brain in collaborative ventures with the left hemisphere.

Optimal mental health depends not only on the appropriate use of the functions of each brain system, but most importantly on their complementary functions. Gilbert Rose is articulate and suggestive on this point. In his attempt to give perspective to the artistic personality he unavoidably addresses important aspects of the black mind.

> Perception organizes the world into global unities with-out boundaries, and at the same time into discrete, delineated objects. Intellectual thought contends with emotional impulses toward immediate action. And time appears to consist of moments that are evanescent, sepa-rate and isolated, and also everlasting, connected into an enduring, cohesive constancy. These dichotomies of time, person, and space, irreconcilable by logic, struggle for mutual accommodation in the mind, and find harmo-nious resolution in aesthetic form.[9]

Aesthetic behavior, as expressed in the intellectual and popular culture of black/African people, represents the confluent use of the two brain systems. Though the impulses and images that give rise to creativity originate in the right brain system, the left brain system must be called upon to make their presentation in aes-thetic form. It has been noted that art is not thoughtless, and thought can be artistic.

The proliferation of aesthetic expression in black society, then, stems from the African conception of *oneness* of all things, a demand for mutual compatibility among all things; this is the main requirement of black/African thinking. The requirement shapes perceptions regarding the inner self and the external world. Perceptual demand for mutual compatibility makes necessary the exclusive and complementary uses of the left and right hemispheres of the brain.

Leopold Senghor's reflection on the nature of African man is confirmative: the black man feels rather than thinks himself through the world in comparison to Western man. But with the African, feeling and thought are one. Senghor explains:

> In short, while a great many Europeans and Americans, especially the French and Anglo-Saxon, think with their head, by concepts and schemes logically connected . . . , Africans think with their soul—I would even say: with their heart . . . formed intuitively in the style of feeling-thinking subject, that is to say, in feeling, sensitivity is thought.[10]

Maurice Nadeau points out the idea of Hegel, which suggests that the African facility with the consciousness system of the right brain represents an advanced level of thought:

> Reason, logic, categories, time, space, two and two makes four, became in the end for [whites] the only living realities, whereas they were nothing more than a convenient framework, practical, provisional means to action . . . nothing more than a stage in *thinking* [emphasis ours] which has to be gone through. . . . Hegel and his dialectics are the answer to what lies beyond this stage . . .[11]

Aesthetic facility heightens one's recognition of reality, Gilbert Rose believes this too. In fact, he suggests that "this may well be the only way to acquire a fuller appreciation of the familiar."[12] Knowing by feeling and moving, an African way, brings greater spiritual awareness to material reality.

According to Geneva Smitherman, "Black Americans believe that soul, feeling, emotion and spirit serve as guides to understanding life . . . and there is no attempt to deny or intellectualize away that fact [use repressive mechanisms]."[13]

Music, instrumental and vocal, is a popular aesthetic form in the black community and clearly expresses the confluence of the left and right hemispheres of the brain. The music is invested with thought, order, and insight, all articulates of the left hemisphere. It is also invested with imagination, emotions, and movement, which are expressions of the right hemisphere. At the point where the two hemispheres embrace, lyricized thought is produced. What better living example than the creative genius of Stevie Wonder, or Quincy Jones, who exemplify this holistic tendency of the black/African mind.

In traditional Western music, however, what we see is a complete intellectualization of music, making it predominantly a product of the left hemisphere. The symphony orchestra is such a product. "Here," Ortiz Walton explains, "specialization reached its peak, for every man had a specific sheet of music to play, the same way each time."[14] No harmoniously spontaneous deviations were allowed, "and an assembly-line type operation [was] set into motion by a foreman, the conductor." Walton is even more graphic:

> Each player, like an assembly-line worker, was expected to contribute his share to the final product. The symphony orchestra is furthermore organized along lines of maximal efficiency, with a division into sections, and a further hierarchy of section foremen or leaders and sidemen. A large clock usually adorns the rehearsal hall and orchestra members are expected to be neat and punctual. In accordance with union rules, members are given a ten-minute coffee break, during which they may discuss their grievances. As in a factory, there is the professional manager who collects the money and pays people according to their relative efficiency and position in the hierarchy. There is none of the romantic conception of musicians playing their instruments in lonely church-

yards in Southern France, like Casals. Nor is there the
freedom that is associated with an artist like Picasso,
casually throwing paint on the wall to discover new
color combinations. Instead there is the awesome impression of gravity, of men having an important mission
to accomplish. Gray morning coats and knee-length tails
are worn, and the facial expressions, rather than reflecting the ecstasy of creation, are severe and strained.
Each note is indicated not only as to exact pitch, but in
terms of loudness, intensity, duration, and even the feeling state that is intended by the composer. One note
may thus have four or five signs concerning how it's to
be played.[15]

With blacks the human voice and musical instruments speak
the language, express the feelings, images, and sensations of both
hemispheres agreeably together, and therefore the music is more
soulful. It is spiced with the spiritual, emotional, sensuous ingredients of the right brain system, ingredients repressed in the
Western mind.

According to Francis Beby, black music "unanimously re-
creates the Universe each time that thought is transformed into
sound."[16]

What emerges here is the ability of unassimilated blacks to
efficiently balance the opposites of nature. These opposites are
replicated in man's biological make-up as represented in the polar
characteristics of the left and right hemispheres of the brain. The
ability to bring balance and synchrony to that which is oppositional in human nature and in the nature of the universe is truly a
measure of optimal mental health.

What's involved in this mental health feat, the ability to balance opposing forces within the self? Two worldviews, two
different consciousness systems must be examined for insight.
When we refer to a worldview or consciousness system, we are
talking about the manner in which an individual, because of his
or her cultural and ethnic traditions, comes to see, experience,
and express what is real to him or her. This manner contains recognizable distinctions that are clearly perceptible to individuals

from other groups who bear their own recognizable distinctions. The worldview to which we subscribe is involved in the decisions and judgments we make, the values we adopt, the cultural practices and the aesthetic forms by which we are motivated to express ourselves, all of which are under the control of the human brain. Our claim here is that the African worldview, in comparison with the Western world view, allows the individual a greater opportunity to acquire and maintain optimal mental health, owing to differences in how each makes use of the brain's two hemispheres. Remember that the Western mind, under the dominance of the left hemisphere, is characterized by the practices of examining, separating, and pulling things apart, so as to logically understand them and make decisions and judgments regarding them. When the mind is predominantly organized to pull things apart or break them down into their various components, all the way down to their fundamental elements, it comes under tremendous mental strain. Physical and mental fatigue are usually the first indicators of this strain, signaling that an overuse of the intellect or the left hemisphere of the brain is causing the person to experience a sort of imbalance within the self, an unhealthy tilt due to increased mental pressure.

We can illustrate this somewhat in terms of a law of physics. If we conceptualize the left-side dominance of the Western mind as a force with an intellectual direction, then we must accept that this force creates an opposite and equal force, representing opposition in the mind. The healthy way to reconcile the opposition, or opposing force, which emanates from the right side of the brain, is to yield, submit to it and carry out its demands as well. Otherwise, when the right-brain force is resisted, the opposition is experienced as a pulling apart of the mind's unity. It is felt as tension and strain in the muscular and brain systems, in the forms of soreness, tightness, or stiffness in the muscles, dizziness, headaches, backaches, stomach aches, and general nervousness, all of which hinders free, rhythmic expression of the body, reducing its efficiency in sexual responsiveness. The opposition in the mind impacts on the total personality of the individual, and this can be very dangerous to one's mental health.

The greater the opposition is in one's personality, the greater the demand is on repressive defenses of the mind, which attempt to ward off the discomfort the mind experiences. In instances where opposition is very strong, the tension and strain break the defenses down and severe psychological disturbances result. When the defenses do not control the pain, Westerners more often than not turn to the "across the counter drug traffic" in search of relief in the form of chemical stimulants.

What we are finally beginning to see is that the compartmentalization of human faculties, by a single culture (Western), then, specialization in the one thought most important, has constrained human potential, and put the forces of the mind at odds with one another. Schizophrenic? Possibly. For certain it is an absurdity which has fostered disunity of the mind. Equipped with its own capacity for synchrony and harmony, the mind requires only a fuller use of the right brain system. It is here that the black/African mind has an edge.

The natural response to opposition in the mind is a quest for relaxation, which synchronizes the body's rhythms with those of the natural order, and calls for a discharge rather than repression of tension, strain, and anxiety. These can naturally and pleasantly be discharged through creative forms such as music, dance, drama, poetry, painting, sculpture, and oratory, which are under the regulation of the right and left brain hemispheres, deriving creative inception, however, from the right. These confluent expressions, we have insisted, are far more evident in the behavior of black/African people than they are in other races. The black/African mind renders this possible through the "oneness" imperative meshed in its worldview. That is, instead of a one-sided dominance, the tendency of the black/African mind is to bring things together—to see, experience, and express the *parts* of things identified by the left hemisphere as whole, complete entities, which is the duty of the right hemisphere of the brain. The right hemisphere is not repressed in the black/African mind and is therefore allowed to freely interact with the left, infusing it with creative imperatives. This is how the wonderful blend known as harmony comes to reside in the personality. The healthy consequence is that when the body builds up tension or strain due to an exhaustive use of the left hemisphere of the brain, the tension and strain seeks dismissal, or at least reduction, through the expressive urges of the right hemisphere of the brain. Human nature is a replica of the natural world. We know that the order of the universe is influenced by forces that can be characterized as positives and negatives, charges and discharges, and at the human level, tension and relaxation. The black/African mind is far more obedient to the laws of nature, evident in the emotional quality of its expressive practices, which act as a balancing measure to thought activity of the mind.

The impact of black expressiveness upon the white world has been an altering one. It has moved the West, unknowingly, toward a recovery of the mind's unity, a recovery of thought, of feeling and sensibility, of rhythm and motion, together. The West has come nearer to "oneness," a parade of steps closer to the Africa within itself.

"For what is the difference," asks Janheinz Jahn, "between Western and African dancing?"[17] After citing such features as rhythm, posture, steps, and gestures, Jahn comes to the point of significance. "But the difference lies above all in the sense; in the meaning of the dance. For all African art the meaning flows plainly from the sign used to express it. . . ."

What Jahn says, in other words, is that the dance of Africa, in the midst of passion, with all its rhythm and sensuality (facets of the right side of the brain) has a sequential, detailed counterpart (contributions from the left side of the brain). The dance talks, tells stories that can be both deeply felt and richly described, making it a product of hemispheric confluence. Illustrative of the point is a description of a dance from Afro-Cuban culture.

In Afro-Cuban religious beliefs, Oshun, the "compassionate virgin," is a goddess. Rivers and fresh waters are under her rule. Strained honey is her drink, and for her flowers are objects of sacrifice. "Her colour is like the gold that is found in rivers; her emblem is the fan," Jahn informs. And further:

> Her dance, with its tripartite choreography, follows in pantomime the legend of the goddess herself. The first part is a dance of the springs. She stretches out as if she

were lying in the dry bed of a river, and calls the
springs to her. They entwine themselves in spiral movement around her. She rises, and with outstretched arms,
jingles her bracelets, moves her hands down along her
body as if water were flowing over her, skips about
gaily, uninhibited and youthful, like bright waters leaping over rapids, or then again rows as in a boat. But she
is not only a river; she is also a maturing woman, who
remembers her duties and grinds the maize with pestle
and mortar to feed her aging family. Then the rhythm
changes; the second part represents the bath of Oshun.
Tenderly she lets the water caress her, she bathes
through the waves, looks at herself in the still water of
the pool and discovers her own beauty. She is the femi-
nine goddess, the divine spouse, who welcomes the feast
of life. In the third part, she adorns herself coquettishly
and, with sensual swaying movements stretches out her
arms with their golden bracelets to the rain, the water
of heaven, the source of all fresh water.[18]

Jahn then quotes Fernando Ortiz' final line of the legend:

'Honey! Honey!' She calls for the symbolic essence of
love, her body is doubled up with passion as she awaits
the mystic drops of conception.[19]

Judith Lynne Hanna, cited in John Lovell's *Black Song*, explains that dance is and has long been a medium of education in
Africa. She says that the dance taught members the prevailing
knowledge, role differentiation, institutionalized goals, and appropriate means of achieving goals. An understanding of fertility
in people, proper roles of special members in the society, binding
ideas and beliefs and laws, and the role of war were all taught.
She noted that there were dances that taught responsibility and
restraint and group cooperation and harmony.[20]

Europeans use words and numbers to teach (communicative
modalities of the left brain), while Africans achieve the same
goal by embodying words and numbers in dance, music, poetry,

drama, painting, sculpture, and similar expressive outlets, effecting a marriage between the two brain systems. The former enlightens with stoicism, the latter enlightens with vitalism.

Black vernacular is both poetic and prosaic. It therefore looms as an artistically expressive medium in the formalized traditions of prose and poetry. Whether written or oral, black vernacular has long been of interest to those captivated by beauty that arises from the artistic sequencing of words. Be it in the form of sermon, rap, dozens, signifying, folk tale, song (shouts, spirituals, gospels, field hollers, rhythm & blues, blues, reggae, jazz), it emotionally stirs and seizes upon transmission. Black vernacular is explosive with emotional power. Its power is generated in the awareness system of the right side of the brain.

Haunting images, symbols, ancestral spirits, and other primitive impulses and sensations all find aesthetic incorporation in black vernacular. Word language we know is the prerogative of the left side of the brain and imagistic language of the right side. What black vernacular does is to bring the language systems of both hemispheres together in a grand juncture of "oneness." It therefore takes on creative properties and is quite unlike white vernacular.

The vernacular of whites is clearly marked by its addiction to rules and standards appealing to functions of the left side of the brain. It is timely to suggest that herein are probable reasons for many of the problems blacks have learning so-called standard English. Westerners do not heavily draw upon the excitatory tendencies and the imagistic and imaginative richness of the right brain's consciousness system. The left brain dominance of the West's language practices presents blacks with learning situations that deny their affinity for the inclusion of stimuli from the right side of the brain.

Some scholars now recognize the superiority of language usage which occurs from the involvement of both hemispheres over that involving only the left hemisphere. Empirical studies on the use of imagery production of the right brain system in learning has been described by Allan Paivio.[21] Imagistic techniques increase the recall ability of students. Paivio contends that imagery is the most significant factor in the determination of free recall.

Free recall is quite characteristic of black/African oral historiographers, and those who are able to recall with exactness and ease song lyrics, texts of sermons, lengthy jokes and tales, biblical passages, raps, dozens, legends, and other media of oratory that are imagistically inspired.

Several other researchers have tested Paivio's findings. One group attempted to determine "if kinetic molecular theory could be taught to kindergarteners and primary school children using pictures, concrete examples, and simple verbal text to introduce and explain the concepts of molecules in motion, stories of matter and changes in states of matter. . . ." Artists prepared for them "several hundred original colored drawings [which] were used to represent molecules, gasses, liquids, solids, evaporation and condensation." After a period of instruction, a large majority of the children had "learned and remembered the concepts one year later."[22] These were concepts once thought too complicated for kindergarteners. Children in the study were below Piaget's symbolic or concrete levels of intellectual development.

More recently, Wittrock taught definitions of vocabulary words to elementary school children. They compared three different procedures:

Read and write the words and their definitions (verbal)

Read the definitions and trace the picture of it (recognize an image)

Read the definitions and draw your own picture to represent the definition. (generate an image)[23]

The researchers predicted and found that the best recall was produced by generating an image; second best was produced by tracing an image; and learning the words only produced the lowest recall.

This indicates that where language is elaborated imaginatively it evokes the operation of the right brain in concert with the left, processing the information in two interactive ways. The result is a heightened recognition of reality, which produces a higher level of learning. Learning in this manner involves the noted psychologist Jerome Bruner's notion of spontaneous surprise, the hallmark of creative language expression.

What is obvious by now is that the culturally nourished method of information processing leading to aesthetic expressiveness, characteristic of the black mind, is the newest and seemingly the best theory of learning. It seems rather clear. Should the processes of education begin to allow for increased interaction between the two hemispheres, the language in educational circles will come closer to exacting the flavor of black vernacular. It is certain to be poetic, picturesque, and full of rhythm, creditable to the naturalistic tendencies of black/African ways.

The action of the brain's two hemispheres is not the only physiological factor influencing black expressive behavior. There is also quite possibly another factor.

Melanin, a dark pigmented chemical substance produced in human cells, is found most abundantly in the skin, hair, eyes and substantia nigra (in the mid-brain). The substantia nigra (black substance) serves as a catalytic agent in igniting starter impulses which facilitate "the rapid and exact movement of specific muscle groups."[24] It is found also, in proportionate relation to its presence in the skin, in internal organs and muscles. Now it looms as a factor in black expressive behavior. Why? The production of melanin has energy-related features that are involved in the regulation of some aspects of human behavior, particularly those falling under biochemical control. That is, much of our behavior, the quality of it (intensity, duration, frequency, etc.), is regulated by secretions from various glands and organs of the body. Melanin is one of the body's secretions and appears to noticeably determine the quality of black expressive behavior, of *soul*. A fuller acquaintance with its nature is necessary for a fuller appreciation of its importance to the point advanced.

"Melanin" as a term derives from the Greek word *melanos*, meaning "black." That is why melanin was described as a "chemical glob" of black substance in the July 2, 1977, issue of *Science News*. The article insisted that melanin is "some of the toughest material there is." Apparently its chemical composition, the article noted, is impervious to destruction even in boiling acid, prompting a reference to it in the article as "weird stuff."

Seemingly, it is unalterable by time. Melanin has been found in archeological findings aged by as many as 150 million years.[25] Clearly there is a paucity of melanin-digesting enzymes existing in nature.[26] Most chemical substances of the body are eroded eventually by the action of enzymes in the environment which feed upon the substances. Melanin appears to endlessly endure.

If it appears that melanin is quite fundamental to the stuff that constitutes the very essence of biological life, it is. Dr. Leon Edelstein, associate professor of dermatology and pathology at the University of California Medical School at Davis, and past chairman of the same department at the University of Massachusetts Medical School, says that melanin in abundance, as in blacks, produces a superior human being, both mentally and physically. In a July 1980 issue of *Sepia Magazine*, Edelstein was quoted as saying that melanin was at the very essence of life.[27]

Melanin protects the DNA of the basal cell from mutational damage, writes Farrington Daniels, Jr., of the Department of Medicine, Cornell Medical College, New York. He is joined in this assertion by two fellow scientists. They suggest that the location "of melanin around basal cell nuclei is consistent with a role of protecting basal cell DNA" from the harmful effects of ultraviolet radiation (UVR) that comes from sunlight.[28]

When ultraviolet radiation from sunlight acts on the skin, the molecules become electronically excited and generate what is known as free radicals, or energized particles with harmful potential. Melanized skin or melanin itself acts as a repository or storage apparatus for these free radicals and possibly converts them to useful energy.[29] For instance, white skin, as a result of UVR, may develop appearances of rapid aging, elastosis (degeneration of the elastic tissue of the skin), telangiectasia (dilation of blood vessels in the skin associated with skin diseases), dark spotting, light spotting, and "disorganization of premalignant skin, as well as benign and malignant tumors." Most importantly, UVR may affect human characteristics by contributing to genetic mutation.

There appear to be definite biological advantages to having dark skin. Protection against vitamin D intoxication, or hypervitaminosis, "enhanced resistance to . . . infections . . . , improved visual acuity in bright light, and . . . protection against the carcinogenic effects of ultraviolet (UV) radiation" are some noted advantages.[30] It goes a bit deeper, however.

It has been established that black skin, because of melanin, is more adaptive to the sunlight and the sun's energy than white skin. But the advantages of melanin extend far beyond the prevention of skin cancer and other dermatological disorders.

Biochemist W. Farnsworth Loomis of Brandeis University has brought attention to light-sensitive vitamins through his research on vitamin D, the "sunshine vitamin."[31] Vitamin D is produced in the skin. Its production is influenced by solar radiation (UVR), and it helps the body process calcium to make bones, and prevents rickets. However, in lightly melanized skin, the radiation can act to overproduce vitamin D. Too much vitamin D, like too little, is harmful. Chalky calcium deposits in arteries, kidney stones, and kidney dysfunctions can occur from long-term excess. It is not difficult to see how these in the long run could be fatal. Melanin in sufficient quantity acts as a natural control against such overproduction. Of course, clothing protects the skin against overexposure to UVR, but it represents only a compensatory adaptation for the absence of black skin. "We suggest that dark skin color may protect critical metabolites in blood and dermal tissues from photodecomposition by solar UV radiation," contend Richard Brando and John Eaton, both of the Department of Medicine, University of Minnesota, Minneapolis.[32]

Brando and Eaton identified several other light-sensitive vitamins, including vitamin E, folic acid, and riboflavin. They have concerned themselves particularly with the investigation of folate. They report that folate deficiency is frequent "and is known to have adverse effects on survival and reproduction."[33] The researchers further suggest that "folic acid, in its various forms, is a requisite cofactor in nucleic acid and protein synthesis and is indispensable to cell growth and replication."[34] They make it clear that folic acid deficiency may sharply decrease one's reproductive capacity, and that dark skin, because of melanin, protects against the destruction of the vitamin by UVR. All of this seems to suggest that without melanin, or black skin, human life would be nearly impossible in the tropics, or at best hazardous.

The presence of melanin in the eye, causing it to be brown in color, gives blacks a probable advantage, particularly in bright light, as melanin acts as an optical filter protecting the iris from solar radiation. Professor Dan Landers and his colleagues at Penn State Motor Behavior Laboratory say that dark-eyed people, without regard for sex, race, or socioeconomic status, have faster reaction times and react more swiftly than blue-eyed people.[35] Landers feels the explanation is "genetically related to the amount of neuromelanin in the nervous system." Neuromelanin is thought to have "electrical properties that can hasten the speed of neural impulses." Allan Markle, a psychologist at the Huntsville–Madison County Mental Health Center in Huntsville, Alabama, was quoted in an article entitled "Why Blacks Run Faster" as agreeing that researchers have "found that the speed of neural transmission increases when melanin is present."[36] It is then reasonable to deduce, as Landers has, that rapid neural transmission is the basis of quick reaction time, which is highly correlated with dark eye color. These studies point to a clear relationship between melanin and the central nervous system and the center of motor coordination in the brain.

Just what is it that melanin does in the cells? Scientists believe that melanin, as earlier indicated, may be a reservoir for highly reactive chemicals known as free radicals, which are generated by the action of UVR upon the nervous system. Moreover, it is believed that melanin may serve as a semiconductor for converting these free radicals, once stored, to useful energy. It therefore is potentially able to discharge disruptive electronically excited molecules.

The article "Why Blacks Run Faster" quoted Leon Edelstein:

> . . . blacks have far more melanin in their muscle cells as compared to whites. When you combine that fact with the biophysical characteristics of the melanin polymer, namely its semi-conductor quality and its ability to trap free radical energy, this gives the cell the ideal

alternate energy generating and energy modulating
pathway, so that the harmful energy produced during
rapid cell activity can be converted to useful energy and
utilized therefore for more efficient muscle function.[37]

As do the researchers on eye color, Edelstein believes melanin
to be the factor that accounts for black athletic superiority, particularly in sports requiring the athlete to react instantly to stimulus situations that are continuously and rapidly changing.

Edelstein is also convinced that melanin, with its resilient poly-
mer, not only activates starter impulses for physical quickness
and mental keenness but actually extends the natural life of
human cells. In a remarkable article entitled "Can Blackness Prolong Life?" Edelstein advanced this view.[38] Historian J. A. Rogers
claimed years ago that blacks lived longer.[39] Of course, Rogers
was guided by statistics on persons living 100 years or longer. He
found that, by a shocking percentage margin, longevity favored
blacks. And now, in "Can Blackness Prolong Life?," Edelstein advances an equally stirring claim, scientifically supporting Rogers'
findings: melanin retards the aging process. Edelstein believes
this to be due to the absorptive capacity of melanin, which allows
it to act in a protective role by nullifying the effects of harmful
energy in cells from internal and external sources, thereby imped-
ing the aging process. What is the basis of Edelstein's belief? He
generalizes from the laboratory. At St. Vincent Hospital in
Worcester, Massachusetts, Dr. Edelstein and his team conducted
research involving melanin and longevity. Using experimental
black mice and white mice, both fed normal diets, the research
team found that the black mice lived twice as long as the white
mice. When material to increase melanin content in white mice
was added to the diet, the general life span of white mice increased to the equal of black mice. Dr. Edelstein reasons, then, if
you eliminate the deleterious effects of nutritional and infectious
diseases, and other ailments owing to oppression and disad-
vantagement, blacks should live twice as long as whites.

How does all of this bear on the nature and general dimensions
of black expressiveness? Expressive behavior is in direct response
to arousal of the nervous system. It does appear that melanin,

through speedy neural transmissions, heightens as well as quickens arousal and therefore triggers emotions or feelings which are fundamental to black expressive behavior. The early research data do seem to suggest that blacks are indeed more emotional, feeling, sensitive, and more soulful than whites as a result of their more heavily melanized pigment cells. A predisposition for action is set forth by arousal, and this action frequently takes the form of artistic expression.

Psychologists Phillip McGhee, Wade Nobles, and their colleagues were among the first black scientists who advised (in agreement with Dr. Francis Cress Welsing, a pioneer in melanin research), "that melanin refines the central nervous system and, in so doing, produces a highly sensitized sensory-motor network."[40] They concluded, as we have, that a positive correlation exists between the intensity of emotional arousal and the action upon the nervous system of enzymes which are born out of the process of melanin production and dispersion in the body. Emotional arousal, the basis of expressive behavior, looms, then, as a positive trait, giving melanin a clear behavioral influence.

Others have hinted at the likelihood that aspects of human behavior may be a factor of melanin quantity in the body. In an article entitled "Pigment Hormone May Color Behavior," carried in the January 29, 1972, issue of *Science News*, the editor introduces readers to the research of Abba Kastin, an endocrinologist at the Veterans Administration Hospital in New Orleans and at Tulane University. Kastin was guided by the world authority on hormones and psychology, John W. Money of Johns Hopkins University, who stresses that "the body's hormones would be expected to strongly influence brain activity and thence an organism's behavior."[41]

Kastin concerned himself with several hormones released from the human hypothalamus, a sort of "executive switchboard" for hormonal releases in the brain "that exert staggering effects on target tissues throughout the body." One of his chief interests was in the hormone MSH (melanocyte-stimulating hormone), which is released from the pituitary but regulated through the hypothalamus by an inhibiting hormone. MSH causes the melanocyte cells of the skin to disperse melanin in the body. The more melanin one's body produces, the more active the melanocyte cells must be, therefore requiring greater quantities of MSH. Looking for the influence of MSH on behavior, Kastin has found "that if one gives some rats an injection of MSH and other rats no MSH, then expose both groups of animals to electrical shock, the rats given MSH will avoid shock better."[42] Moreover, changes in brain waves are effected by injection of MSH, along with "some other kind of electrical activity . . . when MSH subjects are concentrating on something."

MSH, Kastin has established, helps human subjects see and recall better. "When subjects were shown geometrical forms and asked to reproduce them on paper from memory, they did better after receiving MSH injections," Kastin contends.[43] Kastin also proposes evidence suggesting that MSH "facilitates adaptive behavior in stressful situations such as active avoidance . . . , passive avoidance . . . , appetitive response for food when hungry . . . , and escape reversal learning. . . ."[44]

The action of MSH upon the nervous system should give blacks certain behavioral advantages. Included among them are attention and recall (devices of thinking), more probably under selective conditions. Perhaps more noteworthy is the ability to adapt under stressful situations as a result of the quantity of MSH, a contingency of melanin quantity. It is fair then to reason that the remarkable adaptation of blacks to the tropical harshness of Africa, and the horrors of slavery and oppression in the New World (stressful situations), is due to the sheer abundance of melanin in their bodies. Blacks manifesting agility and cleverness (coping skills) in an oppressive world is analogous to rats in an electrical shock cage, aided by MSH injections, successfully avoiding the pangs of convulsive currents.

Black expressive behavior has been the principal weapon in the arsenal of coping skills that blacks have deployed in successfully mastering the many stressful situations forced upon them. That this behavior is made possible by melanin production is the point of discussion. Melanin's energizing nature, arousal and neural propellant capacities would obviously seem to influence the intensity, duration, and frequency of expressive activity within the human being.

Moreover, when we add on to this evidence the advantages from the action of MSH upon the nervous system, which most nearly amounts to heightening intuitive powers—sharpening attention and increasing recall—it makes the point seem case hardened. These powers of intuition, in the forms of active and passive avoidance and escape reversal learning, all quicken the attentive powers of the mind to increase its recall ability, are manifest in quickness and maneuverability of the body and mental agility and alertness; these powers of intuition are readily evident in black expressive forms.

Spirituals, the blues, gospels, sermons, and dance, to name a few forms, all have served as survival vehicles for blacks. Upon careful study of their texts, in many instances, survival messages can be detected. The spirituals have many examples. A popular one, "Sinner, please don't let this harvest pass, and die and lose your soul at last," has a nonreligious message. Unable to engage in active militance, in camp meetings against slavery and oppression, for example, without grave consequences—consequences threatening to survival—slaves used songs like this one to covertly urge fellow blacks not to miss out on an opportunity to strike a blow against slavery, one for freedom. The songs served as code language for planned insurrections.[45] Cleverness and camouflage —hiding the plan from the masters while telling it to fellow slaves —are embodied in the song. Are these not practical translations of active and passive avoidance, escape reversal learning, reflecting increased mental attention and recall? If we accept the findings of enlightened authorities, we must conclude that the feat of black survival has been made possible by melanin quantity, which, with its capacity to spark and fuel human action, is fundamental to black expressive behavior.

Melanin quantity overlays hemispheric specialization, and explanations of black expressiveness come closest to truth when they reflect the dynamic interaction of culture and genetics.

3

DO YOU HAVE YOUR HEAD ON STRAIGHT?

The Healthy Personality and Black Expressiveness

He who cannot dance will say: 'The Drum is bad.'

African Proverb

During the 1820s, when blackfaced white American performers like George Nichols, Bali Farrel, George Washington Dixon, and Thomas Rice toured the nation, performing allegedly Negro songs and dances in circuses and between acts of plays, little did they know the high compliment paid the black community or people of African descent. It was a compliment, in spite of the racist stereotyped acts intended to denigrate black people, because the performers were demonstrating, for all to see, the vital emotionalism, spontaneity, and rhythm unique to black expression. Nor is it likely that the average person who enjoyed the popular entertainment form that grew out of the turbulent 1830s and 1840s, the minstrel show, was cognizant of this subtle inconsistency. The minstrel show was a form of popular entertainment that took the rich music, humor, and dance tradition from black expression, infused it with the most degrading stereotypes, blackened the faces of the performers, and passed this off as representative of the entire black community. The minstrel show was unabashedly popular in appeal, focused on blackfaced characters, and dominated by earthy, vital song, dance, and humor. Every part of the show—its features, form, and content—was hammered out in the interaction between performers and the vocal (white) audiences they sought to please. "I've got only one method," J. H. Haverly, the greatest minstrel promoter, explained, "and that is to find out what the people want and give them that thing —There's no use trying to force the public in a theatre."[1]

Everywhere the minstrel played, it seemed to have had a magnetic, almost hypnotic impact on its audience. "A minstrel show came to town, and I thought of nothing else for weeks," Ben Calton recalled of the first time he saw minstrels in the 1840s in Pawtucket, Rhode Island. George Thatcher, later a minstrel star, had comparable feelings when as a boy in Baltimore he saw his first show. "I found myself dreaming of minstrels; I would wake with an imaginary tambourine in my hand, and rub my face with my hands to see if I was blacked up. . . . The dream of my life was to see or speak to a performer."[2] After Dave Wambold, later a minstrel tenor, attended his first minstrel show in Newark, New Jersey, his parents could not keep him in school because "he was prone to play truant and get up minstrel performances among his companions." Similarly, Joel Chandler Harris, Stephen Foster, M. B. Leavitt, and Al G. Field—all later important in American popular culture—were stagestruck boys who played minstrel in their youth. Minstrels had truly captured the imagination of the nation.[3]

But why was minstrelsy a national sensation? What gave it such great appeal for northern white ordinary people, often called middlings, of all ages? As it evolved into an entertainment institution over the years, it became a major vehicle through which white Americans conceptualized and coped with many of their problems. An analysis of the "deeper" meanings provides the fullest understanding of the reasons for minstrelsy's popularity.

The minstrel's "new" audience first emerged as a by-product of the nation's wildly accelerating urban growth. Between 1820 and 1860, Philadelphia quadrupled in population; New York City mushroomed from 410,000 in 1840 to 910,000 in 1860; by 1850 eight American cities had more than 100,000 residents. In this urban population explosion the rural migrants, who had left Europe in droves, faced an almost totally alien environment that forced them to make fundamental changes in their lives, thoughts, and popular culture. They had to endure dire living conditions, totally inadequate housing, and rampant disease. Furthermore, many of them saw their economic hopes dashed as the ranks of the poor and the wealth of the few rich citizens swelled as never before. This disparity gave urban white people's anti-elitist feelings a basis in reality as well as in ideology. These new American city dwellers had to endure social and psychological anguish that was in some ways more severe than their physical plight. They had to learn to live by clocks rather than by a more natural order of time, to work to the rhythms of machines away from their homes and their families, and to live crowded together as strangers.[4]

These new immigrants found themselves in a cultural predicament. Here they were in a "new world" with the elitists or "highbrows" who indulged themselves in Old World cultural events: European opera, drama, dance, and chamber music. The "middling" Americans, *most* Americans, could not, for obvious reasons, include themselves among the aristocrats who enjoyed the traditional European arts. Almost inevitably, entertainment in America fragmented into "highbrow" and "lowbrow," elitist and popular. From this conflict came popular art forms that were both products of and responses to the way white Americans reacted to their new homeland. Early on, in order to resolve the conflict they simply borrowed from African art forms in the transformation of their cultural lives, resulting in the minstrel show, which became the most important new art form to grow out of this process.

This new art form—the minstrel—emerged central to white America's identity. The minstrel was much more than entertainment; in folk societies verbal arts teach values and norms, invoke sanctions against transgressors, and provide vehicles for fantasy and outlets for social criticism. These shows told people who they were and how to live with their neighbors.[5]

These "new Americans" had to establish new definitions of themselves as Americans and to find new "rules" to govern and explain their situation. They desperately needed amusements that spoke to them in terms they could understand and enjoy, that affirmed their worth and gave them dignity. They needed something that could establish a new sense of community and identity for them and those around them. These needs originated in cities but spread throughout the country as developments in transportation and communication greatly increased the flow of people, goods, information, ideas, and anxieties. By trial and error, popular arts emerged to fill these needs. Minstrelsy ultimately became the most successful entertainment formula.

There are two primary reasons for the success of the minstrel show. One, the lower-class whites, or middlings, had been made to feel the severe shock of class distinction in America. The resulting consequence was one of widespread inferiority feelings. In order to ward off the shock of these feelings, the middlings had to find a powerless and defenseless group who, when compared to themselves, gave them a relative sense of superiority. The minstrel, with its built-in denigration of black people, then, gave them a constant affirmation of this false sense of worth. However, owing to the elements of black expression, the vitalism of feeling, spontaneity, and rhythm, they experienced a second benefit. Their surrender to and utility of these gave them, also, a sense of release from the stresses imposed by the new environment and the feelings of inferiority they had to hide.

However, before the minstrel, or the systematic and programmatic spreading of black expressive dynamics to white audiences, became the norm for popular entertainment in the nation, entertainment in general had become less formal in tone and turned to regional American folk culture for material to construct heroes of common white Americans. There had been a glorification of "plain" white people. Between 1826 and 1836, actor James Hackett established the Yankee as the most significant American stage character. This rustic, Brother Jonathan—morally strong, independent, proud, brave, and nationalistic—delighted audiences throughout the country with his victories over "elitists," effete characters and stealthy, scheming, unprincipled city dudes. Coming out of the countryside, dressed rustically, and speaking in unrefined language, he routinely broke through the hypocrisy and corruption of "civilized" society with biting commentary. He accepted all the cruel jibes directed at common Americans for being uncouth and unrefined and turned them into a debunking counterattack against the bearers of refinement and high standards of deportment. A model of what common Americans like to think they were, the Yankee possessed the good traits of Europeans, stripped of their decadence, pretension, and corruption. He was a blend of fact, fiction, and fantasy; he nevertheless proved to be a model ordinary Americans could identify with and believe in.[6]

Besides the Yankee-type character there were the Backwoodsman and the boasting Frontiersman, Daniel Boone types, who roared of superhuman powers and deeds in so much of the popular literature of the period. Occasionally, the Yankee and the Frontiersman appeared together on stage as part of a trend to combine or unite the two native white folk types. Although they retained their basic differences, the low-keyed understatement of the Yankee and the arrogant ballyhooing of the Frontiersman, both used speech rich in homely metaphors, both boasted of hav-

ing what were supposed to be faults, and both defeated preten-
tious aristocrats. Similarly, in the widely popular melodramas,
rural heroes who were pure of heart and motive inevitably won
out over corrupt, immoral city slickers. These rural characters
with the strength to triumph over every adversity fed the iden-
tity-hungry egos of the growing numbers of Americans who were
experiencing the jolting shocks of urbanization.[7]

In the thirty years after the War of 1812, the forces demanding
a white man's common culture had transformed American entertainment. Virtually all of the old cultural forms, which had tried
to accommodate highly vocal middling Americans into their audiences by making extensive use of European-oriented American
folk culture, had failed. Besides serious literature and art jour-
nals, there were now inexpensive popular books and folksy week-
lies, dominated by greater-than-life American folk heroes. Similarly, in addition to complex drama and comedies of manners,
theaters now offered uncomplicated plays in which simple Americans won out over corrupt, money-gambling schemers and pre-
tentious intellectual types. Led by P. T. Barnum, entertainment
entrepreneurs, sensing the great financial potential of the rapidly
expanding markets produced by the revolutions in transportation
and the explosions in urban population, began consciously cater-
ing to mass audiences and working to create public interest and
attendance. Among all the new, unique, popular-culture art
forms, the minstrel show emerged on the scene and immediately,
virtually over night, became the instant rage and a national institution.[8]

Although the minstrels failed to accurately portray black life or
even black culture, it is of great significance that black expression
exerts such powerful influence on the arts in America. The impli-
cation of the "borrowing" of black expression to serve as the
foundation for popular culture, or the turning to Africans when
one is to become most human (at play), suggests overwhelming
significance worthy of analysis.

On November 10, 1860, the *New York Clipper* reported that
"minstrelsy provided common Americans with folk-based earthy
songs, vital dances and robust good humor as well as with beautiful ballads and fine singing that they [the audience] could enjoy."

Embedded in this review is the core point which highlights the significance of the popularity of black expression in early America, which has spread worldwide and now permeates most popular entertainment art forms everywhere. Why are the "Souls of Black Folks" the fountain for much that Western man does when he is one with the whole world in love and pleasure? Why are black people the prime sources of Western entertainment?

In order to grapple with these questions, we have examined the attitudes and behaviors of black people to discern some explanations for this particular group's proclivity for expressing joy. Black expressions are utilized by all, including the early middling white Americans who, in spite of great disdain for and racial prejudices against black people, all too willingly accepted the expressiveness that emanated from black life-styles and used it for their own creative expression. This gave our social system a personality reflecting injected black feeling which now is an enduring factor in the emotional life of the nation. It follows that black emotionalism is positively involved in the mental health status of our society and warrants analysis.

From the beginning, our social system, like all social systems, required that each member of the society take certain roles. Unless the roles were adequately fulfilled, the system would not have produced the results for which the organization existed. This rule applies to systems as simple as one developed by an engaged couple to those as complex as a total nation among nations. Societies provide institutions—families and schools—which serve the function of training people to take on the age, sex, and occupational roles which they shall be obliged to fulfill through their lives in the social system. Generally, if a person carries out his role suitably, he can be regarded as a "normal" personality. Normal personalities, however, are not necessarily healthy personalities.

More important than "normalcy" is the ability of the individual to integrate all aspects of his personality. Broadly speaking, the major aspects of personality include: (1) cognitive or intellectual aspects, (2) affective or emotional aspects, and (3) psychomotor or action aspects (movement). It appears that one is

deemed to be a healthy personality when the individual responds
to his environment as a "total organism" or "whole being," when,
in fact, all aspects of personality are fused or when the individual
relates to his surroundings with spontaneity and integrity.

Yet, when one observes the Western world, and more particularly elitist early Americans, who attempted to influence the cultural destiny of the young nation (and apparently with much
success when viewing the present status of the nation's mental
health), one is impressed by the propensity to subdue the affective aspects of the personalities of the individual members of the
populace and to encourage intellectualization.[9] Upon closer observation, one sees the same inclination in regard to the action or
movement aspect of human personality. The minstrel, though vio-
lating the elitists' sense of respectful behavior, like no other feature of popular culture brought to the attention of the nation the
vitalism planted in the emotional and movement aspects of
human behavior that are exemplified in African man.

What we see is that optimal mental health is achieved by a fu-
sion and balance of the three complementary modes of experiencing: cognition, affect, and motor or movement.

The Western world has established institutions to tutor the development of cognitive, analytic, linear activity in the human
being;[10] it has left emotional learning and motor expression to be
nurtured by the folkways of the people. Persons whose behavior
expresses their emotions are likely to enjoy a better state of positive mental health. Many theories of psychotherapy concur with
this conclusion. Congruence of feeling and overt behavior are indicative of a healthy individual. The healthy person is more
prone to exude a warm, sincere, empathic attitude in relations
with other human beings.[11] The healthy personality calls for
spontaneous, creative, flexible, actively expressive behavior.[12]
This frees the body of tension and allows it to be open to new experiences. Healthy attitudes toward normal sexual behavior are
implicit among the criteria for optimal mental health.[13] The mentally healthy individual exhibits real, honest, authentic behavior
and has the ability to accept and live in harmony with other
beings and nature.

A. H. Maslow, the renowned humanist, spent much of his life

attempting to understand how human beings develop to their full potential. He came to believe that the gratification of basic needs, a hierarchical sequence that all humans possess, was the key. This hierarchy, from lowest to highest, includes:

1. physical needs—basic needs such as food, water, shelter, and clothing;
2. safety needs—the security needs;
3. belonging and love needs—those needs representing the need for affection and belonging to other persons;
4. esteem needs—those needs related to respect by others for one's accomplishments and achievements; and
5. self-actualization.

Maslow further studied individuals who appeared to meet the criteria for optimal mental health or self-actualization. Certain traits exhibited by the people Maslow elected to study appeared consistently. They show a complementary relation between the thinking, feeling, and movement aspects of personality. The traits appearing most frequently among Maslow's self-actualizing (S-A) selected persons follow, along with commentary by Sidney Jourard from his book *The Healthy Personality*.

1. A more adequate perception of reality and more comfortable relations with reality than occur in average people. His S-A cases seemed to detect the spurious, the fake, and the dishonest in interpersonal relationship and to be attuned to truth and reality in all spheres of life. They eschewed the illusory and preferred to cope with even unpleasant reality rather than retreat to pleasant fantasies.

2. A high degree of acceptance of themselves, of others, and of the realities of human nature. They were not ashamed of being what they were, and they were not shocked or dismayed to find shortcomings in themselves or in others.

3. Spontaneity. The S-A people displayed spontaneity

in their thinking, emotion, and behavior to a greater extent than average people.

4. Problem-centeredness. Maslow's subjects seemed all to be focused on problems outside themselves. They were not overly self-conscious; they were not problems to themselves, and could hence devote their attention to a task, duty, or mission that seemed peculiarly cut out for them.

5. A need for privacy. The S-A people could enjoy solitude; indeed, they would even seek it on occasion, needing it for periods of intense concentration on subjects of interest to them, and for meditation.

6. A high degree of autonomy. The S-A people seemed able to remain true to themselves in the face of rejection or unpopularity; they were able to pursue their interests and projects and maintain their integrity even when it hurt to do so.

7. A continued freshness of appreciation. The S-A people showed the capacity to "appreciate again and again, freshly and naively, the basic goods of life . . . a sunset, a flower, a baby, a person"; it was as if they avoided merely lumping experiences into categories and then dismissing them. Rather, they could see the unique in many commonplace experiences.

8. Frequent "mystic experiences." The S-A people seemed subject to periodic experiences that are often called "mystic" or "oceanic"—feelings that one's boundaries as a person have suddenly evaporated and one has truly become a part of all mankind and even of all nature.

9. Gemeinschaftsgefühl. The German word gemeinschaftsgefühl means brotherly feeling, the feeling of belonging to all mankind (related to the mystic experiences above); the attitude was found to be characteristic of S-A people. They felt a sense of identification

with mankind as a whole, such that they could become concerned not only with the lot of members of their immediate family, but also with the situation of persons from different cultures.

10. Close relationships with a few friends or loved ones. Maslow found that his S-A subjects, although not necessarily very popular, did have the capacity to establish truly close, loving relationships with at least one or two other people.

11. Democratic character structures. The S-A people tended to judge people and be friendly with them not on the basis of race, status, religion, or other group membership traits, but as individual persons.

12. A strong ethical sense. The S-A subjects were found to have a highly developed sense of ethics. Though their notions of right and wrong were not wholly conventional, their behavior was always chosen with reference to its ethical meaning.

13. Unhostile senses of humor. The S-A people had senses of humor which made common human foibles, pretensions, and foolishness the subject of laughter, rather than sadism, smut, or rebellion against authority.

14. Creativeness. The S-A people were creative and inventive in some areas of their existence, not followers of the usual ways of doing or thinking.

15. Resistance to enculturation. The S-A subjects could detach themselves somewhat from complete brainwashing or imprinting by their cultures, permitting them to adopt critical attitudes toward cultural inconsistencies or unfairness within their own society.[14]

It is curious that the Western world presents a dearth of settings or cultures reflecting these sentiments of optimal mental health on a large-scale basis. Note that the healthy personality, as outlined by Maslow in his description of the self-actualizing person, would have a difficult time surviving psychically in the America of today, or in the 1830s when the basis for popular entertainment was formulated. If in this culture an individual exhibits real, honest, authentic feelings and has the ability to accept and live in harmony with other beings and nature, he becomes a target for the more competitive and "creature-comfort" acquiring individuals in the community, who are influenced by a system whose reason for being is to acquire more wealth and control over all—including nature. It is no wonder, then, that such a culture would of necessity have to turn to another culture for its essentially humanistic needs, such as entertainment, and whether it is recognized or not, the "borrowing" from black culture brought the nation closer to its own definition of a civilized society, of which a requisite is mentally healthy behavior. The arts, particularly the popular arts, must derive from people free to exercise the affective (feeling) and motor aspects of personality as one unmistakably observes in the behavior of people of African ancestry.

The affective and psychomotor are powerful domains in human behavior. Affective behavior is the reason there are affecting things and events, those cultural objects and occurrences containing feeling, resulting from human actions directed toward producing them. Affecting things and events (e.g., sculpture, craft, music, dance, drama, poetry, festival, costume) are not accidental but are cultivated in mentally healthy societies or cultures. Further, affect or feeling is with us early and it is articulated earlier than the intellect. It is, in fact, a primary level of existence; and what relationship it has to thought or intellect, to structure and content of behavior that is not affective, one cannot easily say. One can say that many Westerners, in their fervor to acquire more wealth, relegate feelings to a level of insignificance. However, when many pause to enjoy life, to be happy, they must "borrow" from blacks who value feelings and who proliferate feelings in the creation of affecting or artistic items and events. Who can deny, if one is familiar with the format and content of radio and television productions in the West, that popular culture is saturated with the African motif? There are those who believe that the way in which one organizes his feelings and the motifs he stresses are not at all unrelated to the rest of his life.

The affective domain includes felt values, dreams, symbols, natural objects and events to which affect has accrued. The affective or feeling realm is the pivotal part of man's universe, and it compels overt emotional expressiveness. This is exampled in the universal experience of love, hate, loyalty, fear, and other such emotions. Note, however, that the circumstances under which these emotions are characteristically generated, and the means of their expression, are subject to cultural variations. Moreover, subscription to these feeling norms, and the intensity of feeling, are obviously subject to individual differences.

Man has feelings; he expresses them, teaches them to others, and refines them through the environment or the culture in which he finds himself. The resulting arts (music, dances, poetry, etc.) in any given culture are accepted by those native to the culture as being purposefully concerned with their way of being. However, irrespective of such considerations, under certain circumstances and in some cultures such occurrences and events may be admired for the excellence of their own properties; thus, this admiration is in itself of an affecting nature (e.g., to dance for the sheer sake of the rhythmic sensation of movement in space, and not for sexual flirtation as is common to some).

Potency, bravery, and force clearly produce affect, and it is to this affect that the thing or event is dedicated, and thereafter it is the work (music, dance) affecting us when we enter into transaction with it. The totality of expression, such as dance, constitutes a distinct human entity—of thought, feeling, and rhythm. This is the ultimate objective of the creation of things and events (art). Presentation, not representation, is the goal of the healthy creator of things and events. More practically stated, affecting things and events are not valuable because of their price in the marketplace but because they constitute a distinct and significant category of human existence related always to the maintenance and enhancement of the inner self. If an understanding of this category is not achieved, it follows that there is no full understanding of human behavior and its cultural basis.[15] Cultures, like Western culture, that ignore these facts must look to a more affectively

expressive culture for popular art forms that are enjoyed by most
of the people.

It was not an accident, then, that America and the West turned
to African expressiveness for the foundation upon which to build
popular art forms, beginning by imitating blacks, first on a wide
scale through the minstrel, and continuing to "borrow" from
blacks thereafter for the entertaining arts. Black expression appears to epitomize best those criteria of Western psychology indicative of optimal mental health. It is a synthesis of three major
domains of human personality: affect, intellect, and movement.
This propensity is readily observed by the most casual observer
who recognizes among ordinary black people the inclination to
use, for life enrichment, music, movement, folklore, poetry, oratory, and most of the other remaining arts. Such an inclination
should make comprehensible the fact that black people react
more frequently to environmental stimuli in more creative and
satisfying ways. These ways include, but also go beyond, the
usual verbal or numerical responses that enjoy high acclaim
owing to the intellectual strivings of the West. As earlier stated,
blacks seem to perceive the environment and respond to it with
musical notes, movement (dance and athletics), and lines
(graphic arts and sculpture) more frequently than do Westerners, who are more dependent on printed words and numbers
in their search for consonance with the world. However, we do
not claim that black people are unique in this regard. We suggest
that the major cultural groups of the world have developed characteristic modes of intellectual and affective expression that are
clearly recognizable and clearly different from those of other
major cultural groups. Still, it is curious, and not accidental, that
the major portion of the world's population, particularly in the
West, have adopted much that comes from black expressiveness
as the basis for their popular cultural arts.

Black expressiveness, the foundation upon which Western popular art rests, has its genesis in African behavior. The behaviors
and attitudes that flow from African people appear to combine
the feeling or affective aspects with the other components of personality and render them into physical manifestations (e.g.,

dance, music, poetry) which constitute affecting things and events. As shown earlier, feelings in the Western world are suppressed and subordinated to intellectualization. Yet we know, and have already reported, that feeling is with us earlier, far earlier, than intellect. But let us reiterate that feeling, emotion, or affect is most relevant to the status of optimal personality functioning.

Freedom from anxiety is a key indicator of good mental health. Evident, it would seem, is a decisive relationship between good mental health and the complementary functioning of intellect, feeling, and psychomotor responses. Feeling is primary in the expression of the innermost, the self. The fact is, the earlier Americans, when attempting to create for themselves a functional entertainment art form, turned to black expressiveness because the black community brought with it from Africa a ready-made cultural heritage sufficient to elicit from participants/observers spontaneous delight and release from tension. It gave the participants, through the tension reduction derived from physical participation, or assertion, a sense of liberation from the anxiety which is often associated with total or almost total dependence upon the intellect. The minstrel produced what is clearly recognizable in contemporary black expression: humorous stimuli, spontaneity, creativity, and the ability to love other people and nature without the expectation of material gain.

There have been persistent reminders from many that black expressiveness is a viable, real, and deducible phenomenon. Few have been more intelligible than Leopold Sedar Senghor, who writes:

> The Negro is quite different. American psychotechnicians have already confirmed that his reflexes are more natural, better adapted. That explains his utilization in industry and in the technical services of the Armed Forces in a higher percentage than that which he represents in the population of the United States of America. But let us take up again the thread of our story. First, the African Negro is by his colour as in the

primordial night. He does not see the object; he feels it. It is the pure sensorial field of the third day development of a worm. It is in his subjectivity, at the end of his sensory organs that he discovers the Other (Nature): There he is, stimulated, going centrifugally from subject to object on the waves of the Other (Nature). And this is not simply metaphorical, since contemporary physics has discovered energy under matter: waves and radiations. Thus, one sees the African Negro who sympathizes and identifies himself, who dies to himself in order to be reborn to the Other. He is not assimilated; he assimilates himself with the Other. He lives with the Other in symbiosis; he is born again (con-nait) to the Other, as Paul Claudel would say. Here subject and object face each other dialectically in the very instrument of knowledge, which is the instrument of love. "I think, therefore I exist," wrote Descartes. The African Negro could say, "*I feel the Other; I dance the Other, therefore I exist*" [emphasis ours]. Then, dancing is creating, especially when the dance is the dance of love. In any case, it is the best means of knowledge.[16]

Senghor is suggesting that the black man comes to know by feeling. Seeing a probable paradox, he insists that African feeling is "animated by reason." The black man's reason, by way of heritage, is different than that of Europeans whose reason is based on definable, measurable, detectable material or exterior. Reason for African man "comes from the logos more than from the ratio." European reason, through material utility, is analytic; black reason, through experiential involvement, is intuitive. Without exactness in language, Senghor alludes to one of our essential points of emphasis—the interlocking of affect, intellect, and movement exposited in the perceptual and expressive behavior of African man. Enshrined in this style of life, this way of knowing, this way of being, is an internal psychological order which synthesizes the tenets of the healthy personality allowing the giving of ourselves for our own and the world's happiness.

Black creativity, as the basis for Western relaxation and enjoy-

ment, continues, not without improprieties however. Harold
Cruse explains:

> . . . the role of the Negro, as entertainer, has not
> changed since the 1920's. In 1967 the Negro entertainer
> is still used, manipulated, and exploited by whites.
> Negro entertainment talent is more original than that of
> any other ethnic group, more creative ("soulful" as they
> say), spontaneous, colorful, and also more plentiful. It is
> so plentiful that in the marketplace of popular cul-
> ture, white brokers and controllers buy Negro entertain-
> ment cheaply (sometimes for nothing) and sell it
> high—as in the case of Sammy Davis. But there is only
> one Sammy Davis. In the shadows, a multitude of lesser
> colored lights are plugging away, hoping against hope
> to make the Big Time, for the white culture brokers
> only permit a few to break through—thus creating an
> artificial scarcity of a cultural product. This system was
> established by the wily Broadway entrepreneurs in the
> 1920's. Negro entertainment posed such an ominous
> threat to the white cultural ego, the staid Western
> standards of art, cultural values and aesthetic integrity,
> that the entire source had to be stringently controlled.[17]

That the mental health of a society can be assessed by the status of the society's popular art forms is indisputable. It goes without saying that the end goal of all healthy personalities is happiness: a lessening of tension and anxiety that allows the individual
or the society to relax and enjoy the wonders of nature, of whom
we are all creatures. Yet, to experience this unusually human
state of affairs a society must provide an appropriately conducive
atmosphere to allow the affect or feeling component of personality to have free range or at least to have equal significance in
the lives of a society's population. This state, or entity, may be
referred to as soul, spirit, religion, art, or similar affective appella-
tives; whatever it is called, in order that the society enjoy relative
peace, harmony, and balance among the populace and with nature, the feeling component must be in good estate.

Unfortunately Western man, in the mass, appears not to possess this vital spiritual endowment. The truest gift has been arrested. The arrest has left the "mind" hovering over spirit. Western man has wandered far, if ever near, and lost the means of natural satisfaction. He has invented a life void of the deep and satisfying harmony which the soul requires for personal efficiency in human relations. Living a life concocted by his own intellect, he has worn thin his spirit and devitalized his functional art. His art and his life are no longer one and the same as required of the healthy personality. Art has become exotic, a thing apart, an indulgence, a something to be possessed, suspensions of oddity on walls of expensive homes and lucrative museums, imprisoning emotional vitalism. Because his art is not real and vital, there is little harmony between himself and nature, which means little happiness.

Consequently, he has been forced to borrow much of the basis of his popular art, his soul, from blacks, whose tremendous emotional endowment, free imagination, and powers of individual expression have been inherited from ancestors of black people. Blacks have, in superlative measure, the fire which, coming from within, floods the whole world, colors the images and impels expression. Those blacks who remain relatively unacculturated are poets at birth. Their daily habits of thought, speech, and movement are flavored with the picturesque, the rhythmic, the unique. Black art has universal appeal. No matter where one goes, if there are black people there one finds this rich tradition firmly implanted in the soul. As Albert Barnes has stated it:

> The unlettered black singers have taught us to love music that rakes our souls and gives us moments of exquisite joy. The later Negro has made us feel the majesty of Nature, the ineffable peace of the woods and the great open spaces. He has shown us that the events of our every-day American life contain for him a poetry, rhythm and charm which we ourselves had never discovered. Through him we have seen the pathos, comedy, affection, joy of his own daily life, unified into humorous dialect verse or perfected sonnet that is a work of exqui-

site art. He has taught us to respect the sheer manly
greatness of the fiber which has kept his inward light
burning with an effulgence that shines through the
darkness in which we have tried to keep him. . . . His
message has been lyrical, rhythmic, colorful. In short,
the elements of beauty he has controlled to the ends of
art.[18]

It is no wonder, then, that underlying the minstrel, jazz, vaude-
ville, Tin Pan Alley, pop, Al Jolson, Frank Sinatra, Bing Crosby,
Elvis Presley, John Travolta, rests black expressiveness. Agnes de
Mille, the famous choreographer, has said, "Since 1850, there has
been little change in Europe. . . . All further innovations have
come from the United States, Cuba, or South America, and all
broke with previous tradition."[19] Jean and Marshall Stearns add:
"The chief source of these innovations—is Africa."[20] Although the
writers above are referring to dance, their commentary is equally
relevant to the remaining popular arts. Accordingly, blacks' sacred music, spirituals, secular music, the plantation songs, ragtime, blues, jazz, work songs, folklore, plantation tales, and
dances have all gone into and more or less permeate Western life.
Given these facts, and having determined that the level of mental
health of a society can be estimated, to some extent, by the state
and source of its popular arts, the question must be asked, dar-
ingly, "Whose head is on straight?"

4

DO BLACKS HAVE A NATURAL RHYTHM?

Rhythm—The Fundamental Behavior Principle

Rhythm—a basic creative principle
Rhythm—an expression of race memory

Larry Neal[1]

(. . . I want to proclaim out loud///
that life is only rhythm//
and rhythm within a rhythm)

Guy Tirolier[2]

I am the rhythm of my past, my present,
I sing a song of future.
I shall sing my . . . [rhythm]

Eugene Redmond[3]

Blacks have given the nation, and the world, joy and laughter, through song, dance, oratory, and the rest of the arts, providing for life, relaxation and contentment, restoring balance, symmetry, and smooth fluidity to waves of force that are vitally essential for optimal mental functioning. These "waves of force," elusive, bedeviling the senses, and "Roots of Soul" we call rhythm.

From things unknown to man's beginnings, rhythm has predominated and is woven intricately, and intimately, into man's actions and ways. Rhythm is fundamental, fueling the wondrous timepieces of the universe, and is central to its order and organization.

Living things respond to the environment with a rhythm that is near clocklike accuracy. Oysters are known to time their lives to the ocean tides, no matter how far they are shipped from the water's mighty roar. Interestingly, potatoes in sealed containers predict atmospheric pressure trends well ahead of time. Such strange and permeative forces, these waves are, which exert powerful sensations on living things—truly the basis of their incredibly adaptive capacities.

How scientific are these claims? The most recent research is discussed in Edward Mann's book *Orgone, Reich, and Eros*. According to Mann, Dr. H. S. Burr, a leading professor of biology at Yale University until his retirement, and an internationally ranked neuro-anatomist and embryologist, pioneered the research that is now confirming the articulations of African philosophers regarding the rhythmic nature of life. A new way of studying and conceptualizing life, in all its forms, has been made possible through the discovery of electrodynamic force fields.[4]

Around all living things is an aura, or electromagnetic atmosphere, of bioelectric energy that can be detected by electrical measuring devices. Within each aura a rhythmic pulsation can be precisely counted, one not affected by known body rhythms such as respiration or heart beat. Each living thing has its own pulsation rate, or "steady state" (i.e., its unstimulated state). The pulsation rate varies from the steady state, showing increases and decreases, as a result of bodily excitation or emotionality.

The so-called steady state, which represents potential power, is unlike either AC or DC electric currents; it increases at intervals that parallel the occurrences of the full and new moons. It increases and decreases, also, from changes in the sun and other natural objects. We reason that this potential power is analogous to, if not the equivalent of, the African concept of vital force.

In summary, our contention is that human beings pulsate, each at his or her own rate and rhythm, and in relative harmony and unison with the energy systems of other things and beings in the universe.

The research done by Dr. Burr and his associates compels us to accept premises long cited by the wise of Africa, that the emotional, excitatory processes of the body are related to the rhythmic excitations of nature. Rhythm and vibrations, waves of force, are the essential ingredients in the organization of human behavior, and we shall soon see the fascinating likenesses of the scientific claims of Dr. Burr and colleagues to the philosophical claims of scholars on African thought.

Man responds to the same primal impulse that pumps in the heart of the world. The man of African ancestry is the best expositor of the force experienced, and expressed, as rhythm. It is the exposition of rhythm that accounts for the black man's powerful capacity to vitalize human existence, adapt to the unadaptable, and survive the clutches of death (oppression). The common black man puts rhythm into whatever he does—it is so prevalent in the black community, it seems as if only a few actions can be carried out without the help of a certain rhythm. Shining shoes, performing assembly-line routines, washing cars (remember the movie *Car Wash?*), typing, talking, walking, making love, worshipping, or carrying articles on the head (as do the Caribbean people and others close to the folkways of Africa), all require a certain rhythm, which is at the heart of man's basic nature. J. A. Rogers recollects:

> Some years ago while wandering in Cincinnati I happened upon a Negro revival meeting at its height. The majority present were women, a goodly few of whom were white. Under the influence of the "spirits" the sisters would come forward and strut—much of jazz enters where it would be least expected. The Negro

women had perfect [rhythm], while the white ones
moved lamely and woodenly. The same lack of spontaneity is evident to a degree in the cultivated and inhibited Negro.[5]

Melville Herskovits' observations of black behaviors parallel
the account given by Rogers. Struck by the pervasiveness of
rhythm, he marveled:

[Shelling] cereals of one kind or another is ubiquitous
throughout Africa, though of course not confined to that
continent. The way in which these are used, however,
shows a further retention of motor habits, especially in
the tendency to work as rhythmically as possible; in the
West Indies, Guiana, and West Africa, it takes some experience for the visitor to learn to distinguish the alternate strokes of two pestles in the mortar from the beat
of a drum.[6]

Noteworthy historians and anthropologists have stated the
clear probability that human life started in Africa, and, in quest
of that which is fundamental to all behavior, to all men's nature,
an examination of African thought and philosophy is pertinent.
Wilfred Cartey, in his book *Whispers from a Continent,* quotes
Aimé Cesaire who is less tentative in his referral to the black race
as an old one "which dances with the winds, which flows from the
source of waters, which moves from the total rhythm of the
earth."[7] In a powerful affirmation, Aimé Cesaire claims that
blacks are:

truly the elder sons of the world
porous to all breath of the world
spark of the sacred fire of the world
panting with the very movement of the world[8]

Cesaire's rhythmic and flavorful lines mirror African thought and
philosophy, to which rhythm, as a behavioral concept, reduces.
    As the cradle of mankind, Africa conveys a message of rele-

vance for the whole of humanity. Of extraordinary importance, the common black man, separated from the entrapments of artificiality that are propagated by Western ways, offers the richest possible view of human behavior, one unspoiled by the technological domination of the modern world, and very probably one which best answers the questions: WHAT IS THE NATURE OF MAN? WHAT IS THE NATURE OF PERSONALITY? It is reasonable, then, to expound on African thought with obvious overtones of universality in the application to all of mankind.

Rhythm, the fundamental principle in human behavior, reigns as the basic ingredient of black expressiveness. It is most easily transmitted in aesthetic forms that become tangible enclosures for the waves of force (rhythm) that are nourished by that which is "spiritual" in the universe. Clearly a human characteristic, rhythm's vibratory nature pulsates throughout the universe. In human behavior it is expressed sensually, through lines, surfaces, colors, language, music, and movements in dance and other motor responses. Blacks walk, talk, dance, prance, look, cook, play, and pray in marvelous harmony to, and with, the rhythm of the universe.

With rhythm established as a formidable factor in the way people behave, and conceding that African man best embodies the rhythm force, one relaxes to the point of certainty in the conclusion that there is something unusual about the make-up of the black mind, the black man, that is in a very real way, in all men. Black/African philosophy and thought reveals that which is allegedly peculiar, unusual, and different about the black man, something marked by rhythm, and emotional power in expression.

Man, through his procreative and creative capacities, is invested with force, with rhythm, compliments of the universe. That the rhythmic, cosmic union between God, nature, and the universe begot life, and man, is a primary conception of black/African philosophy and thought.

The traditional African worldview holds that "being" is identical with life itself. A vital force, similar to that which rhythmically empowers man, enlivens each item, each object, each thing in the universe.[9] Every tree, rock, animal, or substance in the natural world takes on the properties of life. They reverberate with life's essence—the spiritual gene. "Who killed this tree?" angrily roared Okonkwo, the main character in Chinua Achebe's novel *Things Fall Apart*. Note the quality of "being," of life, in the tree as given in Okonkwo's fiery outburst.

Human personality and identity are psychological derivatives stemming from man's essential union with other things and beings in the universe. "In short," Onwuachi asserts, "the African identity must correlate with the African ideological formulations in the African world."[10] In as much as black Americans and blacks in other parts of the world have retained an essentially African character base, one must consider African ideas about nature, human life, existence, social relations, God, and spirituality as bases for understanding and cultivating black/African identity within the personality of the black man. As a beginning point, recognize that, in spite of man's unique and characteristic idiosyncrasies, in the African world he is never conceptualized as an individual in isolation from the total community that supports his existence. His identity is one that embraces the life force and the character structure of other things and beings in the universe, without regard, necessarily, for the biological requirements of life.

These things and beings that give man his identity, his personality, form a hierarchy. God is seen as the ultimate explanation for the existence of the world and all contained within it. Follow the debate, from Chinua Achebe's *Things Fall Apart*, between a European missionary and an African elder, regarding the ultimate power of the universe:

> "You say that there is one supreme God who made heaven and earth," said Akunna on one of Mr. Brown's visits. "We, also, believe in Him and call Him Chukwu. He made all the world and the other gods."
>
> "There are no other gods," said Mr. Brown. "Chukwu is the only God and all others are false. You carve a piece of wood—like that one" (he pointed at the rafters

from which Akunna's carved Ikenga hung), "and you call it a god. But it is still a piece of wood."

"Yes," said Akunna. "It is indeed a piece of wood. The tree from which it came was made by Chukwu, as indeed all minor gods were. But He made them for His messengers so that we could approach Him through them. It is like yourself. You are the head of your church."

"No," protested Mr. Brown. "The head of my church is God Himself."

"I know," said Akunna, "but there must be a head in this world among men. Somebody like yourself must be the head here."

"The head of my church in that sense is in England."

"That is exactly what I am saying. The head of your church is in your country. He has sent you here as his messenger. And you have also appointed your own messengers and servants. Or let me take another example, the District Commissioner. He is sent by your king."

"They have a queen," said the interpreter on his own account.

"Your queen sends her messenger, the District Commissioner. He finds that he cannot do the work alone and so he appoints kotma to help him. It is the same with God, or Chukwu. He appoints the smaller gods to help Him because His work is too great for one person."

"You should not think of Him as a person," said Mr. Brown. "It is because you do so that you imagine He must need helpers. And the worst thing about it is that you give all the worship to the false gods you have created."

"That is not so. We make sacrifices to the little gods, but when they fail and there is no one else to turn to we go to Chukwu. It is right to do so. We approach a great man through his servants. But when his servants fail to help us, then we go to the last source of hope. We appear to pay greater attention to the little gods but that is not so. We worry them more because we are afraid to

worry their Master. Our fathers knew that Chukwu was
the Overlord and that is why many of them gave their
children the name Chukwuka—Chukwu is Supreme."[11]

It's a foregone conclusion that the domain of spirituality looms
as the principal realm for the formation of all things, including
the personality of man. The spirits, superhuman beings, and the
life forces of ancestors (persons separated from the flesh by
death), occupy the second tier in the hierarchy. There is a mystical power, or order, in the universe. This power comes from God,
who makes it available, in varying degrees, to spirits and to
human beings (those alive and those about to be born), who are
third in the hierarchical scheme. The remainder of biological life,
including animals and plants, follows man, and lastly are phenomena and objects without biological life.[12]

Man's insertion here forms a dynamic order of interdependency in the universe and explains the bases for the African
practice of collective and communal living. "Thus we are," according to Erny, "introduced into a universe of correspondents,
analogies, harmonies, interactions. Man and cosmos constitute
one single network of forces; to grasp one intellectually is to
grasp the other."[13]

Because of this quality, Jean Paul Lebeuf instructs: "Never in
Black Africa does a human being, an object, a plant, an animal,
an insect, appear in only one aspect and detached from other spe-
cies; never is man entirely singular."[14] Meshed with what constitutes the essential, there is an element, a piece, a part, however
small, of the opposed and complementary, of everything that exists. To this point Janheinz Jahn speaks:

> On the basis of African philosophy there can be no strict
> separation of sacred and profane. Since everything is
> force or energy, the orisha [spirit] as well as the human
> being, the sacred drum as well as the profane, and all
> force is the embodiment of single universal life force,
> the boundary between sacred and profane cannot be
> drawn as it is in Europe.[15]

Although the gradations are infinite, sacred and secular, recognizing their essential kinship, warmly embrace each other in the spirit of "oneness." "Oneness of being," of all things, through interdependency, is the overriding dictum. Cartey credited the poets of the Negritude literary tradition, which stressed the essence of black existence, for giving this point more intimacy. Armed with the poets' convictions, he wrote:

> Suffering and joy, like infancy and age, life and death, present and past, are not opposites . . . [They are woven] together, demonstrating the essential unity and harmony between them. One exists because of the other, since to plunge into the essence of one is the plunge into the essence of other. To know the essence of suffering is to know the essence of joy. To experience the passion of hatred is to know the force of love. To know that death is, is to know that life is, also, and that it must be lived.[16]

A perception obviously conditioned by the African worldview. Leopold Sedar Senghor stated, quite explicitly:

> I have therefore lived in that kingdom, seen with my eyes, with my ears heard the fabulous beings beyond things . . . the dead of the village, and the ancestors who spoke to me, initiating me into the alternating truths of night and noon.[17]

Black/African philosophy and thought ascribe life and curative strength to rivers and waters, winds and motions, "accepting the rhythmic pulsation of all elements, each force concatenating to another force, forming an essential unity. They accept the unbroken convergencies of all things and give a total primacy to the strength which comes from the convergence."[18] The individual unites with the family, the family with the clan, the clan with the tribe, and the tribe with the nation. Concurrent with this union is a spiritual merger with other beings and things in the world, all of which make up the ingredients of the universe.

With the elements, Cartey noted, man coalesces. By the elements, he is transformed and invigorated. The merging of man and the elements occurs through a restorative, cleansing, and abiding power that forces the river's water to rise and fall, forming on the water ripples of eternal motion, sweeping the individual with the spiritual properties of life. This power mystically enables people "among other things, to communicate at distance (telepathy), to receive visions," and it can be used "by man for healing purposes."[19] These gifts are bestowed by life forces represented by God and spirits. Because of their closeness to the divine world, certain persons, such as old men, newborns, twins, the very ill, and religious leaders, as well as certain animals, rivers, and high rocks, are affected more keenly or endowed more richly with the spiritual forces of the universe.

For traditional African man, the whole of existence is a spiritual one. In a universe where spirituality occupies the highest realm of reality, it holds that man, living in such a universe, would become, by birthright, a deeply spiritually motivated creature. Man has in him ways of being which describe his idea of God. Concurrently, he has in him ways of being which stem from the natural aspects of the universe. Man is, therefore, both spiritual and physical, having the physical properties of matter, the biological and physiological features of living things, and having values, insights, intuitions, dreams, will, and feelings, all dominated by spiritual forces; it is these forces that elevate him above other forms of life. It is his absorption and recognition of spirit as an entity of intelligence that make him closer to the ultimate life force (God), for God is spirit, for God is intelligent, for God is in man, and that makes man deeply spiritual, soulful, human, and deeply expressive.

Man's expressiveness unclogs his existence of strict cognition, or thought, and allows the spirit to move flowingly, emote sensually, keeping him in tune with the rhythm of the natural order, and is a measure of his mental health.

When the spirit is a part of you, you laugh, you dance, you sing, you love, and make love, celebrating its vital presence, and perhaps, most importantly, you endure. Zora Neale Hurston, revealing Africa's transferrals to black Americans, gave us "High John de Conquer" to explain:

> High John de Conquer came to be a man, and a mighty man at that. But he was not a natural man in the beginning. First off, he was a whisper, a will to hope, a wish to find something worthy of laughter and song. Then the whisper put on flesh. His foot-steps sounded across the world in a low but musical rhythm as if the world he walked on was a singing-drum. The black folks had an irresistible impulse to laugh. High John de Conquer was a man in full, and had come to live and work on the plantations, and all the slave folks knew him in the flesh. The sign of this man was a laugh, and his singing-symbol was a drum-beat. No parading drum-shout like soldiers out for show. It did not call to the feet of those who were fixed to hear it. It was an inside thing to live by. It was sure to be heard when and where the work was hardest, and the lot the most cruel. It helped the slaves endure. They knew that something better was coming. So they laughed in the face of things and sang, "I'm so glad! Trouble don't last always."[20]

Energy is common to all matter, and the African worldview compels us to conceive of life as a spiritual power, an inner power, a force which is present in the movement of the matter that shelters it. This invisible, spiritual force is much more than the energy of matter as manifested in human motion, or movement, it is an energy of the mind. It is involved in one's capacity to remember, to derive meaning from experience, to discriminate among and between sensory stimulation, to work and play inventively and creatively.[21] Whether spoken of as consciousness, spirituality, intelligence, or one's "soul-field," it is the energy or force within man which gives direction and shape to his overt behavior and expressive style.

Taking in man's affinities for judgment, decision, desire, and will, human motivation is affected, in the African mind, by spiritual as well as physical energy. Biology and spirituality converge to form the human being. One does not exist exclusive of the other. The individual can invoke psychological defense mechanisms, such as denial, and rationalization, to suppress or block out of awareness the spiritual component, or the biological component for that matter. Concerning the spiritual component one has only to attend to the unnatural, quieting emotions and reduced spiritual behavior of Western man. Each human being is accompanied by a spiritual self, a double, harnessing the life force. "In every essential being," Jahn states, "there is another essential being: in a man, another little man is sitting all unseen."[22] This "little man" affects operations of the mind, such as judgment, decision, desire, memory, etc., and remains with man always, separated only by the death of the physical body. The inner man, the spiritual double, the rhythm principle, life force, lives on in other men and things.

In man's day-to-day life, the life force is given the beginnings of form in mental perceptions and imagery. Tangibility of form occurs in the creative and artistic expression of such perceptions and imagery, usually through highly contagious, strong emotions. Human motivation, especially in black life and culture, is at the heart of this process.

When does the spiritual life begin in the human being? At conception, the spirit or soul of the child originates, largely, from the spirits of his mother and father. Secondarily, the child receives soul from the family, involving all of his ancestors. Ultimately, the principal part of the personality is "constituted by a 'good' soul of an ancestor who was waiting for the moment of spiritual revitalization in human form."[23] The total personality of the child is composed of a body (biological aspects), a soul (spiritual aspects), and a score of names representative of the ancestral heritage (social aspects). Each of these components expresses a partial view of the self. The self emerges fully from the cooperation and collaboration of the component parts. In this cooperative and collaborative venture, all aspects are made one and are reflected in emotional, aesthetic behavior.

Accounting for certain experiences of the spiritual and invisible, the African searches for concepts to explain the mysteries of life: "breathing, gushing blood, vital growth, beating heart, thought, shadows, an image reflected in the water or in a mirror."[24] This search yields a find in values which make up black culture. The foundations of these values, Senghor explains, are "fundamentally, the sense of communion between the visible and invisible, man, nature, and God; the sense of analogical images, which expresses this communion and finally, the sense of rhythm."[25] Many things contribute to the value base of black culture—priority of group identity (inherent in collective and communal participation) over individual identity; respect for elders (who are closer to that which is divine or spiritual in the universe); acceptance of unseen forces as real, visible elements (i.e., having life, with feelings and intelligence) in the organization of one's behavior; respect for fertility and procreativeness as manifested in praise for generative powers (ability to bring the vital, spiritual force into being)—all combine to create the fabric of black culture and frame black behavior, under the commandership of vital rhythm.

It is the sense of rhythm that gels and expresses human reality. Rhythm, basic, fundamental, synonymous to the life force, is paramount in the black man's self-image as defined in his philosophical conceptions of the world. Rhythm resounds in customs, work, play, war, sex, speech, worship, song, dance, the entirety of life (viewed from the conception of the African principle, "oneness").

Established is an intimate, embryological union between man and the basic forces of the universe, revealing itself most profoundly in man's artistic, creative, and spontaneous renderings. Ben Enwonwu penetrates this union and places black expressiveness appropriately in context:

> Thus the field of so-called African art is really the realm of the ancestral world of images so confined as it were to creativity in a spiritual sense.

> In terms of reference then, African art is not really art in the Western context, but an invocation of ancestral

spirits through giving concrete form or body to them
before they can enter into the human world.[26]

Black art, Senghor said (agreeing with Enwonwu), "is animated by invisible forces that rule the universe."[27] When man is
emotionally affected, the rhythm force increases in intensity on
his being, bringing him in contact with cosmic forces, and man
attempts to give form to these forces in creative and artistic self-
expression. So, in black life, art becomes TRUTH, knowledge and
explanation of the organization, operation, and interplay of forces
responsible for order in the universe.

With regard to rhythm Senghor has advanced a law of African
culture giving full view to its richness:

> It is the architecture of the being, the inner dynamic
> which gives it form, the system of waves which it emits
> to others, the pure expression of the vital force. Rhythm
> is the vibrating shock, the force which, through the
> senses, reaches to the root of our being . . . directing all
> tangible things toward the light of the spirit.[28]

Rhythm endows man with creative power, permitting him ac-
cess to the essence of life—to the seeds of spirituality. Energy
contained in all matter is known to form rhythmic waves that
radiate from all matter, a fact confirmed by physicists. The
world's material, that is all things, are in a constant state of vibra-
tion. They are composed of waves, waves of rhythmic energy.
The black man seeks to be in time with this rhythmic energy, and
when this is achieved, he knows peace, joy, and happiness. It is in
this context that rhythm becomes an instrument of knowledge, in
that blacks only know, convincingly, be it person or object, when
their instincts have seized the waves emanating from the other
who represents the object of knowledge. This poetic line from
Senghor's pen, "Noble must your race be and well-born the
Women of Timbo who rocked you in the evening to the noctur-
nal rhythm of the earth," seems to convey the complete unison of
man with the rhythm of the universe, and the soothing comfort
the union brings.[29]

Rhythm, Francis Beby explains, "is the element that infuses music with a biological force that brings forth a psychological fruit."[30] "Rhythm," he continues, "is an invisible covering that envelops each note or melodic phrase that is destined to speak of the soul or to the soul. . . ."[31] The African tied music to medicine and characterized it as a chain of melodic sounds linking all things. When people heard music, it was believed that the rhythmic sound synchronized the rhythms of the cells in their bodies and minds. Because music was seen as the link to the force of all things, hearing its impelling rhythms placed them in harmony with the rhythms of planets, and other airy bodies, earth, waters, plants, in short, the universe. They thought that this harmony enriched life, giving one abundant health. Through music, biological and psychological forces interact in fruitful ways. This is the message of Francis Beby. They are joined with links of rhythmic waves. No wonder music is such a formidable force in black life and culture, giving the note a foremost place in communication and expressive behavior.

Guided by this knowledge, Beby without reluctance, claimed, ". . . Africans do have a natural sense of rhythm."[32] Whether innately or experientially acquired, their instincts for rhythm have produced a way of being that is clearly distinguishable. Conceptualized in African philosophy and thought, the rhythmic way of being is universally appealing, no doubt it is authentically human, truly the mark of all men's nature.

The poetry of nature is a fitting reference to the essentiality of rhythm. "This music and these pictures of flowing waters, rustling leaves, beating wings, [and] twinkling stars," that Senghor talks about are of nature, and fully poetic.[33] Too, rhythm is the poetry of black flesh. Those who retain at least affinities for the rhythmic vitality of common existence (close to nature) are sensitive to the delicate melting of life, nature, and rhythm that blacks imbue with vivid and striking imagery. Note the force of spirituality, "oneness," and sense of all time, or self-continuity (elements crucial for healthy identity formation), in Gwendolyn Bennett's poem "To a Dark Girl":

> Something of old forgotten queens
> Lurks in the lithe abandon of your walk
> And something of the shackled slave
> Sobs in the *rhythm** of your talk.[34]

The kinship of life and rhythm are plainly apparent in Larry Neal's "For Our Women":

> Black women, timeless,
> are sun breaths
> are crying mothers
> are snatched *rhythms.**[35]

David Diop makes synonymous rhythm, the beginning, and human genes as he extols the life force felt in the sensuous dance of a black woman:

> . . . You are the dance in the naked joy of your smile
> Through the offering of your breasts and your secret power
> You are the dance by the golden legend of wedding nights
> In the new times and the age-old *rhythm** . . .[36]

Rhythm as nourishment for life is assumed in Viriato da Cruz's "Black Mother":

> . . . Through your lap, mother
> Rocking those other people
> spoilt by the voice of tenderness
> and fed on your sustaining milk.
> the good poetry
> . . . of *rhythm**[37]

Sex, defined by psychiatrist Frances Cress Welsing in a speech delivered in Philadelphia, Pennsylvania, at Temple University, as the act of reproducing oneself, is also the clearest expression of the life force. Interchangeably referred to as "love," it is renamed "Rhythm" in the increasingly intense, repetitive urgings of a Roy

* Emphasis ours.

Ayers song styled in the African responsive tradition (solo call
and choral response):

CHORUS	really need your love
SOLO	*Rhythm!**
SOLO AND CHORUS	I need your *Rhythm!**
CHORUS	really need your love
SOLO	*Rhythm!**[38]

Haki Madhabuti sees the rhythm of the universe in black flesh:

> . . . We got motion
> We got motion
> We are the *rhythm** people . . .[39]

Life progresses to death, often an untimely and unnatural one
for blacks. Black survival, having withstood the crudest savagery,
demonstrates that rhythm, like matter, like energy, cannot be de-
stroyed, not even through death, no matter how criminally grue-
some. Death is paradoxically intertwined with life and nature.
Mari Evans' exclamatories are testimonial in "Princeling":

> *Swing sweet rhythm*
>   charcoal toes
> *Swing sweet rhythm*
>   blooddripped knees
> *Swing sweet rhythm*
>   exorcised penis
> *Swing sweet rhythm*
>   My God—my son![40]

The force of oppression is oppositional to, and constantly applies a choke hold on, the rhythm response. The form of rhythm is
so varied, however, that it is only partially negated through
Western assimilation or sometimes through psychological casual-
ties bred by oppression. Rhythm interrupted (the basis of anxi-

---

* Emphasis ours.

ety) by oppression can deny one the attainment of optimal self-
hood, and is seen in Ntozake Shange's poem "Dark Phrases":

> dark phrases of womanhood
> of never havin been a girl
> half-notes scattered
> without *rhythm**. . .
> . . . Sing a black girl's song
> bring her out
> to know herself
> to know you
> but sing her *rhythm** . . .
> . . . Sing her song of life
> she's been dead so long
> she doesn't know the sound
> of her own voice
> her infinite beauty
> she's half-notes scattered
> without *rhythm** . . .[41]

At the essence of man's basic nature, enveloping vital forces,
rhythm is a critical factor in the organization of human behavior.
It is required for the attainment and maintenance of momentary
perfection in human performance, which is the platform for
achieving optimal happiness. To be in rhythm is popularly recognized as a requisite for human efficiency. When a football team
executes each play with precision, a free-throw shooter sinks the
ball consistently, a tennis player serves the first one good, serve
after serve, and the pitcher throws strike after strike, the oppo-
nents know that it is necessary to interrupt, alter, break the
rhythm that allows for the display of human perfection. The
singer sings, the writer writes, the dancer dances, the actor acts,
the speaker speaks, the painter paints, the lover loves BEST
when perfect rhythm is acquired. At such moments, one does not
move in an analytical, step-by-step progression, one *is* the spontaneous, rhythmic unfolding of the progression. One does not try to

---

* Emphasis ours.

do, one happens to be an instrument of the doing. During such moments, nothing is difficult, and there is no anxiety.

So it is with one's inner life. Perfect rhythm brings perfect peace. It brings perfect harmony and joy. And such perfection occurs only during anxiety-free moments.

Why does one lose the rhythm, the ability to be happy, and fall victim to inefficiency, unhealthy gloom and despondency, or ways of coping that subvert a wholesome and natural sense of morality and decency? This question is circumscribed by a larger one, that the majority of counseling and personality theories attempt to answer: WHAT IS THE NATURE OF ANXIETY? Why does man become anxious?

Anxiety is indeed an unpleasant, annoying, and often painful feeling, compelling us to make adjustments, blocking or invoking defense mechanisms of the mind in order to reduce the experience of anxiety. Without rhythm, our behavior becomes artificially adaptive. Having at our disposal psychological defense mechanisms, or coping weapons, human beings can put them into operation so as to adjust without rhythm. But then behavior becomes strained and is characterized by rigidity (bodily and attitudinal). We become inflexible in postural alignments, which is an attempt to curb rhythm sensations. Moreover, thought patterns are characterized by an emphasis on the rational. By ignoring and subduing emotional stimuli, rhythmic signals are averted. Social distance in interpersonal relations becomes a necessary suppressant of emotional behavior and compels gravitation toward a disposition of individualistic independence. Central to the induction of anxiety, such defensive behavior, rational extremity, and individualism are unnatural and are clearly contrary to the rhythmic and collective interdependency of the natural order. The basis for the experience of anxiety is planted in blocking, suppressing, or distorting the waves of rhythm that invisibly subsume us and dominate the universe.

Blocking, suppressing, or distorting the rhythm force leads to overemotionally restrained behavior. In Western man, emotional restriction, a natural way of inducing and maintaining anxiety, usually originates from a supercilious rejection of that which is natural in human behavior and in the universe, like the accept-

ance of invisible forces impacting one's being, like earthy responsiveness and spontaneity, like ecstatic laughter, sensuality and
sexuality, like style, and rich and spirited vernacular, all expressed
in dance, song, drama, painting, poetry, and probably in forms
yet unknown. Black expressiveness encompasses all these and
more, as they serve as vehicles for the dismissal of anxiety.

Anxiety increases in occurrence when the conditions of life
create pressure on the individual. Pressure stifles, and when extreme it freezes rhythm. Anxiety is a consequence of pressure and
is either discharged through creative self-expression or maintained through emotional restriction. It is often hidden from
awareness, however, with the assistance of a Western value position and psychic defenses designed to ward off the sting of anxiety. Moreover, chemical suppressants, or "across-the-counter
drugs," are used to reinforce or take over for the defense mechanisms of the mind.

Pressure on the individual, in the West, stems largely from the
societal style of individualism. It is a practice that pits individuals against each other. Fostered is a focus on the self, ranging
from those characterized by self-rejection, or failure orientations,
to those characterized by narcissistic obsessions, exampled in un-
realistic feelings of loftiness, or superiority complexes. Western
practice awards advantage to individuals based on their aptitudes and physical appearance. Acquiring material possessions
becomes the objective of the individual, a goal with menacing
side effects. Standing out among them is anxiety.

African thought and philosophy disciplines one into the quality
of selflessness, as opposed to the increased selfishness of the West.
The quality of selflessness is necessary for a sense of collectivity.
A collective existence cannot depend upon individual aptitudes
and affinities; rather, it is the collective that protects the individ-
ual from his own faults, shortcomings, and imperfections. Mata
Deren, in her book *Divine Horsemen: The Voodoo Gods of
Haiti*, notes the collective emphasis in black religious worship.

> It [the collective] must provide the generally uncrea-
> tive, often distracted individual with a prescribed move-
> ment and attitude, the very performance of which grad-

ually increases and perhaps inspires him. It must provide the drummer with a beat which will properly unite and pace the proceedings whether or not, as an individual, he might ever have been capable of inventing that beat.[42]

The collective, representing the interdependency or "oneness" emphasis in the African world, supports the individuals, provides for them an optimum measure of personal security, which serves as the most effective antidote to, or killer of, anxiety. Group interdependency, in contrast to individual independence, functions at a supreme level of creativity. By combining the creativity of the individuals who make up the group, the group extends the capacities of its members, conferring upon them grace, knowledge, and an even greater power of self-expression, which expresses the collective.

Invested in the group is a kind of super power that, being stronger than individual members, helps them control their weaknesses as individuals. Therefore individual rascality is restrained by the collective force, minimizing antisocial behavior. What is more, the collective motivates the individual toward worthy endeavors, which contributes to the dynasty of the collective. And yet individuality, as a reflection of personality, is not undermined by collective dominance. Deren confirms:

. . . since one's public behavior is virtually guaranteed and prescribed by the [collective], one's individual idiosyncrasies in personality as a private individual are not understood to threaten the public welfare. There is, in fact, virtually no social inhibition upon private personality and, as a consequence, a group of Haitians is far more "colorful" and diverse than an equivalent group of individuals in our culture; for among us, personal persuasion is directly projected as public policy. . . . And the integrity of the [Western] culture therefore becomes dependent upon a certain standardization on the personal and private levels.[43]

To be different, in a noticeable way, threatens the institutional foundation of Western society, hence the need to curtail the creative force of rhythm. Within black life-styles, particularly where modern individualism does not abound, the individual is freer in self-expression, "since there is no feeling that this idiosyncrasy may be read over into public contexts."[44] Blacks are therefore more in tune with the spiritual domain, the rhythm force, and in turn are more vital, emotional, creative, artistic, expressive, and generally less anxious.

It is the spiritual-intuitive direction of personality that gives perspective to man's emotions and intelligence, which are not aggravated by exhausting anxiety, owing to the degree of security, stability, and quiet certitude that is given by the traditional African community. In a stable, firm universe, where meaning and cause are ascribed (derived from physical and spiritual realities), where the haphazard and unknown do not exist, one could say that the individual is protected by an all-encompassing sense of "knowing" that creates a feeling of freedom—freedom of spirit, inner peace, contentment, relaxation—all oppositional to anxiety.

But the traditional African community has undergone a surgical transformation. Slavery and the take-over of Africa by Europe set off a long history of black subservience to the desires and ways of white people. Forceably imposed upon the African worldview, upon the black mind, were the ideas and ideals of the European. Western conceptions of reality, orchestrated by the principle of individualism, blurred the vision of black people, creating the only possible image of themselves, one against a background of white supremacy domination. It was a background which mirrored reflections unlike themselves, posing conflict deep within the core of their being: Physical objectionableness, cultural backwardness, moral primitiveness, and heathenistic and intellectual incapability, reflections from a mirror fashioned by the white mind. These were forged into ideology and thought from which came theories that paved the way for practices that compel all sensitive human beings to shudder and cringe with utter disbelief.

With oppression came an attack on the values of black behavior, eroding in some instances and forceably transforming in others the philosophical and conceptual aspects of the black mind; and necessarily, to some extent, the flow of rhythm streaming in black veins was coagulated. Anxiety is a natural consequence of an interruption or alteration in an optimally organized rhythm pattern.

Remaining intact, however, particularly among the masses, was vital expression, through which anxious feelings passed. This acted as a restorative agent on the rhythm flow, providing relief for the oppressed soul. But the continuing unhealthy conditions of life created some common mental health problems. Color inferiority, diminished self-esteem, identity conflicts, and other problems generate anxiety states. Fortunately, anxiety stemming from these conditions are, in great measure, dismissed through black expressiveness, or the invocation of rhythm responses. However, in some cases black expressiveness is undermined and suppressed. Attitudes associated with middle-classness, characterized by the suppression of emotion and devaluation of the natural and sensual responsiveness of human beings, serve to stifle the expressive characteristics of many blacks. Yet the features of black responsiveness operate at the base of popular culture and are quite acceptable to Westerners when they become separated from black origins, that is, minus the emotional power which gives momentum to their expression. In effect a veil is created, making these features appear to be of another origin. This way, they seem to be creations of thought devoid of emotional power. However, beneath the veil remains vital black rhythm.

Rhythm is subdued, also, by a sizable class of black people who, most demonstratively, cease to be guided by black/African thought and philosophy. As a reaction to the experience of anxiety, stemming from the white assault on the values, images, and expressive tendencies of black/African man, assimilation into the white world became a common unhealthy adjustment. This adjustment was aimed initially at escaping the blunt wrath of oppression, but it is a way of behaving that favors the emotionally, spiritually dispossessed ways of the West. The assimilated black borrows back his own emotionality after the West bleaches it, attempting to rob it of its obvious origination. But the rhythm colors it in tones of darkness, making its ownership easily recognizable to the world.

Oppression, cast in Western philosophy and thought, places identifiable constrictions on the natural rhythm of man, putting him often at odds and out of phase with the natural rhythm of the universe. Moreover, the philosophy and thought of the West places prominence on behavior that, being artificial, sensually awkward, and rhythmically out of tune, induces stress and anxiety. The restrictions and confinement of the rhythm response leveled by Western thought and philosophy disallows the physical expulsion of stress and anxiety that occurs from free and active expression. Therefore, the behavior of most Westerners approximates the profile of unhealthy behavior, most often labeled as different forms of neurosis. Neuroses, states of mental health most often characterized by unexpressed tension and anxiety, represent a flagrant distortion or interruption of man's natural rhythm, which constantly applies strain on our personalities. A strained personality is one divested of spirit, near emotional death, it is intellectually crippled without the support of requisite affective and psychomotor forces, it is not whole. The personality is in fine order when the flow of rhythm is not dammed by the internalized values or the externalized virulence of the West, in which intellectual addiction and material possessiveness are central.

The West's unnaturalness is appetizingly advertised and breeds black assimilation and disillusionment. The impact on the black mind has been an altering one, shaping it to the alignment of the West's mind. Disillusionment and assimilation are prominent in the current-day mental health problems of black people, and in combination depict the most common strain on optimal ego development or self-development in the black community. We refer to this strain as ALIENATION. Alienation implies a separation from the source, a loss of roots to sustain existence. It is a state of existence that is cut off from the values of the black/African world, having occurred from a forceable interruption of the flow of the essentials that gave reason and purpose to being. It suggests "fear, degradation, disgust, anger—untold states of emotional upheaval," which, all together, deepen the sense of alienation.[45]

In disillusionment, more often the experience of the common man, there is active, vital rhythm, and hence earthy, sensual, emotional expressiveness. But rhythm is sometimes restrained by self-doubt, or it flows uncontrollably, pacing ahead of the natural order as an expression of arrogant indignation to a world that looks on in amused contempt. This arrogant indignation functions to free oneself through violence (self-abuse, and abuse of one's kind), criminality, alcoholism and drug abuse, and immorality, all deriving from the pathos of the West, which is manifested in a burning desire for possession, for material goods, for the trappings of items, objects, and flesh, by any means possible. But in freedom, however gained, rhythm restoratively predominates.

Active rhythm, and brief flashes, deep in the memory, of the traditional African worldview that abides more in black expressiveness than in black thought, allow the majority of the common folk, forceably severed from their roots, to remain closer to the vital forces of the universe. Far more authentic is their art, their style, and their mode of adjustment owing to their closeness to vital forces. Therapeutically, these common folk are enabled, through their expressiveness, to cleanse their spirits, their psyches, of debilitating anxiety, by converting it to song or dance, to strange faces and lines on paper or canvas, and to the production of other art forms, which allows them to enjoy more frequently than others, if only momentarily, anxiety-free states. Feelings of disillusionment are poured out in mournful blues, shouting gospels, inspired spirituals, lively jazz, gusty humor, all combining to give a sensuous rhythm, a rich drama to the burdensome endeavors of life. When degradation colors life, the expressive content can often be hideous and foul. Even so, many times it comes out with a distinctive quality of rhythm, and artful beauty.

Melvin Van Peebles, in his play *Aint Supposed to Die a Natural Death*, captured the pulse of rhythm in disillusionment. He paints a picture in one scene, called "Motherless Old Broadway," a woman yearning, thirsting for love, for someone to hold on to, even a stranger:

HELLO, HELLO, HELLO THERE

A sailor too . . .

Across from a schoolyard with broken basketball rings, "Dee-Dee loves Jack" and a hole kicked in the screen, they set on the skeleton of a car. She likes him. She looks at her husband for the evening and sighs, she realizes already, unlike a lot of folks (sure like everyone else, she wants immortality and she tried more than a few times to get it that way), you can't leave imprints in the sands of time on a piece of poontang. . . . Her bitchy flip brash mask drops away and she looks toward the river. . . . She can't see it but she knows it's that way, all black and oily and wide. People need each other so much. . . .

THE WORLD IS ALL SCABS AND
BROKEN NEEDLES
UNLESS SOMEONE CARES FOR YOU
ANYWAY
WE ONLY LIVE ONCE ANYWAY
YOU KNOW WHAT BALLING IS
IT'S A POOT IN OLD DEATHS
FACE
ISN'T THAT A GIGGLE
I DO LIKE YOU A LOT ANYWAY[46]

Her quest is to be in tune with the rhythm of the universe, to overpower the anxiety inherent in living, and be rendered free through the expression of vital forces stationed in the sensuality of her ways.

Helped by the mirror, "Fatso" lathers his face in another scene from *Aint Supposed to Die a Natural Death*. He wants to be in tune, he longs for the serenity, the harmony that comes from blending with the flow of the universe. But his long gaze in the mirror makes his image linger, and the pace of rhythm flows wildly out of phase; his anxiety flooding, he talks loudly to the person in the mirror:

LOOK AT YOURSELF
YOU BIG UGLY MULE-FACE-MULE
YOU GOT THE NERVE
TO TRY AND CRY
    . . .
DON'T YOU BLINK
YOU LOOK STRAIGHT BACK AT ME
AND YOU GOT THE NERVE
TO HAVE SOME KINDA
CROCODILE TEAR IN YOUR EYE
YOU SURE IS DUMB
AIN'T NO FOOL LIKE AN OLD FOOL
THEY SAY
YOU BETTER BELIEVE IT
MIRROR MIRROR ON THE WALL
YOU EVER SEEN A BIGGER FOOL
    THAN ME[47]

Extracting from the material of his mind, material implanted by the West's crimes against nature, the disillusioned black man sings, with rhythm but a bit out of key, declaring his taste in women:

I don't want no woman
If her hair ain't longer than mine
I say I don't want no woman
If her hair ain't longer than mine
You know she ain't no good for nothing but
trouble
And keep you buying wigs all the time

Yes, you know I carried my wife to the
hairdresser and this is what the hairdresser
said "I stuck that straightner in it,
wig fell off her head."

I don't want no woman
Boy if her hair ain't longer than mine
Yes, you know she ain't no good for nothing
but trouble
And keep you buying wigs all the time . . .[48]*

The disillusioned have as their most common mental health problem diminished self-esteem, or self-rejection, in which color inferiority is principal and, with outrage, echoes the West's disposition. But the common man is not without vital rhythm even in this bold act of self-repudiation, beneath which the beauty of blackness beckons. An excerpt from Joseph Walker's play *The River Niger* is humorous but seriously revealing:

JOHN (To DUDLEY): Why don't we make a little run and leave these black beauties to themselves. To get acquainted—

GRANDMA: Don't be calling me no black nothing. I ain't black! I'm half-full-blooded Cherokee Indian myself. Black folks is "hewers of wood and drawers of water" for their masters. Says so in the Scriptures. I ain't no hewer of no wood myself. I'm a Cherokee aristocrat myself.

JOHN: Go on, Grandma, show us your true Cherokee colors, yes, indeed.

GRANDMA (*She is obviously inebriated—sings at the top of her voice.*):
Onward, Christian soldiers,
Marching on to war,
With the cross of Jesus
Going on before!
(*Begins shouting as if in church.*)
I'm a soldier myself. I ain't no nigger. A soldier of the Lord. I ain't no common nigger. So don't you be calling

me no black nothing. Bless my Jesus. Don't know what
these young folks is coming to, calling everybody black!
I'm going home to see my Jesus.
This little light of mine,
Let it shine, let it shine, oh, let it shine. Do Jesus!
(*Shouting gestures.*)

DUDLEY: What I tell you, Johnny. Crabs in a barrel,
waiting for a hand from Canaan land to lift 'em out.
Each one shoving and pushing, trying to be first to go.
And if Jesus was to put his hand down there, they'd
probably think it belonged to just another nigger crab
and pinch it off.

JOHN: Ain't that poetic. I can just read the headlines:
"Jesus extends his hand to bless his chosen"—'cause we
are the chosen, Dudley—"and a hustling dope addict
takes out his blade and cuts it off at the wrist."

DUDLEY: For the ring on his little finger. Rub-a-dub-
dub, niggers in a tub. Christ extends a helping hand and
(JOHN *joins in and they deliver the end of the line in*
unison) draws back a nub.

MATTIE: WILL YOU TWO PLEASE STOP IT!
(GRANDMA's *still singing.*)
Mama, why don't you go upstairs and take a rest. Ya'll
'bout to drive me crazy.

GRANDMA: My own daughter treats me like a child.
Sending me upstairs. Punishing me 'cause I got the
spirit.
(*Starting for the stairs. Starts singing once again, but in*
a more subdued and soulful manner.)
I know his blood will make me whole.
I know his blood will make me whole.
If I just touch the hem of his garment
I know his blood will make me whole.
(JOHNNY *tries to help her up the stairs.*)

Don't need no help from nobody but Jesus.
(*Starts up steps.*)
I got Minerva and Flora, and Jacob and Jordan—fine
children. Any one of 'em be tickled pink to have me—
tickled pink! I don't have to stay here.

MATTIE: Mama, go lie down for a while.

GRANDMA: And ain't none of 'em black either. Chris-
tian soldiers every last one of 'em. Mattie's the only
black child I ever spawned—my first and last, thank
Jesus.
(GRANDMA *starts up the steps—on the verge of tears.*)
I don't have to stay here—
(*Sings.*)
I ain't got long,
I ain't got long
To stay here.
Ben Brown was black though. Looked like an eclipse—
sho' nuff. Lord, my God, hallelujah and do Jesus—he
was the ace of spades. And a man, afore God, he was a
man—you hear me, Johnny Williams? My man was a
man.[49]

· · ·

He was wild as a pine cone and as savage as a grizzly,
and black! Black as a night what ain't got no moon.
He'd stay out in the woods for days at a time—always
come back with a mess of fish or a sack of rabbits, and
possums—that man could tree a possum like he was a
hound dog. I guess he was so black till they musta
thought he was a shadow, creeping up on 'em.[50]

Joy sprinkles spirited sorrow. With the disillusioned, it is this
way.

In assimilation, a form of reactionary alienation, a constriction
of rhythm occurs; it is more commonly the experience of the
black middle class, whose embodiment caricatures the white
mind. He closes ranks with those who outcast him, he deserts and

disaffects from the disillusioned of his race. Though he knows that the European, forever presented as the model man, at the most authentic levels of his existence despises him. Fine manners and verbal eloquence cannot change the West's conviction that "Negroes are irregardless, niggers." Frantz Fanon has walked the tightrope:

> My blackness was there, dense and indisputable . . . I was walled in; neither my polished manner, my literary knowledge, nor my understanding of the quantum theory mattered. . . . I was repeatedly told about cannibalism, mental backwardness, fetishism, racial defects. . . .[51]

The assimilated personality, though, persists in its own humiliation, its own self-rejection, passed off as refinement in color, that lifts the assimilated into a false sense of loftiness, above their color, above the waves of rhythm, into illusions and delusions of whiteness:

> Quiet
> Pray have I told you or not that you must speak French
> the French of France
> the French of French people
> French French . . .[52]

In this same poem, Leon Damas recalls the ravings of a creole mother with assimilation afflictions, of which artificiality and pretentiousness, the straitjackets of rhythm, are symptoms:

> A banjo
> did you say a banjo
> what do you mean by
> a banjo
> did you honestly say
> a banjo
> No, mister-man

> you ought to know that in this house we allow
> neither ban
> nor jos
> neither gui
> nor tars
> negro people don't do that kind of thing
> leave it to the niggers.[53]

The emotional restraint of the West ironclads nature's pulse—
rhythm—which in turn ironclads one's sensuality, one's motion,
one's sex life, sharply reducing one's natural enjoyment. With
constriction, anxiety infects.

Bertène Juminer's first novel, *Les Bâtards*, as understood by
Randolph Hezekiah, gives an interesting account of the tensions
and anxieties of the assimilated—elite black, whose rhythm
yearns for activation to free him of the West's chains.[54] Cambier,
a mulatto, sports a deep-rooted inferiority complex stemming
from the fact that he does not belong to the white or black group.
He harbors feelings of desertion, of being a traitor to both whites
and blacks. Cambier is overcome with shame and the lack of
confidence when in public with his white girlfriend, Charlotte:

> With Charlotte, he felt like himself only in intimate sur-
> roundings, although their intimacy was not to go be-
> yond a certain point [note the constraints on the rhythm
> response even during intimacy]. In public, he felt a sort
> of inhibition. . . . An absurd sense of shame came over
> him. The acrid atmosphere, the surrounding bustle sud-
> denly weighed heavily upon him. . . . He had to leave,
> escape . . . these people, these witnesses.[55]

> . . . To stroll about almost in broad daylight, in the
> gaze of passers-by, with Charlotte on his arm, gave him
> a stifling feeling [rhythm constricted]. It was pointless
> trying to bury his head in his shoulders, each pedes-
> trian, as if unsure of what he had seen at first, turned
> around to look at them pass by.[56]

. . . This is what his own grandmother used to say. Had
Africa committed such great crimes that she should be
disowned by her own children?[57]

All of the psychological discomforts of Cambier are symptoms
of his confused sense of racial identity, which is a common mental health problem of the assimilated. Cambier's relationship with
Charlotte reflects his struggle to ferret out of his self-doubt, the
basis of inferiority. With Charlotte he found himself impotent, incapable of accepting her offers of herself, despite his own natural
inclination to engage in the sex act with her. With her, his state
of emotional paralysis was escalated, he was without the rhythm,
the vital expressiveness that the aggressive sensuality of the
black/African woman induces.

The anxiety of the assimilated, like that of the European, is
more controlled, less explosive, but far more damning. In achieving optimal mental health (happiness), the assimilated and the
constricted European must first recover or acquire the rhythms of
"niggers," which have been subdued and repressed by defense
mechanisms of the mind. They must dance to the rhythm of
Cesaire's pen, and do:

the break-yoke dance
the jailbreak dance
the it-is-beautiful-and-good-and-lawful-to-be-a-blackman dance[58]

To further illustrate, we present the clinical history of a patient
treated by one of the co-authors several years ago, whose illness
exemplifies the damning effect of assimilation, indeed, of the
West's mind.

Thirty-five at the time she first sought treatment, Mary reflected the radiance of an adolescent girl, slightly contrasting
the accompanying charm that assured the presence of a ripened
woman. She was light-complexioned, with dark, long hair of fine
texture, all of which told of her gene mixture of black and white.
Mary's face, attractively formed, provided a captivating background for her deeply set eyes of a strange brown color. Her nose
and lips, trim, registered impressions of Ethiopian beauties,

though her posture and walking motion were notably aristo-
cratic, oddly conservative, without rhythm, strikingly unlike the
darting of her eyes that hinted at her talent for sly flirtation.

Men had long looked upon her with favor, and stinging desire.
And Mary enjoyed her inaccessibility to those "low-down, common niggers," though admitted repressing fantasies in which she
became sexually excited by the curious, robust maleness of these
plain blacks, a quality not characteristic of men of her class and
standing, or the white men who frequently propositioned her
with added financial enticements. Strangely, but typical of the
assimilated black mind, she was not annoyed or unnecessarily
offended by sexual advances of white men whose regard for her,
evident by the approach, did not surpass that ordinarily accorded
a prostitute.

Her father was a postal worker and her mother a school
teacher. She recalled her ballet classes, but little else that she enjoyed as a child. She didn't have any friends as she was not allowed to play with the mostly poor blacks who populated the
community in which she grew up. Her family was situated in the
community but apparently not a part of the community. Church
attendance, schooling, and what little recreation she enjoyed all
took place in whatever white community was accommodating.

Attending private and parochial schools since the elementary
grades, she held a master's degree in a respectable field of education. Her peers had always been the few middle-class blacks attending school with her and the few whites at her various schools
who accepted her. She had had many painful episodes in her life
as an adult. The first of a pronounced nature occurred when her
husband, a physician, divorced her and married a white woman.
This shattered her. Though she was unquestionably beautiful and
intelligent, she did not have the insight yet to know that a black
woman charading as a white woman does not compete well. It
was a bitter lesson, one from which she did not learn before therapy. Mary blamed the divorce first on their dull sex life, as she
had remained frigid and much of the time he had been impotent
throughout the marriage. Mary finally satisfied herself by believ-
ing that she was not young enough to be considered desirable

anymore, since the white lady the doctor married was far younger.

No longer frigid at the time therapy began, Mary had given in to her girlish fantasies and enjoyed a thrilling and fulfilling sex life with a stable black man of common heritage. "Of course I do not love him," she responded with disbelief to the inquiry. He was not fit for her love, she explained, owing to his social position and appetite. He was her secret lover, hidden from her genteel associates. Naturally when she attended social functions, such as balls and cocktail parties, professional men of class and stature, who intellectually drooled over her, took turns as her escort. Occasionally she tolerated sex with them, exclaiming, however, "it's nothing more than empty boredom."

She came to therapy after experiencing feelings of shocking desperation and panic at her inability to effectively teach and manage her classes in a school located in a low-income, urban black community. She had long known of her inability, but before this critical point she hadn't particularly cared that she was ineffective. It was the presence of a young, ghetto-raised black male in her classes, who had been hired as her aide, that precipitated her attack.

Mack was without formal training beyond high school. After dropping out, he had earned his diploma through evening school attendance. He had a criminal record. He was earthy. His manners approached crudeness and gruffness. Possessing a flair for dress indicative of the "cool and hip," a taste for "rowdy" music, and a great love for soul-food, all complemented with elements of "street" language, Mack was detestable to her sense of refinement and elevation. With all these qualities she deemed unfit, the young man instinctively emerged as a master teacher. The students obeyed him, not her. He got their attention for her. They played, they laughed, with him. They asked, on their own accord, questions of him. But more, they loved him and he loved them. And she could not see either of them worthy of love. She became so anxiety stricken she could not continue work and was given a sick leave.

Mary came to therapy with a bitterness toward blackness. "While driving my car," she reported, "sometimes I try to find music on the radio to suit my taste so I can relax, because I am so tense all the time." And when the dial passed stations playing "that old loud music that niggers like," she found herself whirling the knob, speeding the dial across the band of numbers, away from sounds that horribly disturbed her.

During therapy she learned that her reactions to the music, to her aide, were defensive ones, hiding her real feelings. The sounds of rhythmically inspired music, conjured up images of black sensuality in dance and romance, as did her aide, compelling her body to respond. These were images which violated her twisted sense of decency, and Mary hated herself for wanting to partake of what she called "nigger immorality" but what in actuality were only spiritually provoked rhythm responses, which could be safely sublimated or discharged through feelings of admiration. Admiration is the seed of affection and a prerequisite to the internalization of a new value sentiment.

This music, that poetry, their drama, that dance, this rhythm, which she had despised, became hers as a result of therapy. She learned to laugh with surprise at, and gain an appreciation for, the rich humanity in black expressiveness. She learned to empathize with the woes endured and recognize the gifts shared by all humanity. Eventually, snapping her fingers and singing along, she joined the rhythm of the natural flow of her body's impulses, in harmony with the natural order of universal currents.

All aspects of black expressiveness come to bear on treatment and eventual progress in therapy. Fuller utilizations of feeling, naturalistic attitudes, stylistic renderings, poetic and prosaic vernacular, and motor responsiveness are all employed, as these are the ingredients of technique in our counseling and therapy practices. This therapy we call "psychorhythm." Patients are helped to move through seven stages of growth, from "Alienation" to "Fraternal Love."[59] Self-discovery is the ultimate achievement, which requires the recovery and utilization of rhythm, in connection with the values of the black world. The values allow for the wholesome transmission of the rhythm flow. These are the broad goals of therapy. Involved is a returning, symbolically, to the essence of things, filling in the voids in the mind created through the loss of black/African values, the alienation and confusion of life put upon the individual in the West. These are primary intentions and motives of the counselor/therapist. Individuals are helped to search through themselves to a point of communion with nature, as a result of the therapist's insistence on using that which is natural in the universe as the basis for human conduct. In therapy a "rebirth" is experienced. It is one that links the client to the uninterrupted flow of himself or herself, re-establishing his or her essential connection to the natural order of things, which enables one to flow in rhythm with nature, in rhythm with living things (and in the African world all things live). It is a method that operates on the premise that human beings have a natural rhythm, and that this rhythm is harnessed by their spontaneous and creative arts, which necessarily make up the fabric of our methodology, and are the subject of the next section of this compilation.

Rhythm, the spontaneous, unexpected surprise, the unusual swing that is expressed in song, dance, painting, drama, oratory, poetry, narrative, and the remaining arts, is then vital, and can be used not only for the optimal mental health of the individual, but for the society, the nation, and the world. And it is Africa, and the people of Africa, to which we must turn for models of living, models of therapy, models of learning and instruction that allow for an enduring personal fulfillment and satisfaction, models that vibrate with nature's pulse—rhythm.

PART II

ASPECTS OF BLACK EXPRESSIVENESS

5

WE AIN'T MISBEHAVIN—
IT'S HOW WE GOT OVUH

Depth
of Feeling

. . . the [African] people play, sing, dance with gusto or not at all. The function of the music . . . is to raise both performer and audience far above routine emotion. The sick feel better; the elderly throw away their sticks and dance.

The principle of ecstasy as the result of . . . stimulation is hardly an expression of wild, senseless emotion. It is rather a form of full and deep involvement in life.

John Lovell[1]

Western man has shown a great attraction for the capacity of blacks to express the entire spectrum of human emotions, ranging from the deepest gloom to the infinite heights of exhilaration. But his tendency to borrow the affective aspects of black culture was almost always accompanied by a denial of black humanity, manifested in his scathing cruelty toward blacks. European atrocities in Africa qualify as a madness syndrome. Whatever the category of disorder, it has called upon the full utilization of blacks' capacity for expressiveness, which was absolutely essential to black survival in the New World. Robert Hayden's "Middle Passage" shows, without dimness, the abhorrent cruelty of European perpetrators who seem to be in full possession of untamed vile, and African victims who appear drunk with a "timeless will" propelled by an emotional well whose depths surely extend beyond any capacity to measure. Robert Hayden poetically remembers:

> . . . Sails flashing to the wind like weapons,
> sharks following the moans the fever and the dying;
> horror the corposant and compass rose.
> . . . voyage through death
>   to life upon these shores.
>
> Voyage through death,
>   voyage whose chartings are unlove.
>
> A charnel stench, effluvium of living death
> spreads outward from the hold,
> where the living and the dead, the horribly dying,
> lie interlocked, lie foul with blood and excrement.
>
> > *Deep in the festering hold thy father lies*
> > *the corpse of mercy rots with him,*
> > *rats eat love's rotten gelid eyes*
>
> *But, oh, the living look at you*
> *with human eyes whose suffering accuses you,*
> *whose hatred reaches through the swill of dark*
> *to strike you like a leper's claw.*
>
> *You cannot stare that hatred down*

or chain the fear that stalks the watches
and breathes on you its fetid scorching breath;
cannot kill the deep immortal human wish,
the timeless will.[2]

How blacks survived has been often asked. The "voyage through death" did not end when the slave ships docked at these shores, and an even more commanding question looms. "How are blacks surviving?" In these days of contemporary post-slavery, post-reconstruction, post-Jim Crow, post-depression, post-Harlem Renaissance, post-World War One, Two, post-Martin Luther King, Malcolm X, Amilicar Cabral, Kwame Nkrumah, and on, and on, one cannot declare that the "voyage through death" is an event to be prefixed "post." In fact the question of survival lingers with increasing urgency. Scarred cargo-trademarks of surviving the voyage—are made lucid in Elouise Loftin's smashing lines:

old Black ladies
carryin shopping bags
full of more shoppin bags
memories and dreams
gap their legs
on busses
and say things like
"dont God work in mysterious ways, baby
sweety yours is just startin, sugar"
old Black ladies with wise written
on their faces youth & future
written in their eyes
spread wide open up to me
stretch out their feet
cast down on their legs
and adjust their veins.[3]

How did blacks survive? How are they surviving? Often, black people must have thought that doom was near. So many cries of rage, the screams, moans of helpless women witnessing the persecution of their men and children, feeling that the "lawd" had cursed them with his anger. Frequently registered were the squeals of shrill voices, "Why did yuh take mah man away?" "Mah henry, mah man, oh lawd!"[4]

Several decades ago, St. Clair Drake drafted a portrayal that yet reflects the current-day ghetto. His portrait more than suggests the loitering on the "voyage through death."

> The bedlam of an occasional brawl, the shouted obscenities of street corner "foul mouths," and the whine of police sirens break the monotony of waiting for the number that never "falls," the horses that neither win, place, or show, and the "good job" that never materializes. The insouciant swagger of teenage dropouts masks the hurt of their aimless existence and contrasts sharply with the ragged clothing and dejected demeanor of "skid-row" types who have long since stopped trying to keep up appearances and who escape it all by becoming "winoes." The cheerful rushing about of adults, free from the occupational pressures of the "white world" in which they work, creates an atmosphere of warmth and superficial intimacy which obscures the unpleasant facts of life in the overcrowded rooms behind the doors, the lack of adequate maintenance standards, and the too prevalent vermin and rats.[5]

Clearly the "voyage through death" was/is not without life on these shores. Blacks did and do survive. SURVIVAL? Geneva Smitherman tells us that "getting over" has always been the essence of survival. She saw survival as twofold—spiritual survival in a world of sin, and material survival in a world of white oppression.[6] Material survival was made aggravating by the material greediness and possessiveness of the white world.

Operating from a position of decided unfairness, survival for the black man transposes to a scuffling, hustling, bustling, day-to-day life-style. Reggae artist Bob Marley is graphic in his song entitled "Survival." After questioning the assertion of caring and concern for humanity by the oppressor, in the face of suffering everywhere Marley sings:

> *We're the Survivors; yes, the Black*
> *Survival*
> *Yes we're the survivors like*
> *Daniel out of the Lion's Den*
> *We're the Survivors; yes, the Black Survival*
> *Like Shadrach, Meshach and Abednego*
> *Thrown in the fire but never get burn*
>
> *We're the Survivors, of a Black survival*
> *in the age of technological inhumanity*
> *We're the Survivors, Black survival*
> *Scientific atrocity, we're the survivors.*
> *we got to survive, we got to survive.*[7]

Something distinctively African is at the heart of blacks' ability to survive, their ability to live through the "voyage of death." Already established as the basis of popular culture in the West, it is the ability to feel and express feelings creatively, or through forms touched with artistic sensibilities. We, as many others, have referred to this quality as "soul." Lerone Bennett is descriptive in his conception of "soul," seeing it as the essence of our being, evoking metaphor. Soul emphasizes the feeling involved in the creation of things, the style that defines a man's living, and above all, Bennett believes, soul is "the spirit—a certain way of

feeling, a certain way of being . . . a relaxed and non-competi-
tive approach to being, a complex acceptance of the contra-
dictions of life, a buoyant sadness, a passionate spontaneity, and
a gay sorrow."[8] St. Clair Drake is more illustrative in his description:

> The beat of "gut music" spilling into the street from
> ubiquitous tavern juke boxes and sound of tambourines
> rich harmony behind the crude folk art on the windows
> of storefront churches give auditory confirmation to the
> universal belief that "We Negroes have 'soul.'"[9]

Bennett and St. Clair Drake hint at what we believe to be the
key to black survival of the West's conundrum. Black survival in
the New World is directly related to the stress-reducing characteristics of black expressive behavior. The blacks' repertoire of artistic sensibilities, expressed through a variety of affective forms,
or things and events (music, dance, poetry, narrative, oratory,
movement, graphics, costume, etc.), has served to their mental
and emotional benefit.

Songs were a common form of emotional expression. Like other
art forms, they embodied metaphor (applying Bennett's concep-
tualization), giving shape and dimension to the evocation of the
soul, or spirit, or the rhythm force. These songs and other expressive vehicles are functional, as is black art, in that their utility for
conveying feeling is obvious and numerous in example. Easing
the pain of damaged human spirits and expediting the attainment
of joyous states are noteworthy uses.

During slavery, *songster* was a category of slave employment.
These songsters or singing leaders were paid to instigate singing
by the laborers in order to increase work production upon southern plantations. This practice was common in Haiti also.[10]

Eileen Southern points to another condition of suffering where
songs played a consoling role:

> Singing was for black servicemen not only a recreational
> activity, but a release from the predictable tension in-

volved in fighting a war, particularly one in which the problem of freedom of the race was to be settled.[11]

Those with the skills for leadership in singing have always been sorely needed in the black community, and in a very real but unorthodox way their roles were not unlike those of professionals who provide opportunities for catharsis in counseling and therapy. Note Bobby's role in the family, as captured in Craig Mott's "Folk Song for Langston Hughes":

Isn't it strange how we need each other?
Take my youngest boy Bobby always makin' some fuss.
Playin' guitar and singin' and all that.
Used to takes his plate and go have supper
Out on the front porch. "Robert Franklin can't you ever
eat with your family?" "Now Ma
you know i's courtin' that sunset."
Courtin' a sunset. You ever hear such foolishness?
So we didn't never think that boy was no good.
Paw say: "Sure ain't my side of the family!"
But then one night it snow so bad and everybody
just on edge and getting all upset over little things
when Bobby say for everybody to come on into the big room.
And that boy go to singin' and playin' so good.
Sing this song about the sun, goin' down and
old Man Trouble back up and leave this house right fast
Just like that! And I don't thinks any of us ever
gonna forget the way just how that boy say for
everybody to come on into the big room that night
when it so cold and the wind is callin' us Niggers.[12]

Black aesthetic behavior saturates the common folk community; it is profuse, and it establishes a ready context for emotional catharsis. Among these common folk who leave us this legacy of mental health prescriptions, there was no desire to be white, rather, a sense of good humor prevailed, more often at themselves than not.

Many have noted that blacks endeavor to keep themselves up in spirit through humor. Humor cleanses the heart and keeps it good. If the heart were to weaken, the West's oppression might very well deny black survival. Moreover, from the psychology of the healthy personality we learn that a sense of unhostile humor is a tenet of healthy behavior.

Laughter helped the common folk throw off the burdens of oppression, as in this well-known bit of humorous folklore commonly used among southern blacks: "If you're white, you're right; if you're yellow, you're mellow; if you're brown, stick around; if you're black, get back."

Although the joke is on blacks, forcing laughter at themselves, the laughter eases and makes more tolerable a harsh, cruel reality and thereby becomes the saving grace.

Laughter, a cathartic instrument, serves psychomotor, affective, and cognitive purposes, as do all black aesthetic behaviors. An analysis of the humorous folk idiom just cited should prove revealing. A psychomotor purpose is served by the release of tension through bodily gestures and movement of limbs. An affective purpose is served through the relaxing and humbling of the individual, increasing his capacity for more bountiful living and loving. A cognitive purpose is served through the specification of a hierarchy of racial status, keeping in the forefront of black minds the imperative of survival and the necessity for manipulating the environment to support that end.

Such is the holistic operation of personalities of these common folk, who refuse to be reduced to intellectual zombies void of feeling and rhythm. Spontaneous, artistic gifts are theirs; nonpretentious, they never try to be more than they are, unlike the majority of middle-class blacks who abandon sincere genuineness and freedom of style and expression. Always, with these common folk, there is sufficient resilience to bounce back into what Claude McKay's character Banjo refers to as the "gentle, natural jazz of life," despite the hardships of life that must be daily tackled. Banjo, like Mott's Bobby in "Folk Song for Langston Hughes," strums his instrument, inventing blues-jazz to summon the spirits by way of collective passion that overwhelms those

whose ears receive the "funky" chords. Banjo issues this lyrical
command:

> Shake that thing! That jelly-roll thing! Shake to the loud
> music of life, playing to the primeval sound of life. . . .
> Shake that thing! In the face of the shadow of Death.
> Treacherous land of murderous Death, lurking in sinis-
> ter alleys, where the shadows of Death dance, never-
> theless, to their music of life. Death over there! Life
> over here! Shake down Death and forget his commerce,
> his purpose, his haunting presence in a great shaking
> orgy. Dance down the Death of these days, the Death
> of these ways in shaking that thing. Jungle jazzing,
> Orient wriggling, civilized stepping. Shake that thing!
> Sweet dancing thing of primitive joy, perverse pleasure,
> prostitute ways, many-colored variations of the rhythm,
> savage, barbaric, refined—external rhythm of the myste-
> rious, magical, magnificent—the dance divine of life.
> . . . Oh, Shake That Thing.[13]

By helping to make blacks feel better, the Banjos and Bobbys of
the communities provide them with protective shields that mini-
mize the scars tattooed upon their existence by what appeared to
be a mean world.

These people who aesthetically respond to Banjo and Bobby
with soaring enthusiasm express something characteristically African: emotional intensity dynamiting the New World, blowing it
up, its smithereens timidly reassembling, forming the contour of
the African continent on the entirety of the world's face. This has
been their contribution to health and happiness for the world's
people as well as for themselves. The African presence is universal, streaming through the canals of black humanity journeying
on the "voyage through death" to life upon shores wherever
shores are. A cursory glance at the African heritage, prior to the
voyage, may provide a better understanding of the survival
mechanisms of the so often misunderstood black man of North
America, South America, the West Indies, Asia, Europe, Aus-
tralia, wherever he treads.

There is, without doubt, no people on the face of the earth more naturally affected by the sound of music than the Africans. This was the contention of Richard Jobson. Upon his return from Africa to London in 1623, he published these sentiments in a book entitled *The Golden Trade or a Discovery of the River Gambra and the Golden Trade of the Aethiopians.*[14] Jobson's statement could very well have covered all of the art forms.

Paul Guillaume placed emphasis on sculpture as a primary medium for the expression of the African's aesthetic impulse but advised that there were also many other ways: "Singing of ritual chants, symbolic dancing to the sound of drums, pipe, and stringed instruments, the telling over of marvelous stories of ancestors and the spirits of the forest" were the heritage of every African, passed down, "embroidered" and "slowly recreated by each new generation."[15] Art as a utility in Africa is vivid in Guillaume's remarks.

Without much debate, music is adjudged the principal medium of aesthetic behavior. "Music is the outward and audible manifestation of inward biological functions," Francis Beby suggests.[16] Beby is etching the intricate connection between the physical and metaphysical worlds of the African, placing music in a social role fitting to the visceral and spiritual needs of the individual and his group.

Robert Armstrong has given a more concrete meaning to, and underscored the importance of, the world of feeling that is expressed in the affective form of music. "If we hear a musical composition," Armstrong notes, "which is lyrical, slow, and in a minor key, we are likely to feel a sweet anguish, sorrow, not because those features refer to such an emotional state, but because they indeed constitute the external dimension, indeed equivalents, of the state inevitably invoking it in the sensitive and appropriately cultured-imbued perceptor."[17]

Emotions, sparking aesthetic expressions, are captured and made incarnate in artistic works. These works, or formed artistic sensibilities, have emotions invested in them and provide African people an environmental background for the aesthetic behavior of the collective. As blacks are imbued with the sensitivity and cultural affinity to render them perceptors of the emotions invested in affecting works, such emotions readily transfer to human responses, which reflect the unity of thinking, feeling, and movement. It is this cultural scheme which theories of perceptual psychology have ignored, contributing to the misunderstanding of African-based behavior.

As the minstrel wonder showed, the artistic delights of the African bring to attention the feeling and movement capacities of human experiencing. The thinking capacity is always involved, owing to the unitary or holistic scheme of mental operations that organizes perceptions of African people. Emphasis, however, is given here to the feeling and movement domains in that they are minimized or ignored in Western ways, whereas in black Africa the worlds of feeling and movement abound in expressive practices.

Focusing on the survival utility of music, it is the vitality, which represents the feeling and motor forces, that one finds compelling. Music serves life in all its manifestations. The unborn, the living, and the physically dead are served by music.

The dead, Africans believe, live on, and their music can be heard in the whispers of trees. A Senegalese poet brings us closer to the center of this belief:

> Those who are dead are never gone:
> They are in the brightening Shadow
> And in the thickening Gloom.
> The Dead are not beneath the Earth:
> They are in the quivering Tree,
> They are in the groaning Wood,
> They are in the flowing Water,
> And in still Water,
> They are in the Hut, they're in the Crow.
> The Dead are not dead.[18]

Like those who funeralize in the black tradition of New Orleans, the African confronts death with life's rhythm and music. Tragic moments associated with death are softened by the atti-

tude pictured in the poem, easing the transition from life to af-
terlife.

Music in traditional African society is best seen as the emotional springs that trigger life's quest for "oneness." Beby explains:

> Music is born with each child and accompanies him
> throughout life. Music helps the child triumph in his
> first encounter with death. The symbolic death precedes
> initiation; it is reborn with the child who is now a man
> and it directs his steps along the path of law and order
> that has been laid down by the community.

> On that path, music and truth become one; order and
> rhythm become one.[19]

Because music usually stimulates movement, Nketia states that
musical expression ordinarily occurs in outdoor situations and
takes on the magnitude of public performances. During a musical
performance a special attitude is required of performers and audience. They "are generally not those of restrained, contem-
plative behaviors but more outward and dramatic expressions of
feeling. . . . Music-making is an activity with a dramatic orientation."[20] Appreciation, encouragement, audience responses of
"ululation" and bodily movements are common. Therefore, for
both performer and audience, traditional music brings forth dramatic expression with artistic, social, or religious objectives.[21]

Life is a song, a rhythmic beat. "For women there are recrea-
tional songs, dirges, grinding, pounding, and other domestic
songs, as well as special songs for ceremonies performed by
women or ceremonies which are made the concern of women."[22]
Mens' songs concerned themselves with work, hunting, social
practices, heroic songs, and songs for relaxation. John Lovell in
his book *Black Song* reprints a list given by Elie Siegmeister in
Music and Society:

> Songs by young men to influence young women; songs of
> courtship, challenge, scorn; songs used by mothers to

calm and educate their children, including lullabies,
play songs, song games; songs used by older men to
prepare adolescent boys for manhood; initiation songs,
legends to perpetuate the history and tradition of the
community epics, ballads of famous ancestors; songs
used by religious and hierarchical heads to keep the
community under control; ritual songs to inspire mystery, solemnity, awe, submissiveness; community songs
to arouse common emotions and sense of joint participation; songs used by warriors to arouse courage in battle and to instill fear in the enemy; battle songs, ballads
commemorating past victories, legends of dead heroes;
songs used by priests and doctors to influence nature;
medicine songs, rain songs, bewitching songs, evil songs
to hurt and kill an enemy, good songs to make friends,
arouse love, heal disease; songs by workers to make the
task easier; work songs according to the rhythm of
labor, group songs to synchronize collectively executed
work, team songs in challenge and satire; songs for social occasions; weddings, childbirths, funerals, memorial
services, seasonal holidays, each in its own distinct pattern.[23]

Songs of Africa involve the entire range of human feeling, and
the therapeutic and educational uses are unmistakably clear. In
Roots, Alex Haley provides many excellent examples. He tells of
the African farmers and their sons, some few carrying drums,
preparing for harvesting. Once the work commenced, drummers
walked among them, beating out rhythms to match their movements as everyone joined in singing. Exhilarated farmers would,
now and then, fling their hoes, whirling them up on one drumbeat and catching them on the next. At midday happy shouts of
relief would come as the women and girls, walking single file, also
singing harvest songs, arrived with lunch.[24] Vivid here is the
prevalence of emotion and movement as complements of thought
in the day-to-day activities of African life, while vent is given to
emotional irritants, allowing a disposition of ease and comfort to
predominate the personality.

An intensely emotional capacity, expressed together with the
human capacities for thinking and movement, was the heritage of
every individual of African lineage. Emotionalism is highly valued among African people and rests at the heart of the black folk
tradition in other parts of the world. Every black community
close to its native heritage was equipped with an emotional-spiritual quality that has made possible the task of "getting ovuh," or
surviving the continued difficulties that life in the West poses.
For certain, the black community is separated from its African
roots only by the "Middle Passage." The profusion of emotional
expression, giving rise to a variety of artistic forms, is common to
the black/African experience.

The intimate union between art and man is not a common occurrence outside of Africa, except in those earthy spaces exploding
with the emotional vitality of Africa's descendants. The interactions of art and man are communal undertakings, and individuals
become well-rounded and adjusted from the creative expression
of their emotional sensibility. The expression is not so much from
personal vocation as from the need to fulfill a social mission, one
of spreading joy and happiness, to make life easier, more enjoyable, by bringing relief to weary souls.

During slavery, black "singing accompanied all kinds of work,
whether it consisted of picking cotton, threshing rice, stripping
tobacco, harvesting sugarcane, or doing the endless small jobs on
the plantation, such as cleaning away underbrush or repairing
fences."[25] The music, as in Africa, spirited the work efforts and
summoned the rhythm force of emotions which oiled the coils of
the muscles.

Black performers and audiences of the New World respond
identically to those of Africa. Audience involvement is an aesthetic behavioral sharing not to be found in the performances of
white people, except those inspired by the black presence in the
West. Ortiz Walton encourages us to "imagine a symphony audience snapping its fingers or saying, 'Yeah, baby swing!'"[26] Unlike
musical performers of the black folk tradition, a symphony concert is not a simultaneous and spontaneous sharing of audience
and performer. Rather, it is "a one-way process, i.e., the orchestra

performs for the audience and the only feedback permissible is applause, a quiet stylized form of appreciation, after the performance is completed."[27] Black audience participation, in the forms of verbal approval, verbal commands, hand-clapping, foot-stomping, finger-popping, and other forms, is not only tolerated but is encouraged by the performer and considered a conduit for the flow of the audience's emotional, aesthetic impulses, which in their collective totality form an emotional power that spurs the artist to perform at high achievement levels. It would be well to reason that high achievement for all, in most endeavors, would be enhanced if the collective process was utilized, rather than the individual one that is practiced in the West.

Black survival of the West's purgatory has signaled the flourishing of African culture in the New World. The aesthetic behaviors of common folk are nourished through veins leading straight back to Africa. The presence of African aesthetic behaviors are observed in the common varieties of music and other art forms; in the dramatic emphases in religious practices; in festive and celebrative practices (such as those of the Mardi Gras Indians of New Orleans); in decorative bodily ornamentation—costumes, apparel, hairstyles, etc.; in the submission and obedience to spiritual forces; and in the "call and response" concept (rooted in the performer and "involved-audience" relationships), where themes called by a leader are followed by choral responses of the audience. These observations continue and are numerous and striking.

According to Janheinz Jahn, "The texts of blues follow the African narrative style almost entirely."[28] And John Lovell noted that the rhythms of more than thirty spirituals were likened to songs of the Dahomey people, and many more spirituals were found to have the exact same formal structure of many West African songs.[29]

Lovell also recounts how Geoffrey Gorer traced a dance he observed in Harlem to what he believed to be its original—a dance of Senegalese women.[30] Even the Charleston has been identified as a dance belonging to Africa.[31] Still evident, too, is the tendency to combine dance, drama, instrument, and song in the expression of aesthetic behavior. Dance was a favorite passion of

Africans, and it is vitally present in the New World. Notice the rhythmic bodily movements that are usually present when Afro-Americans of common heritage sing. Ordinarily, a musical-drama will be unveiled, bending and blending with the lyrical sounds of singing.

Instruments are improvised by way of hand-clapping, foot-stomping, or finger-popping when commercial ones are unavailable. Also, the human voice is made to imitate instruments, as in the jazz singing of current-day artists Al Jarreau and Leon Thomas; and instruments are sometimes made to imitate the human voice. It was, no doubt, these types of aesthetic behaviors that prompted an observer to note:

> It is difficult to express the entire character of these Negro ballads by mere musical notes and signs. The odd turns made in the throat . . . seem almost as impossible to place on the score as the singing of birds.[32]

It has been said that blacks can bend the notes with their voices, as they are able to do with instruments. Such is evident in odd sounds that are labeled shrills, cries, falsetto, glissando, vibrato, and melisma, among others.[33] What is of utmost importance is that driving all these African aesthetic responses, now expressed in the New World, is vital emotionalism, which is affected by both physical and spiritual realities, which together represent a broadened concept of reality.

A great many inherited African behaviors manifested themselves, with astounding exactness, in black religious practices. The church atmosphere took on the same dimensions of performer/audience relations. Following scripture and prayer, the preacher moves with a mounting intensity, in an intoxicating cadence, to the heart of his sermon. So responsive is the congregation to this order of service that little time passes before the audience begins exploiting this medium of emotional-aesthetic release (one may surmise that a protocol of behavior conditioning exists here). Something akin to blessed bliss is expressed in the seizurelike attitudes of shouting women, exemplifying what we refer to in contemporary psychology as "peak" experiences.

These experiences include those of a "spiritually possessed" disposition, providing for the individual a high degree of emotional discharge. James Baldwin, in *If Beale Street Could Talk*, provides a lucid sketch:

> Teddy had the tambourine, and this gave the cue to the piano player. He attacked the keyboard like he was beating the brains out of someone he remembered. The church began to rock. And rocked me . . .[34]

Witness the apparent appropriate displacement of anger that Teddy is able to unleash, aesthetically, on the piano rather than on somebody's head, and the emotional build-up ignited by the musical stimuli.

Aesthetic behaviors serve to discharge the body's pent-up hostility and other feelings, through forms which constitute affecting works (music, dance, drama, poetry, narrative, oratory, movement, graphics, costume, etc.). G. E. Lambert quoted Duke Ellington on this point:

> My men and my race are the inspiration for my work. I try to catch the character and mood and feelings of my people. The music of my race is something more than the American idiom. It is the result of our transplantation to American soil and it was our reaction in plantation days to the life we lived. What we could not say openly we expressed in music. The characteristic melancholic music of my race has been forged from the very white heat of our sorrow and from our gropings.[35]

Ellington was, like others of high aesthetic sensibility, without a doubt a therapeutic catalyst forging the minds and the emotional lives of black people sensitive to the black ethos.

The achievement of joyous states is a frequently sought experience. Not only are the states achieved for the sake of joy, an African propensity, but they also insulate blacks against morbid forces of oppressive conditions. Unhealthy depression and gloom —unexpressed, subdued, or repressed—are dissolved, or at least minimized, in the expression of their opposites: joy, happiness, and ecstasy. This can be observed during moments of merrymaking, as blacks seem to forget or lose awareness of their miserable conditions. Applying aspects of contemporary psychology, we know that such emotions as depression and hostility, which stem from anxiety, can be inhibited, blocked, warded off, or overshadowed by a competing, opposite response, such as joy, cheer, or delight. Expression of the relaxing response partially, if not completely, reduces the strength of the connection between the experience of anxiety and the situation, or event, which causes one to feel anxious, depressed, or hostile. In psychology, we refer to this therapeutic principle as reciprocal inhibition, systematic desensitization, or counterconditioning. The African affinity for joy serves to reduce feelings of gloom in spite of the preponderance of oppressive conditions; the condition of suffering invokes a natural coping response. The affinity for joyous responses strengthens or increases the occurrence of the therapeutic principle known as reciprocal inhibition.

Sometimes in the black church or in church-related activities this phenomenon can be noticed. One of the writers attended a black gospel concert in the famous Lincoln Center complex in New York City. The renowned gospel singer James Cleveland was appearing. At the concert a very poised, exquisitely groomed, and attractive young woman was seated nearby with her friend. At the beginning of the recital she sat very quietly; however, as the program progressed she became more animated. Near the end of the program, when James Cleveland slowly and movingly sang "You brought me too far to leave me," the young lady, with raised hands and tears flowing, screamed loudly through much of the song. Then, when Rev. Cleveland's solo ended and the backup choir immediately burst into shouting a swift and highly rhythmic hymn, the young lady leaped to the center aisle and gustily danced for ten minutes. When the choir ended the songs and she stopped dancing, she returned to her seat and said to her companion, "With all my problems, I needed that." An excellent cathartic experience (letting off pent-up emotional energy).

Hymn singing, a method of achieving and expressing feeling states, was a favorite song style of the slaves, arousing all who heard them. According to Eileen Southern, Samuel Mordecia, a local historian of Richmond, Virginia, remarked:

> Many of the negroes, male and female, employed in the factories, have acquired such skills in psalmody and have generally such fine voices, that it is a pleasure to listen to the sacred music with which they beguile the hours of labour. Besides the naturally fine voice and ear for music which seems to have been given to the black race . . . many of the slaves in Richmond have acquired some knowledge of music by note, and may be seen, even in the factories, with their books of psalmody open on the work-bench.[36]

The mundane, sterile, cold aspects and duties of life are enlivened by the expression of black emotionality or aesthetic behavior. The life-giving elements of black emotionality provide warmth, vigor, color, humor, or feeling to a world trapped in thought, logic, and rational processes.

The healing, curative benefits of expressing pent-up feelings have long been known. Expressive avenues were abundant in African reality, finding an outlet in nearly every human activity, and singing remains a favorite expressive outlet of the black community. Martin Delaney's comments in *Blake: or the Huts of America* (1859), about the songs of boatmen, are powerfully touching:

> In the distance, on the levee and in the harbor among the steamers, the songs of the boatmen were incessant. Every few hours landing, loading, and unloading, the glee of these men of sorrow was touchingly appropriate and impressive. . . . If there is any class of men anywhere to be found whose sentiments of song and words of lament are made to reach the sympathies of others, the black slave-boatmen are that class. . . . They are seemingly contented by soothing their sorrows with songs apparently cheerful, but in reality wailing lamentations.[37]

Delaney describes a process of consolation that is well known in black communities all over the world. Our travels throughout the United States, the West Indies, portions of South America, Europe, and Africa bear testament to Delaney's articulations and the fact that this process of comforting the human spirit is one prevalent among people of African origin. The ability to transfer emotions or posit them in affecting works is the basis of psychic uplift in the black community, gained from the unrepressed affinity for the free expression of aesthetic impulses. Expression of these impulses involves the concept of rhythm and, no doubt, keeps blacks in tune with the metaphysical or spiritual forces that dominate African existence.

A frequent sight during our travels was that of blacks performing work tasks in time and in tune to a hum, chant, or explosions of breath ("hanh!"). Feeling, thinking, and movement functions were all commingled in the behavior, revealing the unifying nature of the black expressive style.

Common to the black/African folk community, universally, are paraphernalia that individuals carry around with them, or extensively use, in the case of fixed articles. These include musical instruments (guitars, harmonicas, percussion pieces, horns), radios or recorders, carving tools, sketching pads, and other expressive articles. (It is not an infrequent sight to see black automobile drivers reeling and bobbing to sounds not audible to you, but clearly titillating to the driver observed.) All these form the web of black expression and provide momentary retreats from the agony of troubled existence.

Solomon Northup, a slave whose narratives give us a peek into his psychic survival operations, could not even imagine having to endure the "weariness, and fear, and suffering, and unremitting labor" of slavery in the absence of his violin:

> It was my companion—the friend of my bosom—triumphing loudly when I was joyful, and uttering its soft, melodious consolations when I was sad. Often, at midnight, where sleep had fled affrighted from the cabin, and my soul was disturbed and troubled with the contemplation of my fate, it would sing me a song of

peace. On holy Sabbath days, when an hour or two of leisure was allowed, it would accompany me to some quiet place on the bayou bank, and lifting up its voice, discourse kindly and pleasantly indeed.[38]

We see in Northup's sentiments therapeutic moments that aided his survival, and indeed enriched his living "on these shores."

The Northups, the Bobbys, the Banjos are abundant in current-day black communities, still practicing an African tradition that must be considered self-healing and self-enhancing. Black aesthetic behaviors have long been the primary channel of escape from living conditions that did not support human decency. Curative powers are inherent in the disposition to express, through art forms, one's troubles. The ability of blacks to express their horrors prevented widespread gloom and despondency and effectively sublimated suicidal impulses, impulses which are triggered by excessive depression from which the individual knows no relief.

Blacks, through their expressive capacities, can display behaviors which reveal, as Frederick Douglass observed, at once the highest joy and the deepest sorrow.[39] The expressive behaviors of blacks are driven by emotions, and emotions ride on and out of the behaviors expressed, freeing the body of sensations which impede optimal functioning.

There is something enduring about black affectivity, and it affirms the presence of the "timeless will." An existential notion, "timeless will" contributes to one's capacity to endure, to persist, to prevail against frightening odds; and it seems to be meshed in the belief that the human soul lives after the material reality has expired. Instilled in the black psyche, Smitherman reasons, is "the firm commitment to the triumph of the human spirit over adversity, the certainty that there's a God on high who may not move mountains but will give you strength to climb. . . ."[40]

How blacks got "ovuh" necessitated psychological operations that provided the body with physical release, that freed the soul of disabling emotions. It was made possible by a mental set that included the reality of rhythm forces, soulful experiences, spirit forces, and the like, together referred to as metaphysical reality.

Precepts of the black mind include what is commonly referred to as a "spiritual component," a point on which Naiam Akbar, formerly a professor of psychology at Morehouse College, and others have theorized.[41] It is a world of unseen forces, but forces powerfully felt. Herein lies the womb of gestation for the sharp aesthetic sensibilities of the African. These sensibilities derive their sharpness from the domain of feeling. A full belief in God (spirit forces) calls for a trust in things unknown. Trust is demonstrated in the ability to completely surrender to the demands of God as communicated by way of the feeling sphere of human behavior. "I know he (God) lives, for I feel him moving in my soul" is not an unusual declaration of those sensitive to the other side of physical reality—spiritual reality.

The way of surrender, then, is the route to communication, and therefore contact, with the metaphysical world, and it requires a trust in one's instincts. Emotional freedom is attained through "giving up," or "letting go," which is the way of surrender. Surrender of the self can be viewed on a scale. On one end is the unquestioned acceptance of oneself as a creature of the universe, under the regulation of its laws. On the other end is complete emotional surrender to the forces of the universe, which constitutes "spirit possession." Psychological operations along the scale dictate the degree of affectivity or feeling that is emitted in aesthetic or expressive behavior. The end of the scale characterized by "spirit possession" must be understood in order to more fully understand the black mind and the process of "how blacks got ovuh."

To begin, the body and the satisfaction of bodily senses were condemned by edicts of the European worldview. Austerity was thought to be the most elevated form of life one could live. The African view encouraged full acceptance of the body and bodily drives and endorsed the spiritual link with nature, culminating in unrestrained emotional and bodily dispositions which yielded freedom of expression. Free expression permits feeling states which transcend physical reality, such as the trancelike states experienced during the expression of aesthetic impulses. In these states the highest levels of emotional catharsis occur, making for an anxiety-free or anxiety-minimized condition on return from the trancelike state to an ordinary state of workaday consciousness.

Fortunately, African tradition organizes individuals in such a way as to induce these trancelike states through religious practices and most other celebrative practices. Their transfer to the New World is apparent in the worldwide similarity of black expressiveness. For instance, at Congo Square in New Orleans, drums were rhythmically pounded by drummers at ceremonies to help bring about the trancelike state known as "spirit possession." The repetitive urgings of the drummers, the swelling intensity, would prod one to a voluntary state of emotional surrender. The spirits are seemingly ordered to appear by the narcotizing rhythms of the drums.

Jahn suggests that such surrender "occurs in the African cults, in Haitian Voodoo, in the Cuban santería, in the Jamaican pocomania, in the Brazilian macumba, in the Winti cults of Guiana, and the Negro churches of the United States."[42] Baldwin was profoundly exacting when he, on two occasions, wrote:

On Sunday mornings the women all seemed patient, all the men seemed mighty. While John watched, the Power struck someone, a man or woman; they cried out, a long, wordless crying, and, arms stretched out like wings, they began to shout. Someone moved a chair a little to give them room, the rhythm paused, the singing stopped, only the pounding feet and the clapping hands were heard; then another cry, another dancer; then the tambourines began again, and voices rose again, and the music swept on again, swelled with the Power it held. . . .[43]

The silence in the church ended when Brother Elisha, kneeling near the piano, cried out and fell backward under the power of the Lord. Immediately, two or three others cried out also, and a wind, a forestate of that great downpouring they awaited, swept the church. With this cry, and the echoing cries, the tarry service moved from its first stage of steady murmuring, broken by moans and now and again an isolated cry, into that stage of tears and groaning, of calling aloud and singing. . . .[44]

As Baldwin has shown, in the black church the essential elements of an African seed have been planted and are now woven into the fundamental fabric of conventional black worshipping behavior in the New World.

Gospel, spirituals, jazz, and blues chords seize their listeners, and through exaggerated repetition, which in effect is the physical manipulation of the rhythm force, compel surrender, allowing the dismissal of tension and anxiety, both approaching the trance-like state and while suspended in it. Lovell proves the point of the surrender emphasis in spirituals:

> The possession theme in the Negro spiritual of North America seems a good deal closer to the vigorous dramatic concepts of the Africans. These songs do not describe a pale exercise. When the spirit captures an individual, according to the song, it is a memorable event. The spirit endows the individual with great powers; it transforms him physically and mentally. Expanding his whole role in life and death, the spirit gives the individual new strength, new direction, new motives and occupations, new capacity for wrestling with life, and above all a new sense of grandeur. The spirit sees to it that the natural world cooperates in all these new grand endeavors and performances.[45]

The black minister, choir, entertainer, or situationally emergent leader represents powerful forces in the theatrical gatherings of black people, whether in churches, concert halls, nightclubs, athletic arenas, or on street corners. In communal settings, predilections for spontaneous surrender are nearly always just short of the initiation point. There is only the need for an orchestrator to stir the bubbling rhythms that are held in check by ordinary restraint. When the occasion blooms, collective emotional discharge occurs as in Baldwin's and Lovell's examples.

A concert performance of Gloria Gaynor will further illustrate.

Failing to arouse the audience to its satisfaction, it appeared she might fail as an artist during this performance. Then she announced the last tune, "I Will Survive," and the females in the audience erupted in hysteria, surely and spontaneously aroused by the emotional states captured in the imagery and meaning of the lyrics that spoke so keenly to the black imperative in America, and more immediately to strained love relationships between black men and women, while declaring the indomitable "Will" of the black female. It was a therapeutic moment, a moment of "spirit possession" for thousands with this order of affectional dissatisfaction.

Very probably it was the recognition of relationships between performers and audiences in the black community that prompted Paul Carter Harrison to opine:

> The word "theatre" clearly needs redefinition where Black people are concerned. We call "church" CHURCH, but its spiritual manifestations among Blacks reflect a ceremonial form of worship (despite the mystic constraints of the New Testament) that often seems inspired by a sense of African memory. It is liberating; however temporary, a visceral release is spiritually achieved.[46]

The visceral release about which Harrison speaks invokes visionary experiences (similar to those drugs induce), the release of dormant physical energies through bodily twitching and jerking and other automatic motor responses, and spiritually inspired utterances (similar to what psychoanalytically persuaded psychologists would refer to as free association of unconscious conflicts).

Care needs to be taken here not to make synonymous the inspired utterances of "spirit possession" with free association of unconscious material. Remember that the concept of unconscious motives was founded on the Euro-societal idea of body rejection and suppression of the basic human impulses and drives, which compels censorship of these in the mind. This involves a distortion of the natural emission of human drives and impulses which have to be denied awareness and therefore occupy an area of the mind designated as the unconscious. To maintain the unconscious, which constantly threatens the conscious mind, necessitates an arsenal of defense mechanisms. These are designed to ward off anxiety stemming from the hidden or censored psychological material. These materials are freely emitted through utterances and bodily gestures when the defense mechanisms have been successfully lifted or slackened. This can be made to occur by using such methods as hypnosis, chemical injections, or other psychological surrender induction methods such as free association.

Recall that the Afro-societal ideal requires full acceptance of the body and its basic impulses and drives, as these represent God's creations and are therefore good. Moreover, communal living, which relied upon oral communication and active memory for articulating individual, family, tribal, and clan histories and other relevant societal matters for community maintenance and governance, made it necessary to be minutely intimate regarding the day-to-day details of community life. Beyond this, without human activity being dichotomized into sacred and secular schemes, afflictions of guilt regarding the body's natural drives were unlikely.

This kind of life-style fosters truth and order, in rhythm with nature, which gives the individual a genuine quality of honesty and sincerity, suggesting that the African's personality is not likely to incorporate a massive unconscious component to serve as a storehouse for unacceptable impulses and behaviors that have violated some sacred or moral ethic. The individual is oriented toward truth as it is perceived. The predisposition for truthfulness is a direct outcome of trusting in things unknown, or in one's instincts.

The closest parallel of this orientation in European societies rests, perhaps, in the ways of children, who have not sufficiently matured to have established in their psychic structures distinctly demarcated unconscious regions of the mind. Even Europeans agree that children have healthier personalities. But considering Freud's dominance in Western psychological thought, children are further seen as creatures with an inherent evil capacity (which is thought to be the mark of all mankind, in the West's psychology) who must be morally shaped and given direction by the civilizing elements of society (churches, civic and fraternal societies, schools, etc.), or at best as reverent, savored protoplasm with only potential for good or evil. So in America and other parts of the Western world, the period of childhood is one of incubation for the contaminants of civilization. These same children will express themselves in adult life as carefully transformed experts of pretense and artificiality, far short of their once healthy personality status.

The African view stresses that the child is a messenger of God —presented in the image of God—pure and perfect. The child is related to everything in the universe that is growing, becoming, or entering maturity. Through limitless analogies the child is integrated into the universe, becoming a cosmic symbol linked to spiritual forces and therefore worthy of emulation in many of his or her spiritually transformed states.[47] One must remember, too, that the overriding dicta of Christianity are closer in keeping with the African disposition, with respect to the profile of man that is biblically prescribed. Consider the book of Matthew, Chapter 18, verses 1–4:

> At that time the disciples came to Jesus, saying "Who is the greatest in the kingdom of heaven?" And calling to him a child, he put him in the midst of them, and said, "Truly, I say to you, unless you turn and become like children, you will never enter the kingdom of heaven. Whoever humbles himself like this child, he is the greatest in the kingdom of heaven."

This view of childhood is in closer agreement with the African conception than it is with that of the European.

Observe the gospel genius of Danniebelle Hall as she fashions the same biblical passage into a song that illumines the African way and the healthy personality:

A little child will trust you
He will believe in what you say
He is honest and he hasn't learned the games that grown-ups
  play

He won't pretend to be your friend
And laugh when you're not around
Or wait until you leave
And then begin to put you down.
And when they asked him
Who's going to be the greatest in the kingdom
Jesus brought a little child for them to see
And if you really want to be the greatest in the kingdom
Then like this child you got to be.

A little child is lowly
Not much does he require
The simple thing can satisfy
His longings and desires
He's so in touch with what is beautiful and pure
And if he knows he has your love
He'll always feel secure
A little child is loving
That's just the way he lives
And he can't hold a grudge for long
He's willing to forgive

TRUSTING, LOWLY, LOVING, FORGIVING, is the key
To enter into God's kingdom
Like a child you must be.[48]*

Humility, loving, and forgiving invariably involve trust. These human traits belong to the dominion of feeling and are essential dimensions of the healthy personality. The ability to trust begins with an unconditional acceptance of nature and natural processes. These include the human body and bodily drives and impulses. Remember, trusting one's feelings and instincts can be seen on a scaled incline, beginning with unconditional acceptance of self and reaching the realm of infinity in "spirit possession." Africa has passed on a conceptual way of knowing or experiencing the universe that is critical to survival. It involves intuitive knowing,

* Like a Child" by Danniebelle Hall. Copyright © 1976 by Lexicon Music, Inc. ASCAP. All rights reserved. International copyright secured. Used by Special Permission.

or affectively derived knowledge, triggered by both physical and spiritual realities, and is expressed with rhythm in affecting works and ceremonies through which stress, anxiety, frustration, and other irritants exit the body to be replaced by the experience of joy, happiness, bliss, ecstasy, or other satisfying emotions. Such a capacity makes blacks a remarkably special people.

Armed with their spirituals, their jazz, their blues, their ditties, their dirges—their *feelings*—blacks have survived possibly the cruelest treatment ever accorded a family of mankind. While surviving, blacks have enriched the planet; the curative, healing, or therapeutic aspects of their cultural art forms cannot be overly stressed.

A perceptive grasp of the purposes inherent in the spirituals should reveal their therapeutic aspects. Lovell cites these:

1. To give the community a true, valid, and useful song.
2. To keep the community invigorated.
3. To inspire the uninspired individual.
4. To enable the group to face its problems.
5. To comment on the slave situation.
6. To stir each member to personal solutions and to a sense of belonging in the midst of a confusing and terrifying world.
7. To provide a code language for emergency use.[49]

Providing a code language for "emergency use" is a striking example of how black intelligence (as it is narrowly defined) is organized by feelings and oriented toward the survival imperative. A relevant concept of intelligence for blacks reflects the three principal domains of human behavior—movement, feeling, and thinking. Moreover, both physical and metaphysical realities must be taken into consideration. Frederick Douglass is enlightening in this regard, as he emphasizes several aspects of the spirituals that augmented survival:

We were, at times, remarkably buoyant, singing hymns and making joyous exclamation, almost as triumphant in their tone as if we had reached a land of freedom and

safety. A keen observer might have detected in our repeated singing of
    "O Canaan, sweet Canaan,
    I am bound for the land of Canaan,"
Something more than a hope of reaching heaven. We
meant to reach the north—and the north was our
Canaan.[50]

In this light, the spirituals cast a reflection that shows artistic
and intellectual genius. To construct a song to carry the bitterest
of sorrows without making known in regular words the depth of
the sorrow is ingenious. It is a masterful feat to carefully veil in
biblical images, in the intonation of moans, the true nature of
one's unuttered grief. This can be nothing less than collective intellectual giftedness, which inspires high achievement by individual members when supported by the collective intelligence of the
group in which one holds membership.

The blues, no less than the spirituals, represent a form of social,
aesthetic therapy. The motivations, attitudes, interests, conflicts,
and other emotionally and intellectually based concepts of psychological thought, as they pertain to black people, are constantly presented in blues lyrics. Included are life's hardships,
sexuality, loneliness, boasting, rebellion against oppression, love
relationships (affirmation of love, infidelity, suspicion, jealousy,
reconciliation, lauding the looks and ways of one's lover, etc.),
mystical practices, stimulants, gambling . . . the list is endless.
The blues thus constitute a musical form that allows for the aesthetic and therapeutic expression of one's innermost feelings,
ranging from throbbing pain to spirited joy. Oftentimes, these
two opposing feelings are conveyed together. We have already
shown a method of reducing anxiety that operates on the basis of
expressing together, or in close proximity, two opposing feelings.
What Douglass said of spirituals is also applicable to blues. Ortiz
Walton discusses the capacity for expressing contradictory feelings or forces in song:

It is a music of this earth and of all its paradoxes, where
both its joys and pains are synthesized and resolved into

an emotional-spiritual unity that help make possible life's continuance.[51]

Walton's statement "help make possible life's continuance" translates in psychological terms to a reduction in the anxiety response. Anxiety leads to the experience of painful emotions. The difference here is that the relief gained comes from naturally emitted, African-inspired aesthetic behaviors, intensely expressed while approaching the world of spiritual forces. On return from nearness to metaphysical reality, one suddenly discovers that much, if not all, misery is replaced by a sense of ease. A bluesman muses:

> It's a lot of times we can get worried and dissatisfied, and we can get to singing the blues and if we can play music and play the blues we may play the blues for a while until we get kind of pacified. That cuts off a lot of worry. . . .[52]

And as the bluesman further points out, persons in the audience might be struck by a tune that tells something of what they are going through, and these persons will also experience emotional relief resulting from the special dynamics of the audience/performer relationship, those African tendencies of collective and communal participation. It is the force or power in the collective emotional ceremony, on approach to "spirit possession," that expels annoying irritants of the body.

Ralph Ellison, referring to the blues, offered an inviting view calling it "an impulse to keep the painful details and episodes of a brutal experience alive in one's aching consciousness, to finger its jagged grain, and to transcend it, not by the consolation of philosophy, but by squeezing from it a near-tragic, near-comic lyricism.[53] Gil Scott-Heron more fully explains:

The blues grew up in . . . the singing of Bessie, of Billie, of Mom
The blues grew up in Satchmo's horn, on Duke's piano,
     in Langston's poetry, on Robeson's baritone
The point is that the Blues is grown.[54]

In the face of calamity, misfortune, and pain, the blues lift the collective burdens of the common folk and replaces feelings of helplessness with powers of endurance, making tolerable the incapacity to solve life's perplexing problems. B. B. King's rendition of "Chains and Things" is more persuasive. Sorrowfully, he sings:

> *Woke up this morning*
> *After another one of those crazy dreams*
> *Oh nothing is going right this morning*
> *The whole world is wrong it seems*
> *Oh I guess it's the chains that bind me*
> *I can't shake a loose these chains and things . . .*[55]*

Even in the "Chains and Things" blacks have survived.

Jazz, sometimes referred to as the only true American art form developed in this country, beats out chords all over the world, sounding the bell of African tones. Like the blues and spirituals, jazz has played a therapeutic role in the lives of downtrodden blacks. Each of these musical forms affects the community on both individual and group levels, but jazz has been credited with performing a catalyzing role in resolving interracial conflicts arising from tensions of identity confusion.

The very birth of jazz in New Orleans, claims Walton, rather than in another city of similar density, is not accidental.[56] The social structure consisted of the original citizens, native Americans, settled Spanish, French, Africans, and vestiges of other immigrant groups, all marking the city with their distinctiveness. Through intermarriage and sexual intermingling, the "Creole" was spawned, bearing the dominance and perceived stigma of Africa. It was common practice for white males to possess, in addition to their own families, two or more black concubines.[57] Children born to mothers of different races bore striking resemblances, owing to common paternity. This situation provoked a mania regarding racial identification. Walton's instructive point is that "this biological integration, coupled with massive foreign immigration, led to intense competition and group identity crises. Jazz helped to create a sense of common cultural identity and up-lift of morale in Afro-American communities where conditions had been made ripe for intragroup conflict."[58] What Walton has shown is that black expressiveness, through jazz and other forms, has healing powers that go beyond the relief of individual unhappiness. Rather, they can be counted upon to ease tensions between different racial groups by providing for them a common basis for making sense out of the space that keeps them apart. This has been the achievement of black expressiveness as a dominant ingredient of American popular culture, minimizing strife through shared enjoyment.

Jazz bears an unorthodox image that is like the life circumstances of blacks in America and throughout the Western world. Richard Wright captured the pulse of paradox in jazz and in the lives of black people when he penned:

> Blues-Jazz was the scornful gesture of men turned ecstatic in their state of rejection; it was the musical language of the satisfiedly amoral, the boastings of the contentedly lawless, the recreation of the innocently criminal.[59]

Jazz, accused of being vulgarly obscene, sexually promiscuous, and morally decadent, carries the image of the black man in the New World. And blacks, with their jazz, in spite of their violated and slandered images, have a popular mission to perform. That mission is to spread joy all over the world. People who indulge in merriment (laughing, dancing, singing), lurking in holy and unholy places, are far richer than persons who do not. Langston Hughes, the eminent black poet, fully grasped jazz's mission when he referred to it as "the eternal . . . tom-tom of revolt against weariness in a white world, a world of subway trains and work, work, work, the tom-tom of joy and laughter, and pain swallowed in a smile."[60]

So it is with jazz, a creation of black people that stands on its own beside black people, both as paradoxes made simple, easy and free, warming the coldness of a world with too little passion.

The African source has, without doubt, Africanized the Americas and Americans, as it has other parts of the world. On this point, Lovell sheds more light:

> To the African, singing and dancing are the breath of the soul. No matter where he goes or what kind of life he is forced to live, these two things he will do; and basically in an African way. . . . The literature of the past three hundred years is filled with expositions, descriptions, narrations, and dramatizations of the way in which the African imposed his singing, his dancing, and his instrumentalizing upon the people of the New World. According to this literature, in most instances it was sheer imposition. Very few peoples matched the African in his high estimate of music as a weapon for living. Very few peoples approach the African in the vigor and dynamics of his music. Thus, when he went into a new area, even when he was dragged into it, his musical domination was in great contrast to his social and political subserviency.[61]

This has resulted, primarily, from the special ability of black people, which infuses both physical and spiritual realities, to convert traumatic feelings arising from oppression to comforting and consoling feelings in the form of affecting works, artistic productions of "beautiful things."

Enlarging the significance of this ability, the "beautiful things" contain health-inducing properties. Martha Cobbs was insightful when she proclaimed that "out of the encounter [with oppression] have emerged the trauma of a black skin in a white world, the culture of black survival, and the influence of black aesthetics acting in and on Western civilization."[62] Her insight also asserted:

> Whether the experience has produced spiritual and jazz in North America or santeria and the rumba in Spanish America; whether protest and rebellion produced the underground railroad or the cimarron community; and

whether black aesthetics flowered in the Harlem
Renaissance, French Negritude, or the Afro-Cuban
movement and poesianegra; the roots have been profoundly similar because each within its distinctive character represents the African source from which it
originated.[63]

While the spirit of Africa has transformed Western civilization,
it should be re-emphasized that this transformation has moved the
West closer to its potential for humanness.

The irony in all this is that segments of the black population,
owing to the trauma of oppression, have abandoned the African
ethos and have grafted on the profile of less healthy behavior,
while white cultural entrepreneurs steal black culture for their
own commercial benefit. James Weldon Johnson's statement is
still true:

> There are a great many colored people who are
> ashamed of the cake-walk, but I think they ought to be
> proud of it. It is my opinion that colored people of this
> country have done . . . things which refute the oft-ad-
> vanced theory that they are an absolutely inferior race,
> which demonstrate that they have originality and artis-
> tic conception, and, what is more, the power of creating
> that which can influence and appeal universally. . . .
> The intricate cake-walk steps have taken up the time of
> European royalty and nobility.[64]

Harold Cruse underscored Johnson's statement when he remarked that "the Negro has turned his back on his own native
American dance forms and refused to cultivate them—he the creator of all American popular dance forms from the foxtrot to the
twist."[65] Cruse's remarks can be updated to include the "disco
craze" and all of the popular "crazes" which will follow. What we
see is that black dance, emerging from spiritually inspired motor
responses to aesthetic stimuli (as seen in African tribal life, black
churches, voodoo rituals, secular places of relaxation), has grown
to a Western mode of enjoyment and catharsis, with multiethnic
and multiracial meanings.

During every black creative era, from slavery to our contemporary times, whites have taken careful notice of black aesthetic behavior and then imitated it, making themselves financial heirs to black creativity. The minstrel songs, we have seen, represented an early example of cultural piracy. The American public, upon becoming acquainted with these black melodies, demanded more of them, and many a white writer responded to the demand, infusing the music with remnants of his own ethnic peculiarity. But black aesthetic sensibility was the creative force behind what became an American musical form. J. Kennard focused the point in 1845:

> Who are our true rulers? The negro poets, to be sure. Do they not set fashion, and give laws to the public taste? Let one of them, in the swamp of Carolina, compose a new song, and it no sooner reaches the ear of the white amateur, than it is written down, amended (that is, almost spoilt), printed, and then put onto a course of rapid dissemination, to cease only with the utmost bounds of Anglo-Saxondom, perhaps with the world. Meanwhile, the poor author digs away with his hoe, utterly ignorant of his greatness.[66]

Ragtime fared a similar fate. Commenting on the music of Scott Joplin, a publication of the Toronto Ragtime Society commented that "many had tried to copy Joplin with little enough success."[67] A young white man, Joseph Lamb, was best, and his musical career led to the same conclusion that Walton has drawn: "Classical ragtime, though of Negro origin, had become with Joplin a music for all America."[68]

What Joplin is to ragtime, William Christopher Handy is to the blues. The Memphis blues created a force, emanating from emotional combustion, upon its first presentation to the public during campaign activities for a mayoral election in Memphis, Tennessee. It has been written that "once the playing began," the spectators and Handy's band "went"![69] There was dancing in the streets and in the offices. Whites picked up the intoxicating beat, and clerical staff were said to have danced with their bosses.

Handy was invoking what whites may view as pandemonium, but it was only the African phenomenon of "spirit possession" affirming its presence in the West. After "St. Louis Blues" was published, the blues became the world's music, adopted and adapted everywhere, constituting a conveyor, or a form for feeling states, for the achievement of "spirit possession." And yes, white folks, with Handy's blues and Joplin's rag and Waller's jazz and JuJu's dance and Ellington's swing, went and got the spirit, and had their oppressive vileness toned down by black expressiveness, or what had become American popular culture.

The acceptance and use of these black aesthetic behaviors by whites was not without reluctance. Accompanying the attraction for such behaviors there was a psychologically necessary repulsion. Ambivalence became the state subdued by vital African aesthetic sensibility. An editorial from the *Musical Courier* in 1899 read:

> Society has decreed that ragtime and cake-walking are the things, and one reads with amazement and disgust of historical and aristocratic names joining in this sex dance, for the cake is nothing but an African dance du ventre, a milder edition of African orgies.[70]

The dances of Congo Square, New Orleans, were prohibited. One must recall that these spiritually pulsating dances demanded body movements in the area of the hips, with fertility meanings in the African tradition. The threat that these aesthetic behaviors presented rests in the historical alienation of the European from his body and bodily drives. These dances compelled whites to confront primitive drives within themselves that had been ruled objectionable to their cultural ego-ideal and warped sense of decency. Moreover, there was undoubtedly a seething resentment for having to rely upon a racially excluded class to feed the starvation for aesthetic stimulation.

Black aesthetic sensibilities could be accepted with less conflict if they were "white-washed" and made to appear as if they belonged to a European tradition. Because of the interplay of racism and psychological repression, imitators of Fats Waller, of

Jelly Roll Morton, of Chuck Berry, of Muddy Waters, of James Brown, of Howling Wolf, are crowned "King and Queen," embellishing the given names of Paul Whiteman, Benny Goodman, the Beatles, Elvis Presley, Janice Joplin, "Wolfman" Jack, and the like, who simply bear needle marks of an injected black style. Eileen Southern quoted from Don Heckman who, writing in the summer 1969 issue of *Broadcast Music,* came within the coverage of this point when he stated:

> To say that the Beatles were influenced by Chuck Berry, that the Rolling Stones listen carefully to Muddy Waters, that Eric Clapton and Mike Bloomfield know the work of Sonny Boy Williamson, is to state the obvious. The influence of rhythm and blues in the 1960's has come in a series of impressive waves from the earliest rhythmically primitive Beatles recording to the recent arrival of albino bluesman Johnny Winters. There is no sign that the influences will diminish, as the recent wave of blues-infused groups—both English and American—makes clear.[71]

John Lennon, slain former Beatle, whose pop music brought him and the Beatles extraordinary popularity and wealth, credited black rhythm and blues artists for his fame and fortune. However, the white press and scholars on American popular culture continue to ignore or underemphasize this fact. Upon Lennon's tragic death, the press and popular media gave wide coverage of his life, including his rise to musical fame. None we reviewed, including those of prestigious stature, mentioned the primacy of black emotionalism, spontaneity and rhythm as the bases of Lennon's and the Beatles' popular appeal.

In a *Jet* magazine cover story of October 26, 1974, and reprinted in a later issue following Lennon's death, he said the second most profound experience in all of his life was when he first heard black music. He insisted that every popular white group had been influenced by black artists. "I'm still based in black music," Lennon stated, and added, "I still feel it. To me nothing has really happened to me since 1958 when I heard black rock and roll . . . That changed my life completely."[72] According to

Lennon he dropped his art classes, dropped out of school, he dropped everything. "I got me a guitar," he said, "and that was the end of it. So black music was my life and still is."[73]

But the element of riddle in all of this, Cruse points out, is that Europeans in America have nothing in their "Native American tradition that is aesthetically and culturally original, except that which derives from the Negro presence."[74] And, African given, black American indigenous music is "the aesthetic ingredient, the cultural materials, the wealth exploited by white American cultural imperialism."[75]

It is a situation that has produced feelings of chagrin among black artists. Charlie Mingus, seeking just recognition and reward for his talent, retorted, "It's the American Negro's tradition, it's his music. White people don't have a right to play it, it's colored folk music. . . . You had your Shakespeare, and Marx, and Einstein and Jesus Christ and Guy Lombardo but we came up with jazz, don't forget it, and all the pop music in the world today is from that primary cause."[76] Thelonious Monk was on the same rhythm with Mingus when he talked about the way white dance bands "had carried off the healthiest child of Negro Music, and starved it of its spirit until its parents no longer recognized it."[77] In response, blacks began to "bend" notes, as in bird chirps, so as to safeguard their aesthetic sensibility. "We'll develop something new!" Monk exclaims, "something they can't play."[78] Gil Scott-Heron, the musician/"bluesician," was no less adamant in "Bicentennial Blues":

[The blues has been] ripped off like donated moments from the
     past 200 years
Ripped off like the Indians
Ripped off like jazz
Ripped off like nature
Ripped off like Christmas
Man handled by media over-kill
. . . violated by commercial corporations
It's a bicentennial year
It's a bicentennial blues
And America has got the blues.[79]

Ellington summed it up best. Registering protest against white exploitation of black creativity, he referred to his own band as "The Famous Duke Ellington Orchestra"; and then striking a dissonant chord at the piano, he pointed out: "That's the Negro's life, hear that chord. That's us. Dissonance is our way of life in America. We are something apart, yet an integral part."[80]

Through their aesthetic sensibilities, blacks have survived the cruelty of the West, and have contributed to its moral, spiritual, and aesthetic uplifting. More than that, blacks have packed America, indeed the world, with an emotive style loaded with healing power. Though our society boils in its neurotic afflictions, it would be far worse off were it not for the creative and curative forces of Africa beating in the pulse of Western civilization. The "original man," as the African is often called, clearly has a monopoly on originality that makes use of aesthetic sensibility. It is only he who can claim a surplus of health-releasing properties such as spontaneity, colorfulness, rhythm, and FEELING.

Those of African heritage who have abandoned the African ethos appear to make up the majority of blacks who are suffering, increasingly, stress-related illnesses, and are causing the alarming increase in the rate of black suicide. The woes could very well be outgrowths of increasing assimilation of blacks and the concurrent suppression or "watering-down" of the healthy ability to express feelings beautifully. Few could be more persuasive than Langston Hughes in urging blacks to rejoice in "their own beauty":

> Let the blaring Negro jazz bands and the bellowing voice of Bessie Smith singing blues penetrate the closed ears of the colored intellectuals until they listen and perhaps understand. Let Paul Robeson singing "Water Boy" and Rudolph Fisher writing about the streets of Harlem, and Jean Toomer holding the heart of Georgia in his hands, and Aaron Douglas drawing strange black fantasies cause the smug Negro middle class to turn from their white, respectable, ordinary books and papers to catch a glimmer of their own beauty. . . .[81]

And in the well-known rejoicing words of the black folk community, SING:

Done got ovuh
sooooh glad
Done got ovuh
sooooh glad
Done got ovuh
sooooh glad
Done got ovuh
sooooh glad
Done got ovuh

I done got ovuh at last!!!

6

SWEET AS FUNK CAN BE

Naturalistic Attitudes

. . . [Blacks'] dark skin and tropical habitat fixed for many generations the delusion [in the minds of whites] that they were . . . an essentially dirty and smelly people.

The idea of the allegedly distinct smell of black people has fused with their unmistakable skin color into this potent white fantasy. . . . The question of immense importance is this: why should whites blow up what is at all odds one of the most objectively insignificant qualities of a human being into a massive . . . justified fantasy, the very condition of human disgust?

Joel Kovel[1]

The Dells, on their album *Sweet As Funk Can Be*, recite in modulated rhythms:

> *Say Man!*
> *Can you tell me what is funky*
> *Well uh!*
> *Funky used to be fonkey*
> *and that kind rhyme with hon/donkey*
>
> *Is that right!*
> *Then the word got changed*
> *and the scene was rearranged . . .*
>
> *Is that right!*
> *. . . But funk can swing*
> *Funk is on the case*
> *Funk is out in space . . .*
> *Funk can be sweet.*
>
> *I repeat*
> *Funk can be sweeeeeet!*
> *Now that we've taken it back*[2]

Living close to nature, root black people have inherited and maintained a disposition of comfort with nature and natural processes. In mainstream culture, dirt or earth (the womb of nature) is psychologically analogous to "funk," or anything that can pass out of the body. Emerging from the analogy is a view of the body as objectionably befouled. The West is repulsed by the natural excretions and protectives that the body forms. As one of Toni Morrison's characters notes in *The Bluest Eyes*, Westerners are disquieted by the natural scents of the body, of breath; "the sight of dried matter in the corner of the eye, decayed or missing teeth, ear wax, blackheads, moles, blisters, skin crust . . . ,"[3] mars the body and diminishes its acceptability. Sweat, tears, mucus, pus, equalizes in the West's mind to the color black, offensively "funky," abominable to the West's sense of cleanliness. All of the mentioned offenders can be cleaned away or artificially replaced, except the color black, allowing Westerners to realize semiredemptive relief from their poisonous view of the body. A neurotic striving forces its way into their search for sanctity from themselves, one that is passed on to middle-class blacks. Morrison's description is more applicable:

> The careful development of thrift, patience, high morals, and good manners. In short, how to get rid of the funkiness. The dreadful funkiness of passion, the funkiness of nature, the funkiness of the wide range of human emotion. Wherever it erupts, this funk, they wipe it away; where it crests, they dissolve it; wherever it drips, flowers, or clings, they find it and *fight* it until it *dies*. They fight this battle all the way to the grave.[4]

Ordinary blacks, viewed by whites, are forever "depraved," particularly since the black mind does not condemn the body's natural aromas. These aromas affirm God's creations. What God created is the way it is supposed to be. This affirmation encourages a tolerance for the unpleasants of nature, as well as a healthy preference for the thrills nature gives. When confronted with the black attitude of comfort with the natural processes of the body, the white association of body with dirt, in the form of disgust, is projected onto black naturalistic tendencies. But, the psychology of the healthy personality argues for an acceptance of self, nature, and natural processes. From this acceptance natural behavior is emitted.

The one-dimensional quality of black/African philosophy and thought allows for a paradoxical unity between the unpleasant and the pleasant fragrances of nature. Such unity in opposition is poetically represented in the conception "sweet funk."

Funk became fashionable after blacks made it sweet. "Funk Is in the Eye of the Beholder" is the title of an article by Henry Allen that appeared in the January 11, 1973, issue of the *Washington Post*. Stephen Henderson provided an astute analysis of the article with gripping commentary. The article cited the various meanings of funk, establishing a continuum ranging from "a shameful condition shunned by millions," to the "hottest cultural property since organic food." Allen wrote, "Funk is a way of life that only yesterday you considered tacky, old-fashioned, obnoxious or irrelevant." Funk is, he continued, doing the unexpected, like getting high on cheap wine, listening to the ball game while naked to the waistline, and drinking beer from the container it came in.[5]

What Henderson points out is that a term having deep, historical meaning to the black community becomes useful in satisfying the sensually bankrupt needs of the white community. He noted, too, that a process of justification and sanitization is initiated by media critics, and eventually scholars, who combine their efforts to purify the new usage of its original blackness.[6] What has been the reaction of blacks to whites canning their naturalness? It has been, Henderson states:

> . . . to ignore it, to show Whites what the real thing is by appearing to share it with them, to go back to the original meanings which defy white acceptance, or to discard the expression altogether and take up another. Thus many Blacks didn't care whether white people said that they had "soul" or not, and black D.J.s even invented the term "blue-eyed soul." And James Brown diplomatically allowed that Merv Griffin just might have "soul." And Dionne Warwick said that Dick Cavett had it. Aretha said Frank Sinatra had it too. And Jesse Jackson taught Mayor Daley the handshake. Finally, *Liberator Magazine* got mad and said to hell with it, and declared that soul was useless—officially dead—and printed a picture of the gravesite to prove it. And so we became "funky"—like calling ourselves niggers in public.[7]

Parasitically keying in on the energy of the black community, white students, women's libbers, gays, and even fat white people began referring to themselves as "new niggers," infected with funk. Wild Cherry, a singing group, recorded a song entitled "Play That Funky Music White Boy," and Latimore, a rhythm and blues artist, in one of his songs lauds "A Redneck in a Soul

Band." Indicative in all these instances is the manner in which whites have cashed in on the naturalistic aroma of the black community, or the "nigger identity," for the "sweetness of its funk."

The funky nigger reference does have limits, however, and Henderson pointed to some of these when he indicated that Dick Cavett hadn't referred to Bill Russell as my "main nigger" on TV yet. "And Johnny Carson hasn't called himself 'funky' yet, and one doubts that any of the presidential candidates would address black voters as 'My fellow funky Americans.'"[8]

Black popular artists began ascribing curative, healing dimensions to the quality of funk, again emphasizing its confectious quality. The singing group Parliment gives us directions:

> Now this is what I want yall to do
> if you got any faults, defects, or shortcomings, you know,
> whatever part of your body it is—lay it on the radio—
> let the vibes flow through
> funk not only moves, it removes—dig
> . . . somebody say, "is it funk after death?"
> I say, "is 7 up?"[9]

George Clinton, a member of the group, in a July 1978 *Ebony* magazine article, assures that "All you got to do is acknowledge funk and it frees you instantly, right there and then."[10] You can't abandon your instincts, Clinton insists, stating that some people place too much emphasis on intellect, which disables them in important life endeavors like releasing yourself. Popping your fingers, letting the natural, the raw, come forth is the way of funkiness. "You don't have to get it, all you do is let it," the Brothers Johnson assert in their song "Get the Funk Out of My Face."[11]

So what we see is that the naturalistic affinities of black people are expeditious to the proliferation of their expressive arts, and thus we could say that "funk" rests at the root and stem of popular culture in America. From beneath the arms, the crotch, a sensuously fragrant, musky perfume has arisen, activating an affective force that provides for life, enjoyment, enrichment, and regeneration. It is the most natural force in the universe.

It is important to note that it is not the unclean body that is being celebrated here, it is the naturalness of the body and the attitude of comfort with that which is natural in the universe. Many writers have highlighted cleanliness as part of the traditional everyday hygienic development of the African, back through many generations. Equiano, the first African in the West to write his autobiography, described the practices of cleanliness that were conventional to the point of ritual in African ways.[12]

Any current-day participation of blacks in practices that appear not to meet sanitary standards clearly is not to be credited to the African inheritance. Rather, it makes lucidly visible the abominations repressed in the mind of the West. That is, Westerners create conditions that produce obscenity in the lives of the oppressed for their own neurotic purification needs; at the same time they can be abundant consumers of "funky" enticements, slobbering lewdness, while they consciously deny the existence of the pools of shame in which they swim deep beneath the scummy surfaces.

What is unique and praiseworthy in the black response to these conditions is, in many instances, their ability to transform the disgusting conditions into wonderful delights, as in "sweet funk." They are aided by the black/African value position that increases tolerance for the unpleasants of nature by not viewing them as aspects apart or separate from the pleasants of nature, of life, of God, as they are all of each other, one.

Blacks are in touch with the earth, and this intimate contact generates an unusual perception of reality, one which roots them firmly in the forces and gifts of nature, for all time.

A poem reflects this feeling of continuity:

> Here we have watched ten thousand
> seasons
> come and go
> and unmarked graves atangled
> in the bush
> turn our own legs to trees
> vertical forever between earth
> and sun.[13]

"The custom of planting a tree after the birth of a child," Pierre Erny confirms, "especially at the spot where the placenta or umbilical cord has been buried, is common in Africa."[14] If the tree, whose shadow protects the child, becomes tall and strong, it is a sign of vigor and posterity for the developing child.

From the forces of nature common blacks draw their essence, an essence which makes them a natural people. For them the body and spirit are not entities apart and opposed to the West's conception of mind.

Closeness to nature, to the earth, to dust, suggests an affection for the natural world that is not exceeded in other races. Because of this affection there is an attitude of surrender to, and complete acceptance of, the forces and wonders of nature. In nature the highest knowledge exists, therefore wisdom and truth are acquired only through surrender to nature. A song popularized by the Four Tops expresses this:

> . . . *Do you know how long a tree lives*
> *or the reason it grows*
> *You may ask me all these questions*
> *But darling no one knows*
> *Do you ask the Lord above you*
> *why he made the sky clear blue*
> . . . *it's just the way mother nature planned it.*[15]

Blacks' affection for the natural world is apparent by the frequent references to objects of nature in their songs, poetry, oratory, folklore, dance, etc. John Lovell sheds more light on their sensitivity to the natural world:

> This sensitivity is, first of all, a wide-eyed wonder and appreciation. It expands to love. It even becomes kinship, for often the spiritual poet compares his fate with that of some other natural being. His references to nature are not casual; they are full of wonder, awe, and delight. It might be remembered, also, that some African religions have invested natural objects—sun, moon, sea, rocks—with deistic qualities.[16]

Roland Hayes depicted elements of the naturalistic thrust displayed in his father's ability to communicate with animals in the natural world:

> . . . I admired so much [his] wonderful gift for making music. I believed there was no sound in nature that he could not imitate. His voice brought deer, bear, and partridge within range of his gun. He taught me to identify the songs of birds, urging me to harken to them—himself repeating and answering their melodies, over and over again. I learned to distinguish between "true songs," which the male birds sing . . . and the less highly specialized "recordings" as the songs of lonely females . . .
>
> When my father called a deer, he was a buck himself. In transactions with untamed life he made an offering of his whole nature.[17]

In this same manner blacks communicate with other elements of nature. Heavenly bodies and forces, waters, other airy and earthly elements, plants, all are targets of black communication with the natural world. The West has regarded such behavior as ridiculously superstitious, ferociously attacking these naturalistic tendencies in the ways of black people. But it is not the super- and supranatural that is problematic for black folk; it is the unnatural, the pretender, the imposter, the contriver, that opposes their natural instincts. It is within the context of this opposition, this restriction of vision, that problems of the black community ferment.

The black community confronts its problems with its naturalistic impulses, giving what Melville Herskovits calls a "magicomedical" element to the personality.[18] The West African practice of deriving concoctions from roots, herbs, and other curative plants has continued in the traditions of blacks in the West. For instance, patented medicines are of little use to the Haitian of peasant heritage. Mata Deren tells us that

> . . . the average Haitian peasant knows which leaves to

brew for indigestion, which for a headache, which a
cold. If he wakes up without a voice, he chews on a
strong parsley root and this restores it rapidly. If someone is suffering from shock, the Haitians soak coarse salt
in a small jigger of rum and let the person drink it. If
someone is bleeding badly, they apply a spider's web to
the wound and the blood coagulates immediately. . . .
If a wound is infected, they rub it with garlic, and
sulphur is an effective antiseptic. . . . They are proud
of such knowledge and the remedies are passed down in
the family.[19]

Nature's products, and God, the highest force in the universe,
are firmly believed to be superior healers to professional doctors,
whose medicines are devoid of feeling, products purely of intellect, unnatural derivatives. Faith healing and the intervening
force of God in the solution of personal problems make professional mental health services a peculiarly strange commodity in
the black community, particularly when these services make use
of methods which run contrary to their every natural instinct.

We talked with Joseph Walker, author of *The River Niger*,
about another of his plays, *Yin Yang*. In the play a black psychiatrist is presented rather mockingly, and we questioned Walker
regarding his views on the role of professional mental health
workers in meeting the needs of the black community. He assured us that psychologists, counselors, social workers, psychiatrists are needed greatly. He even told of encouraging his drama
students to get into therapy so they could begin to know when
they were being real or phony. "But most . . . professionals who
serve in these capacities," Walker argued, "by virtue of their
training and the models they adopt, are in an occupational
dilemma. . . ."[20] These models that Walker mentioned were ones
alien to the black community. The mental health specialists, too,
were said to be alien. This is what the psychiatrist in *Yin Yang*
represented, with his restrained, unnatural objectivity. His dress,
speech, and every gesture told the root black people in *Yin Yang*,
like those in real life, of his human detachment from them, which
suggested to them a potential irresponsibility toward their wel-

fare and elicited the reluctance to submit their minds to his analysis. In a sense, the psychiatrist in the play, like mental health workers in agencies and schools across the nation, appeared weird to these root people. It is the unnaturalness of these professionals that contributes to their being perceived as odd, if not crazy. Walker went on to say that common blacks are very much in touch with their intuitions, emotions, and instincts. This suggests that they are very responsive to forces unseen in the natural world, forces which are powerfully active in their expressive arts. The professional skills of mental health workers, developed on Euro-American premises, make for a dissonance between them and the culture of black people. Having become what Walker called pseudointellectuals, owing to the abandonment of their instincts, and relating to their clients from mental chambers of grandeur all contrary to the naturalistic behaviors of the community, these professionals are relegated to the lowest levels of ineptitude. "At that point," Walker correctly insists, "you are bullshitting—absolutely bullshitting!"[21] And because of their refusal to be natural and to utilize the naturalness of their clients, too many social workers, counselors, teachers, psychologists, ministers, and others supply the black community with a useless commodity.

What more does it mean to be natural, to act natural, to exhibit natural behavior? We have identified at least six manifestations that make up these naturalistic tendencies.

An *aversion to formality and standardization* is one, of which time orientation is a major emphasis. Toni Morrison provides an example in *Sula:*

> A real wedding, in a church, with a real reception afterward, was rare among the people of the bottom. Expensive for one thing, and most newlyweds just went to the courthouse if they were not particular, or had some preacher come in and say a few words if they were. The rest just 'tookup' with one another. No invitations were sent. There was no need for that formality.[22]

The absence of invitations to many happenings and occurrences in the black community is a clear example of disregard for Western formality. The "grapevine," like the drum for the African, is a natural way of communicating en masse, or at a distance. So when there's going to be a party, a church celebration, a community supper, a little gambling, a wedding, or when a child is born or a person dies, official announcements, if made, are old by the time they are received; the grapevine moves messages swiftly and with surprising accuracy.

"'Use blues rhythms,'" Sam Greenlee writes in *The Spook Who Sat by the Door*. "'Your poetry, doggerel, anything catchy that people will remember and pass along; we want to plug into the ghetto grapevine.'"[23]

With the grapevine, as opposed to formal announcements, there is vital affect or force. The vine, like the drum, collects the enthusiasm, the joy, the excitement, the sorrow, the mournfulness that accompanies the message, and passes it on to induce the same in the receivers of the message.

When Gladys Knight or Marvin Gaye sing, "I heard it through the grapevine, that no longer will you be mine," or when Billy Paul croons, "Word sure gets around, talk is all over town," they affirm the existence of the communication network that is most common in the natural world—pass the word, the beat, the tone.

A similar disregard for formality is evident in the eating of certain foods. Southern blacks, in particular, love to eat greens and cornbread, mixed up, with their hands, as well as many other foods. The hand is the most natural eating utensil in the universe. Moreover, many of these connoisseurs of southern delicacies declare that the food doesn't taste as good when it's eaten from contrived utensils. This practice derives from Africa. Chinua Achebe, in *No Longer at Ease*, depicts the African prototype of the southern black:

> They were eating pounded yams . . . with their fingers.
> The second generation of . . . Nigerians had gone back
> to eating pounded yams . . . with their fingers for the
> good reason that it tasted better that way. Also for the

even better reason that they were not scared . . . of being called uncivilized.[24]

The absence of formality permits one a certain freedom, a relaxed way of being, without stress or strain that grips the natural flow of one's rhythm. Ralph Ellison in *Invisible Man* gives a fitting account. Having been stopped on the street by the smell of yams cooking on hot coals, the character remembered, after purchasing one from the old man who sold them:

> I took a bite, finding it as sweet and hot as any I'd ever had. . . . I walked along, munching the yam . . . suddenly overcome by an intense feeling of freedom—simply because I was eating while walking along the street. It was exhilarating. I no longer had to worry about who saw me or about what was proper.
>
> . . . This is all very wild and childish, I thought, but to hell with being ashamed of what you liked. No more of that for me I am what I am! I wolfed down the yam and ran back to the old man and handed him twenty cents. "Give me two more," I said.[25]

Ellison was right when he shaped this episode into a guide for living a healthy life—"Continue on the yam level and life [will] be sweet."[26]

Formality requires reduced stimulation, accustoming one to the same thing over and over and over. It creates a sameness to life that is repulsed by common black folk. To be creative, productive, and regenerative, new stimulation is required. Human beings constantly need new stimulation for their highest efficiency and are, fundamentally, sensation-seeking creatures. We adapt and dull our senses to the routine, the old, the commonplace. Like a new tune, we love to play it over and over. After a period, however, it graduates to the status of old and becomes unstimulating. Where formality is involved, we listen, but with a kind of sterile, automatic awareness. It is not unusual to have a black popular recording artist sing the American national anthem before major sports events. And suddenly a song, emotionally flat from age and endless performances, is revitalized and invested with new vigor as a result of the naturalistic tendency to shun the boredom that formality induces.

Related to this repulsion of sameness is the difficulty black youths have in adjusting to the many sterile, repetitive dynamics of formalized instructional processes. The retainers of formality suppress affective and psychomotor expressions, fastening the individual into a pattern that is orderly, controllable, and predictable. These patterns violate the naturalistic acculturation of black youth.

When one lifts the formal restraints on his being, he is given to a more spontaneous and natural existence. He applauds, yells approval, or boos disapproval spontaneously, in collective ceremonies such as those held in theaters, churches, clubs, or concert halls.

A group of counselors in training (mostly white) were taken to see a drama on black life, so as to enrich their learning as it pertained to counseling the culturally different black client. The audience at this Broadway production was mostly black. And the power of the drama kept them murmuring, moaning, groaning, gasping, gesturing at the action on the stage. These behaviors frequently erupted without notice into thunderous applause. What our white students didn't understand was that when a feeling impulse registers on the nervous system, it is natural to express that feeling through verbal or physical conveyors. Because common blacks are a natural people, the theater was without its formal applause at scheduled intervals during that evening, to the amazement and distress of our white students and those few blacks whose identity confusion was aggravated by the spontaneously responsive audience.

We all, on that evening, experienced a bit of annoyance at all the late arrivals who had to be seated by thin streams of light provided by the ushers. Our annoyance was minimal by comparison, because we knew already what many of our students didn't dare think in our presence: colored people are always late.

The time orientation in the black community is not formalized and standardized as it is in the white community. The concept of

"Colored People's Time" is one that has its roots in African antiquity.

During our visit to an African country, it was our privilege to interview a ranking member of the nation's Educational Affairs Bureau. Already we had observed African People's Time (APT) to be clearly leading Colored People's Time (CPT) in degrees of lateness. But then no one was ON coffee, cigarettes, aspirins, or other tension-reducing stimulants, and after about five days in Africa, just before our interview, we both marveled at how absolutely relaxed we felt not having to worry about the expiration of time. We were enjoying pure peace the day we called the educational officer for an appointment. He was delighted to give us one, between the hours of 12:00 and 2:00 the next day. We were perplexed by the time span in which the appointment was to occur. Through informers we discovered that the practice was not uncommon, and after thoughtful reflection it made sense to us. It was obviously a compromise between the West's specificity of time and the African's relativity of time. The compromise did not place the individual in a press for exactness, which is naturally more stress-inducing.

Lateness, the result of Western exactitude, is clearly naturalistic. Time, as related to when a person does something, is more naturally governed by feeling states or an affective readiness to engage in an act. It is unnatural to eat breakfast at 8:00, lunch at 12:00, and dinner at 6:00. It is natural to eat when you are hungry, when the natural rhythm of the body signals the need for nourishment. Getting up in the morning to be at work or class by 8:00 goes against one's every natural instinct, especially if the work or class activities hold no promise for excitement or spirited, emotional stimulation. Proceeding at such tasks when one has acquired a certain affective readiness is a naturalistic response. It is the unnaturalness of work schedules in America that rests at the core of massive job dissatisfaction.

Lateness can pose problems, however. Punctuality in our culture is highly valued and is favorably rewarded. If one is to participate in the reward system, one must be conscientious with respect to punctuality. What happens with probably far too many individuals is that the time compulsion practiced in the West creeps into the organization of their lives outside of obligations to jobs or school. That is, their personal time becomes equally obligated, denying the opportunity for vital spontaneity in the consumption of personal time.

A comedian on a popular television show described the typical executive's daily pattern: arise at 6:00, breakfast at 7:00, arrive office at 8:00, break at 10:00, lunch at 12:00, break at 3:00, off at 5:00, dinner at 6:00, sex at 9:00 (possibly), and sleep at 9:01. Formality reduces one's efficiency in some most important areas of life, owing to the inducement of annoying irritants.

Formalizing and standardizing the time that large numbers of people should do things or the mass synchronization of human behavior is contrary to individual variations in the flow of rhythm, and it becomes a clear imposition upon the basic nature of human beings. Lateness may reflect not irresponsibility and passive aggression against authority, but stout resistance to compulsive, mechanical responses that violate and suppress one's natural sense of time. Giving in to the compulsions of time regiments one's patterns, sharply reducing if not eradicating vital spontaneity. Pioneers in the work world may be catching the hint. The introduction of such innovations as flextime schedules, and other self-pacing work schedules and task behavior, recognize that efficiency increases if workers perform when they are more in tune to their own rhythms. This recognition reduces the element of formality in work behavior, and returns us nearer to the Africa within ourselves.

Anxiety, tension, and frustration are natural consequences imposed by formality, and these impair sexual responsiveness and the general ability to enjoy life. Lateness often reduces these inner irritants, as it decreases the amount of time that one's free spirit has to be squeezed within the self.

John Mbiti has been most thoughtful on the philosophical conception of time in the African mind. "Time," in the Western world, "is a commodity which must be utilized, sold and bought." Mbiti explains that "in traditional African life, time has to be created or produced."[27]

Westerners are made prisoners of time, having their freedom markedly reduced through the repression of a naturalistic tend-

ency, which is replaced with a mechanical compulsion. According to Mbiti, the time orientation of the black/African world is
governed by two main dimensions, present and past. These time
spans are critical to an understanding of black/African behavior,
as they are fundamental to their conception of the universe.
Mbiti instructs:

> Time has to be experienced in order to make sense or to
> become real. A person experiences time partly in his
> own individual life, and partly through the society
> which goes back many generations before his own birth.
> Since what is in the future has not been experienced, it
> does not make sense; it cannot, therefore, constitute
> part of time, and people do not know how to think
> about it—unless, of course, it is something which falls
> within the rhythm of natural phenomena.[28]

In the black world, time is not an academic or economic thing.
"For them," Mbiti assures, "time is simply a composition of
events which have occurred, those which are taking place now,
and those which are immediately to occur."[29] That which has little chance of an immediate occurrence is placed in the category
of "no time." "What is certain to occur, or what falls within the
rhythm of natural phenomena, is in the category of inevitable or
potential time," Mbiti stresses.

Actual time is what is taking place "now," though "now" certainly foretells of the future, and fully embraces the past. But like
tomorrow becomes today and today becomes yesterday in actual
time, the future becomes the present, and the present becomes
the past for the African. All these time modes are experienced,
however, as an ongoing, forever "nowing," a sense of timelessness
like the universe, like nature, like eternal force.

Timelessness becomes linked with the duration of the black
world. It creates within the psyche an acceptance of things which
are impervious to change, for those things are timeless. The African mask has been seen as an article that contains the "all-time"
wisdom of the ancestors, which nourishes the living. It is constant
in spite of lived time. The mask is of the beginning, scores of life-

times removed from actual time, but profoundly in time, immediate, now, here.

Recall that living in the here and now, with a reasonable degree of frequency, is an indicator of optimal mental health, which is clearly satisfied by African tradition and clearly opposed by the time mania of Euro-American practices.

For the black man, time moves according to the rhythms of the earth, the flow of rivers, which transfers to the emotive rhythm of man. The point of conciseness is this: Time, in the black mind, is not solely a mathematical construct but is associated with, and more principally affixed to, natural events in the universe. The vision of time as a sequence of mathematical units superimposing its pattern upon human activity is contrary to the natural rhythm of the universe. The event, the activity, is focal, the time sequence is relative and marked by the pulse of the natural world. So, as Mbiti has pointed out, it is more important to be *in* time than *on* time in the black world.

Malcolm X pointed out that when questioned by policemen blacks are hard pressed to pin down the exact time something occurred.[30] This typifies the clock of the black mind. The management of time, in keeping with the West's imperatives, has not been the easiest task for blacks. It is a compelling phenomenon, often associated with the reduction of freedom and the intended undermining of one's basic sense of dignity. So that, for blacks of common heritage, in those realms of life that are not heavy with consequence they perhaps choose to be LATE, or be *in* time, for a momentary retreat from the West's addiction. "To hell with being on time," they probably say, not as an expression of indignation but as a celebration, the celebration of being natural, pleasing and consoling to the ancestral spirits.

Frankness of manner is a naturalistic tendency of the common folk. It umbrellas an earthiness in human conduct and represents a stern refusal to deodorize life's occurrences so as to make them more palliative to the senses. Dealing with the raw, the unpolished, the rough edges of life, is not shunned.

Underneath this tendency, which on the surface is smeared as crudeness, is the courage, the honesty, the unusual audacity to express the uncut TRUTH of one's perceptions and experiences. Euphemisms have little use in black expressiveness, and because of this, common blacks are often viewed as a people without sophistication or diplomacy. These esteemed character traits of Middle America necessarily distort truth, compromise integrity, and expose one's essence to lethal agents, therefore robbing experience of vital zest and potency.

George Davis, in his short story "Coming Home," has his character compare the expressiveness of his experience with that of a lettered man:

> Already the day is hot. I don't feel like taking a shower. I have sweated in my bed and I feel funky in my pits and groin. I feel the sweat, perspiration, a Harvard man would say, [note the comparison] along the side of my body, and along the inside of both arms so that my arms stick to my body when I press them against me. [But as a man who jerks the "nitty gritty" from his experience] I feel myself funky.[31]

Direct and aboveboard, common folk usually say straight out what they want, and insist upon the same in another. "You're asking for something, so stop beating around the corners and tell me what it is you want!" is a retort from Lonnie Elder's *Ceremonies in Dark Old Men.*[32] It is a demand for honesty in one's expressiveness. "Trying ain't enough! You be honest, you hear? Promise me. You be honest like your daddy."[33] These are strong lines from *Dancers on the Shore,* by William Melvin Kelley. They have their origin in the naturalistic aspects of black existence.

This matter of truth in one's expressiveness is no small thing. It is an essential ingredient for optimal mental health and stands out, with importance, as an ingredient essential for the transformation of our mentally weary society. Malcolm X was adamant in his exemplary comments. "I'm for truth, no matter who tells it. I'm for justice, no matter who is for or against . . . I'm for whoever and whatever benefits humanity as a whole."[34] "Tell it like it is" and "I calls em as I see em" are common black elocutions. Authenticity, truth, and a strong ethical sense are bounded in these expressions. "The TRUTH shall set you free" is clearly the punch line, and is, psychologically, a profound dictum, by which the largest lot of the common folk abide in the organization of their expressive behavior.

It is the freedom in black expressiveness, given dominance by adherence to truth, that accounts for its colorfulness. When off-duty from "playing the game," or being cast in roles that hide the truths of oneself, frankness of manner, a naturalistic attitude, becomes unmistakably apparent. A dazzle of a "lady in red," on duty, into her role of night and life in Ntozake Shange's choreopoem:

> & she wanted to be unforgettable
> she wanted to be a memory
> a wound to every man
> arrogant enough to want her
> > she waz the wrath
> > of women in windows
> > > fingerin shades/ol lace curtains
> > > Camoflagin despair &
> > > stretch marks
> > . . . & allowed those especially schemin
> tactful suitors to experience her body & spirit tearin
> so easily blendin with theirs
> & they were so happy
> & lay on her lime sheets full and wet
> from her tongue   she kissed
> them reverently   even ankles
> edges of beards . . .[35]

Then, off duty, when night edged day, the lady in red, "painted with orange blossoms and magnolia scented wrists," was through playing the game:

> & now she stood a
> reglar colored girl
> fulla the same malice
> livid indifference as a sistah

worn from supportin a would be hornplayer
or waitin by the window
   & they knew
   & left in a hurry . . .[36]

Frankness of manner is a naturalistic tendency that most Westerners fear and find subversive to their rules and regulations,
which generally do not consider TRUTH in their shaping. The
expulsion of black children from schools, which has increased
demonstrably since desegregation, the frequent firing of black
workers from their jobs, the frequent arrests of blacks when no
cause is apparent—all these are linked to the refusal to subdue
the tendency of "frankness" which shapes their responsiveness in
all human relationships, not omitting those that are strained by
adversity.

Speaking one's mind and expressing one's feelings are not practices reinforced by our system of social transactions, which rewards the ability to conceal the ulterior motive, or hide the truth
so as to conclude the transaction with an advantage, the upper
hand, in control. When control is one's motive in expressive behavior, frankness of manner becomes a threat to the attainment
or maintenance of control and becomes cause for invoking the
force of authority; hence the frequent authoritative dismissal of
blacks from white-run settings, because, in the interest of their
own integrity and optimal functioning, they retain this naturalistic tendency.

The currents created by this tendency are electrifying, not only
in verbal expressive behavior but in nonverbal aspects of behavior as well. Tone in vocal expression is a nonverbal quality that
joins affect and intellect in the speech of the black community. It
is tone, echoes of drum passions, that airs the spirit of frankness
about one's experience of reality, and it can threaten the controlling listeners. "Don't speak to me in that tone of voice" is a common demand by the controller in such a transaction, who is obviously rebuffed and setting up defenses against the penetrations
that frankness, the drumbeat, achieves.

The psychomotor aspects of frankness appear in how a person
looks at you and in gestures, signals, and other nuances of motor

expression. When a child sticks his tongue out at another with appropriate facial grimaces, a "frank" psychomotor expression of defiance or rejection, with obvious affect and cognition, has been transmitted. Whereas the statement "I don't think I like you very much right now," particularly uttered with reduced or sterile tonality, one of flat intellect, expresses little of the frankness inherent in the person's experience. This leaves the person plagued by left-over anxiety and tension, and the creation of a gap in communication invariably occurs.

It is the frankness that grabs the receiver and makes him aware of another's truths. When a girl gaily sticks out her tongue at a boy, he is far more certain of and provoked by her interest in him than he would be if she were to dryly proclaim, "I like you." The drumbeat is missing. The telescope to the inner core of existence is powered by the drumbeat, without which TRUTH is left open to suspicion.

Casualness in social transactions is another naturalistic tendency. It is one that gives rise to an element of modesty and appropriate humility in human transactions. It not only reduces to a position that is nonthreatening to another, but provides a wave of human warmth and acceptance, which relaxes the other, lowers his defenses, and puts him in a state of comfort or an anxiety-free state.

This tendency is epitomized when the human being is in a relatively unprovoked or minimally stimulated condition. An easiness like "Sunday Morning" for the Commodores, a time when the screeching noises of cars and unkind voices of irritable drivers, and the roaring of trains and buses are unheard. A quiet, peaceful stillness prevails. A poem captures this quality of easiness that makes the individual casual in his approach:

> How sweet is it to lie beneath a tree
> At eve-time and share the ecstasy
> Of Jocund birds and flimsy butterflies;
> And rise towards the music of the spheres,
> Descending softly with the wind,
> And the tender glow of the fading sun.[37]

Casualness in social transactions is a quality akin to the feeling of being lightly "mellow." Lowered aggression is evident, replaced by gentleness in flesh-to-flesh contact. This tendency seems to spring from the recognition that nature is forever, it is like the river, never hurrying, and this recognition gives birth to patience, affirming the belief that there is no need to rush, as all things are in their own time.

"Worrying isn't part of my nature," Millie Jackson quipped. "I never did see where anything got solved by worrying over it. I believe in making the best of what is."[38] Her expressions here embody casualness with the full recognition that there are forces in our lives over which we have little or no control. A capacity for "untiring waitin" (for better times, a better day) is effected in the virtue of patience, which is a prime requisite for persistence and endurance. Replicated in the human being is the enduring quality of nature and the vital forces of the universe.

"I done put it in the haynes of the Lord" and "I've thrown up bof mah haynes" are common expressions of the black folk community concerning unmanageable problems of life; they affirm the attitude of "letting be" when taxing endeavors become too much. This casual attitude of "letting be" is essential for the maintenance of functional and optimal mental health. It only thrives in individuals who are aware of the limits of their control and not bent on controlling things and beings at the obsessive level characteristic of the West. When one accepts that the river's flow is voluntary, that the moon and sun and heavenly bodies have their way in the sky, that it rains when it wants to, that hurricanes decide their own path, then one can become endowed with the infinite power of "letting be."

"Letting be" leads to self-acceptance, acceptance of others, acceptance of nature and natural processes, which have been shown to be salient features of optimal mental health. To accept suggests a cessation in one's attempts to control, change, or predetermine that which is unalterable in the universe, in human nature, in the self. The quality prevails when one stops trying to be, and simply "bes." It is not unlike the state achieved when one is seductively ordered to "be cool," which relaxes effort and allows things to be their own way without the imposition of control

which often requires exhausting effort and understandably induces more stress, strain, and anxiety in the human being.

Contempt for artificiality and falseness in human conduct is
another naturalistic attitude. Oneself is next to that which is
divine and therefore is all right as it is, without artificial addi-
tives. "Behold the only thing greater than your self!"[39] Such was
Kunta Kinte's exclamation to the babe he held high, closer to the
heavens, to the divine force. The only thing greater than oneself
is divine, vital force, and therefore one has no need to be other
than what one is. It is the natural way to be. To cast oneself in unnatural role behavior, such as imitating other races so as to feel
better than others like yourself, or superior to them, overlooks the
essential wisdom of Kunta's vocal deliverance. Only the divine is
greater than oneself.

A character in Achebe's novel *No Longer at Ease* remarks with
overtones of contemptuous sarcasm, "If you see a white man,
take off your hat to him. The only thing he cannot do is mold a
human being."[40] Mockery, insulated with disgust, is made of the
white man's superiority strivings, which contaminate his being
with artificiality, thereby subduing his capacity for humaneness,
for feeling, and gives him qualities associated with the sterility,
emptiness, and mechanicalness of his supreme invention—robot
man.

Superiority striving is a goal which allows human behavior to
become infiltrated by pretense and falseness, in keeping with an
invented human profile which "elevates" one above the profile of
naturalistic man. It is a striving that subverts the true self, and
among common black folk such artificiality and falseness in
human conduct is held in contempt.

What is observed is a preference for "something real" in people, something genuine and unconcocted which does not need
the affirmation of shabbily fabricated, grandiose delusions that
are usually characteristic of "unreal" people. A description of
Ray Charles' authentic resonance is applicable:

> His reactions to the day's events are always genuine: He
> is genuinely angry, genuinely upset, genuinely moved

by a piece of music, genuinely grateful for a call from an old friend. He is incapable of faking a feeling. He is pleased with his own singing. He makes no bones about it. "I like myself," he says. After hearing himself sing and hearing a particularly nasty lick he will say, "that's me," or "that's stupid" or ask—rhethorically, "does that stink enough for you?"[41]

It does appear that as blacks increase their exposure to white institutions, there is a tendency to suffocate the naturalism of their ways. This is largely the downfall of the black middle class, who quite often have no true self—empty people who are white when they see white and black when it's fashionable. Frantz Fanon, in *Black Skin, White Mask,* noted the unhealthy adaptation of blacks after exposure to Western ways:

Even before he had gone away, one could tell from the almost aerial manner of his carriage that new forces had been set in motion. When he met a friend or an acquaintance his greeting was no longer the wide sweep of the arm: With great reserve our "new man" bowed slightly.[42]

When a black man starts making nearly the money that a white man makes, he starts "to act foolish like a white man," a character asserts in Kelley's *Dancers on the Shore.*[43] "Acting foolish" suggests the abandonment of TRUTH, which is embedded in the make-up of nature, for the sake of dwelling on the rational to the level of irrationality, on the logical to the level of illogicality, leaving one unguided by the natural flow, the natural rhythm of things. At the everyday level, it converts to preoccupation with the trite and trivial which subsumes the entirety of one's being. The ways one walks, talks, postures, become unnatural, phony, rather comical, foolish perhaps?

"Hey lady," the lead singer from Harold Melvin and the Bluenotes conversationally roars, "can I say something to you for a minute, please?" He stresses the urgency of their talk, in the monologue to a song, saying his lady's phoniness has reached a level of annoyance that cannot be ignored. "Why is it that every time . . . we get around my friends, you always talkin bout what you got, how much money I make, where our children go to school, all the fancy clothes, and fancy cars, big diamond rings, and fantastic mink coats?" he asks, his patience exhausted. Compelling her to "sit down!" he seeks to explain her behavior, sharing wisdom passed down to him from the sayings of his mother, then he continues with depictions of her pretense and superiority yearnings. "You standing up in the corner with a bottle of champagne, talkin bout Harry, Dick, and Joe, and Bobby, and what they ain't got, and they live down in the lower development homes." He pleads, exasperated, "Don't make your own brothers and sisters feel bad . . . BE FOR REAL."[44]

The cultural interest of the "ego-elevated" black shifts to the emotionally subdued arts of the European. Eileen Southern comments:

> The kind of music cultivated in the homes of middle-class blacks was the trite and rather superficial music favored by white society. . . . The music historian, Gilbert Chase, has used the phrase "music in the genteel tradition" to apply to this type of music, which was . . . characterized by the cult of the fashionable, the worship of the conventional, the emulation of the elegant, the cultivation of the trite and artificial, the indulgence of sentimentality and the predominance of superficiality.[45]

Visiting such a home, one usually shrinks from the pervasive chilliness that does not disappear with "formal" gestures of welcome. One is ill at ease, guarded in speech, restrained in movement, and conscious of appropriate "formalities." These collectively contribute to strain and discomfort.

A greater feeling of warmth and comfort is experienced when one visits "real people." Note Malcolm X's comments:

> Not only was this part of Roxbury much more exciting, but I felt more relaxed among Negroes who were being

their natural selves and not putting on airs. Even
though I did live on the Hill, my instincts were never—
and still aren't—to feel myself better than any other
Negro.[46]

Lou Rawls growls, singing a Gamble and Huff tune, "I like
groovy people." These are people who do not "put on," those
without an "attitude." People "walking around with their noses
in the air," Lou assures, "them kind of people I just can't use."[47]
When around such people, the song points out, one cannot be
relaxed or put one's mind at ease.

Many blacks, after exposure to Western ways and after a period of trying to be other than themselves, become repulsed by
their unnaturalness and emulate Ntozake Shange's "lady in
green," who asserts:

i want my arm wit the hot iron scar
and my leg wit the flea bite i want my calloused feet and quick
    language
back in my mouth
fried plantains
pineapple pear juice
sun-ra & joseph & jules
i want my own things
how i lived them
& give me my memories how i waz when i waz there[48]

It is a grand gesture of self-acceptance when one gives up
phoniness and pretentiousness. When the "afro" hairstyle (before
it became style) was first worn, particularly by black women, it
was clearly associated with self-image, a black self-image. "Kink-
iness draws the line, helps us to define what it is we're about.
The dark skin, broad nose, what-have-you," commented a young
lady in a discussion group.[49] "I'll be glad when the afro goes out
of style," another young lady remarked, "then the people to
whom it means something can still have it."

Our society could be aptly described as a "false" one, with its
escalating proliferation of artificial articles: hair, bust, hips, teeth,

limbs, eyes, scents, fingernails, colorations for hair and skin, sexual organs, and the list could go on. Moreover, surgical procedures for face lifts, nose and ear realignments, sex changes, hair transplants, and other transformations all mirror unnatural elements festering in the personality of Western man. Falseness becomes, in our society, a lucrative commodity, consuming untold expenditure by persons unhappy with nature's gifts to them. From the shopping malls of our minds we purchase plastic faces, with false smiles. Jazz artist Hubert Laws lyrically explains:

> *When you see those smiling faces*
> *can it be for real what they say*
> *are they as happy as they seem to be*
>
> *Did you ever wonder when you looked*
> *at someone straight in the eye*
> *if what you see is their reflection inside*
>
> *Your expression should reveal*
> *what you really feel*
> *it can be so hard to hide*
> *what you feel deep inside*
>
> *See those False Faces*
> *smile when they're sad*
> *leave those False Faces*
> *make your heart glad*[50]

Billy Paul, spurred by the musical genius of Kenny Gamble, Leon Huff, and Carl Gamble, echoes the urgings of Hubert Laws:

> *False faces—you're such a phony*
> *False faces—you're full o'baloney*
> *I never know how you feel*
> *You keep holdin' back*
> *You won't reveal*
> *The way you really feel inside*

The real you—you're trying to hide
Why can't you be for real—why can't you be for real
So much better you would feel

I never know where you're comin from
I never know where you're really at . . .

Why can't you be for real—why can't you be for real
So much better you would feel[51]

It should be remembered that one mark of the person who is "together" is a satisfaction and pride in the natural self, and the courage to be that self, for he knows that "everything is beautiful in its own way."

The body, for many, is still a dominion of unacceptable drives, urges, and feelings, which many people fight untiringly to subdue, highlighting the absence of *relaxed, fluid body movement,* a naturalistic tendency. Those who are able to subdue the body's impulses achieve, psychologically, a removal of themselves from their bodies, usually through extreme religiosity and compulsive work. The acquired state of being, resulting from the psychological removal of mind from body, is one of "unembodiment."

Sidney Jourard proposes that "upbringing in the Western world produces a partial sense of unembodiment in the majority of persons so socialized."[52] "This unembodiment," he continues, "manifests itself in interpersonal duplicity (play-acting, pretense, role-playing, pseudo-self-disclosure) and in diminished awareness of one's own body."

In the extreme or complete removal of the nonmaterial mind from body, according to British psychiatrist R. D. Laing, the individual is beset with a profoundly severe mental disturbance.[53] It is the experience of being out of one's body, usually beginning with an abhorrent rejection of bodily sensations, bringing about a gradual reduction of mental awareness, anesthetizing the mind of the body's presence. The body becomes devoid of rhythm, rigid and mechanical. These are marks of somatic repression and are known factors in both physical and mental illnesses. Relaxed and fluid body movement and posturing combine as an index of good mental health, and as a naturalistic tendency.

The slippery, liquid walk and the free, unrestrained bodily gestures of the black community point to the state of "being in one's body," blending mind and body into a wonderful melodious harmony of rhythm vibrations. Achebe's character Okonkwo displayed such a blending, and was said to walk with a resilient stride: "When he walked, his heels hardly touched the ground, and he seemed to walk on springs."[54] Such blending allows for oily movements of the body's connecting points.

Movements of a rumba dancer, poetically captured, give the body a kind of intelligence of its own:

> Your belly knows more than your head,
> and as much as your thighs.
> That
> is the strong black charm
> of your nakedness.[55]

It is the looseness and fluidity of the body that give evidence of being in one's body, and therefore tuned in to perceptual sensations that enter awareness through the antennae of the body. Somatic perceptions affirm the body's own mode of intelligence, of knowing, and of expressing.

Deren, in this regard, writes of a Haitian dance which expresses the vitality of water: "Before me the bodies of the dancers undulate with a wavelike motion, which begins at the shoulders, divides itself to run separately along the arms and down the spine, is once more unified where the palms rest upon the bent knees, and finally flows down the legs into the earth, while already the shoulders have initiated the wave which follows."[56]

Note the graceful movements that are pictured in the dance, movements replicated wherever black communities exist. These pictures of graceful, sensuous movement compel artists to create in the fervor of folk blues singers, who often whine, "Everytime my baby walk, it just like a leaf shaking on a tree." Truly the motion of elements, its inertia disturbed only by the winds of the spirit.

What Deren observed were spiritual winds directing the circular movement of the dancers' shoulders that seemed to send them forward, drawing the rest of the body after the shoulders, over and over and over. Erect in posture at the beginning of the dance, the "winds" bend the dancers toward the earth, "the undulation becomes more and more horizontal, until all figures blend into a slow flowing serpentine stream circling . . . with a fluency that belies the difficulty of the movement." And finally, Deren asks in self-reference, "What have they found there, on that central ground, that their limbs should move with such ease and such perfection while, on the exiled outskirts, my own limbs are burdened with muscles, must ponder [think! think!] and delay my every will to motion?"[57]

It is the interference of thought, isolated from affective and motor responsiveness, that acts to bungle the natural expression of sensuality, locking in the body tension or tightness that forbids the pleasant condition of relaxation to permeate the body.

"Muscular armor" is the name psychoanalyst Wilhelm Reich gave groups of muscles frozen by tension. While muscularly armored, the individual guards himself against vitality, sexuality, and other sensuous emotions. Such emotional prohibitions are inherent in the process of unembodiment.

Unreleased tension and anxiety in the body act as a concrete cast, forcing the body's skeletal alignment off the course of its natural development while nullifying vital spontaneity. Postural problems, such as hunched shoulders, forward droop of the head, and a compacted chest cavity which prohibits deep, full breathing, are characteristic of the muscularly armored individual. Moreover, whether sitting, standing, walking, running, or lying down, more than average mental and physical energy is consumed, and the individual experiences a disconcerting strain.

Western psychology has responded to such body ailments with a number of systematic massage techniques, or methods of re-embodiment. The best known of these is called "Rolfing," for the physical therapist who introduced the technique, Ida Rolf. Rolf and other advocates of the method believe that deep manipu-

lation of the muscles actually realigns the skeletal frame, effecting a change in posture, from which results improved "sleep, energy level, elimination, sexuality, and overall health."[58] Reports
indicate that persons having undergone the treatment stand
taller, are more zestful, and more rhythmically coordinated in
their movements.

Rolfing and other relaxation methods, usually involving variations of hypnotic intentions, are designed to free the body of
stress, replacing it with comfort. The major aim of all therapy
methods is to reduce stress and anxiety, which serve eventually,
Ida Rolf tells us, to unnaturally alter the skeletal frame.

Relaxation is the end product of expressive behavior. Black
expressiveness, often requiring convulsive physical involvement,
empties the body of stress, strain, frustration, or other body irritants, making for a calm, restored, zestful, perhaps slightly eu-
phoric disposition following the dismissal of irritants from the
body. Relaxation is necessary for the maintenance of a graceful
posture and locomotive style. It increases vitality, sensuality, and
sexual responsiveness, and it is achieved through black expressive
behavior, which involves the creative utilization of the muscles
and the imaginary channel of the mind. These act to dismiss tension and instill relaxation. It is a more pleasant and natural route
to good health than the relaxation methods offered through the
many different therapy practices, which more often than not are
conscious, deliberate, uncreative efforts to shut off thinking activity in the mind that acts to constrict the muscles.

Running or jogging achieves much of what is physically and
psychologically accomplished through black expressiveness; that
is, jogging exerts the muscles, freeing them of tension, and
runners report the achievement of a meditative state of mind. It
is, however, void of creativity and spontaneity. Whereas the end
achievement, with respect to physical and emotional health, are
meritorious, the process is quite often a very painful one. The felt
pain, however, is no doubt lessened through the psychological
adaptation that occurs from constancy. Felt or not, the actual
physical pain is real, often very annoying, giving the process overtones of masochism. As an expressive vehicle, running or jogging
of the marathon variety has no creative value inherent in its proc-

ess, and is therefore uncharacteristic as a medium of expressiveness. Avoiding encroaching danger or speeding the transportation of oneself to a designated place for reasons of emergency give running purpose. But running for the sake of running or endurance running is a contrived event, without inspirational feeling. One simply decides that a certain amount of time spent running will constitute one's activity, and it is thereby an activity deriving from deliberation. It is quite a different practice from running as an aspect of track and field sports. Track running, particularly in the events in which blacks excel, involves graceful maneuvers and emotional charges that quicken the reactions aimed at the achievement of speed. Involved here are elements characteristic of black expressiveness, such as feeling, style, and creative movement. Moreover, it is a competitive activity, winning is its purpose. It is not an expressive activity of a pastime nature, or a venture in sheer endurance. Running as a pastime requires no agile, spontaneous, or creative moves, just linear strides. Perhaps the strictly cognitive, uncreative basis of endurance running is the reason for its wide and growing acceptance as an expressive mode in the Western world.

The grace, ease, and comfort evident in the bodies of average blacks are the result of life-styles that are more in keeping with the natural laws of the universe. It is natural to express feelings. Whether they are expressed directly or sublimated, as in artistic expression, the body is renewed by health-inducing involvements that contribute to and satisfy aesthetic necessities for an enriched life.

Could it be that Larry Neal is right in his poem "Kunta," in which he declared, "I am descended from Drum"?[59] For Neal the drum was the first formation in the universe. The beat of the world, the rhythm of the cosmos, is of the drum. It is "the pulse that formed the word." From the first form, which was "formless sound," the drum originated, creating a pulse that gave birth to man, who took the pulse of his experience and "formed the word and the earth and linked them into dance." Recognizing the allegiance of common blacks to his constructed law of creation, Neal, with the excitement of discovery, poetized:

No wonder we float so lightly in Summer
we float high, drifting on the rhythms of Drum
do air-dances O so lightly,
the Drum reforming our lives . . .[60]

Sensuality and sexuality, without misplaced shame or guilt, are
a naturalistic tendency, one clearly intertwined with relaxation
and convulsive, expressive capacity of the body. Wilhelm Reich
has argued that a healthy personality is one that has the capacity
to enjoy a healthy sex life. By healthy sex life he means the ability of the body to convulsively discharge sexual energy "in the
embrace of a beloved partner."[61]
Elaborating upon this postulate, Reich states:

> The orgasm is a fundamental biological phenomenon;
> fundamental because the orgastic energy discharge
> takes place in the form of an involuntary contraction
> and expansion of the total plasma system. . . . The out-
> standing phenomena an intensive biological excitation,
> repeated expansion and contraction, ejaculation of body
> fluids in the contraction, and rapid reduction of the bio-
> logical excitation . . . In its quickly alternating expan-
> sions and contractions, the orgasm shows a function
> which is composed of tension and relaxation, charge
> and discharge: *biological pulsation.*[62]

Reich's biological emphasis puts in clear perspective the tension reduction derived from lovemaking, which finalizes in deep
muscle relaxation, the state necessary to activate the proper physiological responses of the body so as to begin the process of
lovemaking. That is, the tense, constricted body opposes physiological responsiveness to sexual stimulation.
Because vital expressiveness, profoundly characteristic of black
life and culture, relaxes and spiritually revives the body, common
blacks enjoy a rich sexual life, a fact long known.
Another component of human behavior is manifest, however,
in this rich capacity of blacks for the expression of sensuality and
sexuality. The spiritual component of personality predominates,

particularly at the orgastic pinnacle. According to Fanon, "coitus is an occasion to call on the gods of the clan. It is a sacred act, pure, absolute, bringing invisible forces into action."[63] Fanon makes use of a premise deeply embedded in African thought and philosophy.

For the African, the world is flesh. He finds, Jahn claims, the warm silk of skin "in the belly of the sand, in the thighs of heaven, it is himself he is caressing."[64]

Jahn writes more fully on this premise:

> Man, therefore, is constructed for reproduction, he is put into the world in order to perpetuate himself by re-production.
>
> To leave no living heirs behind him is the worst evil that can befall a man, and there is no curse more terrible to put on a man than to wish him to die childless. But the whole weight of an extinct race lies on the dead. The worst of evils, the irremediable catastrophe falls on the dead ancestor who came before him. For they have all, for the whole time of their infinite deathlessness, missed the goal of their existence, that is 'to perpetuate themselves through reproduction' in the living person. Thus everything is concentrated on the precious existence of the living, in whom the life that was transmitted to them from their ancestors is carried on.[65]

It is evident that in sexuality blacks celebrate the "mystery of being," and this celebration is woven into the fabric of custom and mores. For instance, when a girl reached puberty it was the tradition of many African societies to celebrate the occasion. News was drummed to all villages. The celebration was marked by the singing of menstruation songs by old women. "As the girl sat in the street," Fisher tells, "others of her sex paraded and sang bara [menstruation] songs of congratulations."[66] Similar celebrations occurred for young men, who upon adolescence were initiated into secret societies as tributes to their manliness.

What emerges for the African is a kind of complementary

merging of virtue and sensuality. "To be sensual," Phyl Garland poses, "is to respect and rejoice in the force of life, of life itself, and to be present in all that one does, from the effort of loving to the breaking of bread."[67]

From the traditions of Africa the common black responds to sexuality and reproduction with neither shame, surprise, nor guilt. Early development in this regard is unmarred by complexes. Since its presentation is quite natural, black children learn that sex is a natural and even commendable activity, in that its ultimate end, procreation, satisfies the yearnings of the ancestors.

Sex, then, is positioned in the regular rhythm of life, just like eating, drinking, and sleeping. Fanon summed it up well, calling sexuality and sensuality "that youth of spirit, that innate respect for man and creation, that joy in living, that peace which is not a disfigurement of man imposed and suffered through moral hygiene, but a natural harmony with the happy majesty of life."[68]

Affection for the natural world seems clearly associated with romantic feelings. The earth, moon, stars, sun, heaven itself, all are infused with expressions of love, surfacing sexual feelings. Examine this passage from *The River Between:*

> Nyambura was fascinated and felt attracted to the river. Her breast, glowing with pleasure, rose and fell with a sigh: she felt something strange stirring in her bowels. It was an exhilaration, a feeling of acute ecstasy, almost of pain, which always came to her as she watched the snaky movement and listened to the throb of the river.[69]

Here the "gurgling" sounds of the river become equivalent to the lyrical sounds of sensually inciting music, which is naturally seductive to human beings and underlies much of expressive behavior: dance, rapping, poetry, song, or other aesthetic forms.

Black sensuality and sexuality, a natural tendency, has long threatened the psyche of the European and has been depicted in many literary masterpieces. James Baldwin's *Blues for Mister Charlie* quite aptly unfolds that threat, and Calvin C. Hernton's analysis of the play is instructive.

Hernton uses the literary review of Tom Driver, which appeared in the *Negro Digest, The Village Voice,* and *Christianity and Crises,* to make his point. Driver, in his review, affirmed "the essential reality of the play: that the white man (and woman) in America has a sexual hang-up about himself vis-a-vis the Negro, and it is this hang-up that terrifies the white man whenever he encounters the Negro, and that causes so much violence and bloodshed."[70] Driver depicted the white male as "sterile and sexually insecure," while depicting black males as "virile and lusty."

What writers have long shown is that sexuality for the common man of African heritage is not viewed with inhibition or shame, but rather as a natural process. They are therefore rendered as passionate, vital, and creative in the conquest of sexual release.

There are many therapies in psychology that view psychological cure as a factor in sexual release. In this connection, we earlier cited the work of Wilhelm Reich. It is fair to say that a healthy sex life, or at least effective means of releasing sexual energy through expressive forms, is crucial to the maintenance of good mental health. In fact, many in the black folk community feel that expressions of irritation such as complaining, grouchiness, and depression are relievable through sexual release. Even such ailments as headaches, bachaches, and other pains deriving from muscular tension are thought to be curable through sex.

When one considers the spiritually induced state of relaxation achieved during an orgasm, and the physical and psychological comfort derived, the conclusion must be drawn that this folk belief of common blacks, articulated in the persuasive moans of Aretha Franklin and the crass mellow tones of Johnnie Taylor, cannot be discarded as empty talk. Sex for common blacks is a kind of medicine, positing a curative, erotic dynamic unavailable to whites or to middle-class blacks, who are often bonded in a class-conscious aristocracy and who are frequently depicted in literary expression as sexually repressed, having defected from the naturalistic fervor that is woven in the fabric of man's basic nature.

Sex, then, a practice enabled by a naturalistic attitude, is a kind of music with its own distinctive beat. It is a beat that thumps away pretense and the entrapments of modern life, a beat that ignites flames of passion, hot beads of sexual excitement, burning pools of "sweet funk."

7

WHEN SUSANNA WEARS RED

Stylistic Renderings

When Susanna Jones wears red
Her face is like an ancient cameo
Turned brown by the ages . . .

When Susanna Jones wears red
A queen from some time-dead Egyptian
    night
Walks once again.

And the beauty of Susanna Jones in red
Burns in my heart a love-fire sharp like
    pain.

Langston Hughes[1]

Self-embellishment, with ornaments and behavioral nuances, gains distinctiveness in the ways of common black folk. Such adornments and idiosyncrasies seem to reflect the individual's attempt to extend the self, or insure its union with nature, through marking the environment with the blueprint of one's essence, one's style.

Johnnie Taylor, a popular recording artist, sings with puzzled delight:

> . . . *it ain't what you do, it's the way you do it*
> *Baby what you're doing I can plainly see but just*
> *How you do it is a mystery to me*
> *Always bringing out the best in me, baby keep,*
> *Keep the . . . [recipe]*[2]

Generalizing, "it ain't what blacks do, it's the way they do it." The way you do or say something shows your uniqueness, your individuality, your style. Style is opposed to that which is faked in human behavior. Rather, it is a naked public declaration of who one is. And who one is, is different from who any other is in the universe.

Optimal mental health requires us to possess the courage to be ourselves, to display our style, the unique characteristics of who we are. To have style, then, is to gamble with one's image in terms of how others see you. You may be seen as sensationally "together," or amusingly odd. The apprehension at being seen as amusingly odd prohibits courage and persuades many to safeguard their images by seeking invisibility, dissolving their individuality into the human glob of conformity, the mainstream, or into profiles of zestless behavior adjudged socially acceptable. Whereas the risk or criticism or rejection by others is sharply reduced or nullified, a tremendous loss of individual identity is incurred, and hence a reduced state of optimal mental health.

In spite of the bombardment of ridicule by whites and middle-class blacks, a bold, humbly arrogant style prevails in the common black folk community. It is a style that is not to be denied by the technological mania of a society bent on forging assembly-

line, standardized humans, humans who are controllable, predictable, regulatable, or otherwise divested of essence.

To be divested of essence is to be desensitized to one's impulses or unguided by one's inner signals, the drumbeat of one's
inner nature. It is a too frequent occurrence in our society, induced by a desire to avoid the display of that which is innately
conspicuous in the self, which, if refined and accentuated, copy-
rights for one a polished, personal style.

Westerners are fortunate to have the examples of free expression in the black community, from which a black style has clearly
derived. It is a style that now, in contemporary times, is imitated
and pirated by Westerners far more frequently than it is cas-
tigated. Whatever styles Westerners enjoy in their popular arts,
and in their personal lives, are borrowed, without consent of
course, from the common black folk community, where the pulse
of Africa is most authentically alive. Only in this community do
style and standard go their separate ways.

Characteristic of the style and interesting flair of black behavior is "the lazy amble with which Jimmy Brown used to return to
the huddle," notes George Frazier, a white writer.[3] The basket
catch of Willie Mays, the basketball dribbling of Earl "The
Pearl" Monroe, the shuffling dance of Muhammad Ali, the steady
unperturbability of Bob Gibson, and the frequently seen triumphant open palm slap of athletes, all reflect black style. There is
also the matchless grace of Nina Simone on stage, and the shoe-
leather-burning antics of James Brown on stage, the smoothness
and fluidity of a youth strolling, the pontifical platform command
of Jesse Jackson, or the spellbinding, poetic drama of Martin
Luther King, Jr. Frazier provided more examples:

> The formal daytime attire (black sack coats and striped
> trousers) the Modern Jazz Quartet wore when appear-
> ing in concert; . . . the delight the late "Big Daddy"
> Lipscomb took in making sideline tackles in full view of
> the crowd and the way, after crushing a ball carrier to
> the ground, he would chivalrously assist him to his feet;
> the constant cool of Satchel Paige; the chic of Bobby

Short; the incomparable grace of John Bubbles—things
like that are style. . . .

The black man has an air about him—Adam Clayton
Powell, so blithe, so self-possessed, so casual, as con-
trasted with Tom Dodd, sanctimonious, whining, an absolute disgrace. What it is that made Miles Davis and
Muhammad Ali, Sugar Ray Robinson and Archie Moore
and Ralph Ellison and Sammy Davis, Jr., seem so special
was their style.[4]

Attire is style, or at least an intricate manifestation of it. "Our
own style," Amy Gross contends, "is our costumes consciously or
unconsciously arranged to present us in some desired light."[5] Costume or dress is indeed an artistic expressive form, Robert
Armstrong argues,[6] and in the black community it is made saucy
by hair and cosmetic decoration. The attire of the black community can be expected to be colorful and visually stimulating,
arousing surprise and interest. What we see is art on limbs,
unleashing upon the world enticing delights, as "When Susanna
Wears Red."
     "Put on your red dress, baby, cause we're goin out t'night," are
lines that folk bluesmen can often be heard wailing, hinting at a
preference for a clothing style that is hot and tangy, agreeably
exciting to the senses. When one "Goes out," he goes in the style
of the times, ready for action. Maya Angelou's poem is fitting:

> Funky blues
> Keen toed shoes
> High water pants
> Saddy night dance
> Red soda water
> and anybody's daughter.[7]

Visualize Melvin Van Peebles' kaleidoscopic description of
"Frog":

His knit is red on red and expensive, his hat is floppy and

red and stylish for days. His slacks are velvet and red
and black, high-heeled, and the envy of his peer group.
He is clean and together forever. Don't be trying to
ignore him, he wants action.[8]

The brilliance of red and the colorful schemes of the black community command attention rather than elicit it. Eliciting attention involves effort by the one enshrined in color and smacks of
pretense. Brightness in fashion evolves from a black style that
needs not the assistance of "putting on"; it compels onlookers to
stare. The wearers of such fashion are engaged by their own visi-
bility and are conspicuously apparent, stirring exciting forces in
eyes that cannot turn away. Zora Neale Hurston gives an applicable example in *Mules and Men:*

Tookie Allen passed by the mill all dressed up in a tight
[skirt—it must have been red]. She must have thought
she looked good because she was walking that way. All
the men stopped talking for a while. Joe Willard hollered at her.

"Hey, Tookie, how do you like your new dress?" Tookie
made out she didn't hear, but anybody could tell that
she had. That was why she had put on her new dress,
and come past the mill a wringing and twisting—so she
could hear the men talking about her in the dress.

Lawd, look at Tookie switchin' it and lookin' back at it!
She's done gone crazy thru de hips. Joe Willard just
couldn't take his eyes off of Tookie.[9]

Freeman, Sam Greenlee's character in *The Spook Who Sat by
the Door,* felt that red "threads" queenly adorned his whore,
who, beneath her occupational status, was indeed a beautiful
black woman. "She smoothed her red dress," after being gripped
on the thigh by a police accoster, "walked to the bar and ordered
a drink, fixed her hair in the mirror and straightened her dress on

her shoulders," and wondered if the "loud" style had really made her beautiful:

> She had never worn red before, she had been told all her life that she could not, because she was too black, but Freeman had told her that she should wear it because she was a Dahomey queen. . . . She had found that he was talking about Africa and at first had been angry. But there was the picture of a woman in the [library] book that had looked enough like herself to startle her, hair kinky and short-cropped, with big earrings in her ears. She had taken the book out of the library and painfully read it in its entirety. Then she bought a red dress and, later, several others when she found the tricks liked it, but mostly because Freeman liked her in red and said so. She wore big round and oval earrings like the queen in the picture, but she could not bring herself to wear her hair short and kinky; but sometimes she would look at the picture and see herself there and for the first time in her life, she began to think that she might be beautiful.[10]

Loud colors and silky textures have long marked the cloth of preference in the black community, and now they have gained wide acceptance among whites, who in addition to consuming these styles for the enjoyment of greater self-esteem also market them for their own commercial gain.

In the loud-hot, colored clothing of the black community, something of Africa is stylized in the stitches. This connection is obvious in one of Helene Johnson's poems. She writes of a black man "dressed fit to kill in yellow gloves and swallow-tail coat and twirling a cane." Onlookers laughed at the man until he began to dance in a "dignified and proud" manner to the jazz of an organ grinder. Happiness was in his face. The poetess transformed him:

> And somehow, I could see him dancin' in a jungle . . .
> And he wouldn't have on them
> Trick clothes—yellow shoes and yellow gloves

And swallow-tail coat. He wouldn't have on nothing.
. . . and he'd be dancin' black and naked, and gleaming.
And he'd have rings in his ear and on his nose
And bracelets and necklaces of elephant's teeth . . .[11]

"The African cult taught Negroes to dress their finest," Fisher explains.[12] The attire of Africans included clothing of "cotton, silk, and velvet beautifully ornamented with embroidery and jewelry of gold and silver."[13] So beautiful was the attire of black women in the West Indies, a law of 1540 forbade their wearing jewelry, pearls, and silk unless they were married to whites.[14] In 1735, a law in the state of South Carolina renewed the confiscation of the finer clothes slaves wore.[15] "Indeed," J. S. Buckingham indicates, "Negroes often dressed more elaborately than Caucasians in the United States or working people in England."[16] Note the finery at a camp meeting in Indiana in 1829:

> One tent was occupied exclusively by Negroes. They were all full-dressed, and looked exactly as if they were performing a scene on the stage. One woman wore a dress of pink gauze trimmed with silver lace; another was dressed in pale yellow silk; one or two had splendid turbans; and all wore a profusion of ornaments. The men, in snow white pantaloons, with gay coloured linen jackets.[17]

What is of special note here is that clothing for African people, whether in African garb or European designs, is used primarily for a sense of embellishment, accentuating the personality, rather than from a feeling of shame regarding the human body or as protective veneer. Attire, as style, then, emerges as a feature of personality, a self-declaration. Observe the characteristics of personality in the stylistic apparel described in Achebe's book *No Longer at Ease:*

> He wore a smart palm-beach suit and appeared unruffled and indifferent.[18]

She was dark and tall with an enormous pneumatic bosom under a tight-fitting red and yellow dress. Her lips and long fingernails were a brilliant red, and her eyebrows were fine black lines. She looked not unlike those wooden masks. . . .[19]

Obi slowed down as he approached three drummers and a large group of young women in damask and velvet swivelling their waists as effortlessly as oiled ball bearings.[20]

As soon as Lagos had been sighted he had returned to his cabin to emerge half an hour later in a black suit, bowler hat, and rolled umbrella, even though it was a hot October day.[21]

Mabel Dove-Danquah, in her essay, "Anticipation," in *An African Treasury*, depicts "a scene of barbaric splendor." Under state umbrellas diversely colored sat chiefs and their governing clan on native stools. Gleaming in the sunlight, young women, "like tropical butterflies, looked charming in their multi-colored brocaded silk, Kente and velvet, and the Oduka headdress, black and shiny, studded with long golden pins and slides." Males, equally dashing, "paraded the grounds, their flowing clothes trailing behind them, their silken plated headbands glittering in the sun."[22]

Loud-hot coloration is distinctively African in style. Umbrellas (like those seen at the New Orleans and Trinidad Mardi Gras) and canopies, like their clothing, have been described as brilliant in effect. Thomas Edward Bowdich indicated in 1819 that the umbrellas and canopies of a king's entourage were "made of scarlet," and of brilliant colors, and that they wore "the most shewy [showy] clothes and silks. . . ."[23]

It is the brilliance of passionate colors that makes the black/African style a compellingly seductive one. You cannot help but notice it, and therefore we can argue that this style has command over one's powers of attention and induces moments of respite as well as imitation.

Hair decoration crowns one's attire and is said to reach a high

point among people of African ancestry, even though it is con-
taminated by the practice of straightening out the kink in imitation of white hair. The object of decoration, however, is unmistakable, and comes to the Americas by way of Africa.

For a hairstyle to truly captivate, it must be complemented by
other body ornaments and appealing costume. Achebe, in *Things
Fall Apart,* has presented the perfect profile:

> She wore a coiffure which was done up into a crest in
> the middle of the head. Cam wood was rubbed lightly
> into her skin, and all over her body were black patterns
> drawn with uli. She wore a black necklace which hung
> down in three coils just above her full succulent breasts.
> On her arms were red and yellow bangles, and on her
> waist four or five rows of jigida or waist beads.[24]

"'How should we style it?'" Great Grandmaw said:

> Style it fancy
> Style it simple
> Style it with seeds on cowry shells.
> Style with ribbons,
> Style with ivory,
> Style with beads on tinkly bells . . .[25]

This poetic passage from Camille Yarbrough's *Cornrows* introduces one of Africa's most popular hairstyles. She tells us poetically:

> You could tell the clan, the village
> by the style of hair they wore. . . .
> Then the Yoruba people
> were wearin thirty braids and more. . . .
> You know the princess, queen, and bride
> by number of the braids. . . .
> You know the gods they worshipped
> by the pattern that they made.[26]

Deep in African antiquity the braided hairstyle is buried, only
to be worn in recent years by white women and renamed "10
braids," from the movie 10, in which a white actress sported the
African hairstyle. Without shame or apology, white women of
America and the West gleam and glitter in the style of Africa,
while unwillingly and perhaps unknowingly paying compliments
to an appealing black style.

As the "10 braids" preposterously dominated the media, blacks
grew incensed at the broad-daylight thievery of white America
and demanded a forum seeking to halt the subversion of truth.
Clearly it was time to put in the proper historical perspective the
culturally parasitic, ungracious ways of the white masses in the
appropriation of black style.

Louie Robinson quoted columnist Dorothy Gilliam of the
Washington Post, who poetically set the record straight:

> Cornrows don't belong to no
> [European stylistic tradition]
> They belong to women selling
>   Yams beneath a
>   sweating sun in Senegal.
> They belong to H Street
>   Northeast
> And to Auburn Avenue in
>   Atlanta.
> They belong to the blues of
>   Jimmy Rushing
> And to the frenetic energy of
>   John Coltrane.
> They belong to the Women in
>   Howard University dorms
> And working mothers styling
>   their little girls'
>   hair on Saturday to
>   last all week . . .[27]

What we see is that the cornrow hairstyle belonged to times

preceding the "middle passage" by centuries. The totality of the black style is similarly dated.

Frobenius found traces of sameness throughout Africa. Egypt, the Congo, South Africa, Dahomey, Nigeria, Senegal, and the Sudan were visited during his travels of twenty years on the continent. He swore that a civilization "bearing the same stamp" was in all of Africa. "Everywhere we recognize a similar 'spirit,' 'characteristic,' 'essence.' "[28] And style.

The definiteness of aim is the main characteristic of the African style. Purpose and function dominate the entirety of Africa and are therefore the elements of essence in the black style. It is articulate in gesture, talk, walk, dance, religious fervor, song, and other expressive forms of blacks, or, to sum it up, in their total mode of existence. Within this context, any black who remains in touch with the powerful vibes of Africa, vibes that have given buoyancy to the once stoical quality of Western life, develops a characteristic style catalytic to the attainment of a fully functioning self. He or she attains self-identity, self-acceptance, self-glorification, and other indices of ego (self) inspiration leading to fulfillment (happiness). We can safely say that self-fulfillment or self-actualization is indicated by the fruition of a personal style.

In the folk community, style is also characterized by behavioral peculiarities that set the individual apart from the group, giving him his individuality. The unusual decoration of a bicycle, an automobile, a house, indicates a personal style. Paraphernalia (items, objects, musical instruments, and trinkets of all sorts) take on stylistic features in many instances. In *Mules and Men*, Zora Neale Hurston recorded this indicative bit of dialogue:

> "Man, you know Ah don't go nowhere unless Ah take my box [guitar] with me," said Johnnie in his starched blue shirt, collar pin with heart bangles hanging on each end and his cream pants with the black stripe. "And what makes it so cool, Ah don't go nowhere unless I play it."[29]

Many may view Johnnie with polite or outright disdain. A

closer examination, however, permits one a view of the self-satisfaction and esteem he derives from his trademark, his style. Ac-
cruing to Johnnie, owing to the unashamed exhibition of his style,
are health-releasing properties manifested in appropriate self-
glorification or exaltation.

Hurston, in this same work, mentions watching some members
of a swamp crew handle axes. "I didn't doubt for a moment," she
wrote, "that they could do all that they said." She further explained:

> Not only do they chop rhythmically, but they do a
> beautiful double twirl above their heads with the de-
> scending axe before it begins that accurate and bird-like
> descent. They can hurl their axes great distances and
> behead moccasins or sink the blade into an alligator's
> skull. In fact, they seem to be able to do everything
> with their instrument that a blade can do. It is a
> magnificent sight to watch the marvelous coordination
> between the handsome black torsos and the twirling
> axes.[30]

In this example a point of critical importance surfaces. Respected individual styles are modeled or imitated. If imitated at a
high enough level, they take on the characteristic of a group style
or a group trait. Therefore, modeling, a learning principle
(though not an expressive form), is essential in considering the
style of a people and the stylistic ingredients essential for optimal
learning within a culture. The isolation of these stylistic ingredients is what lends credence to the often-referred-to notion of
"black learning styles." It is the concept of preferred group behavior that allows us to talk about a black style, varying at the individual level with personal touches. Motivation, or affective
readiness for learning, is clearly a factor of style.

Consider the black "talkin style." Pertaining to language
usage, Smitherman explains, it "refers to the way speakers put
sound and grammatical structure together to communicate
meaning in a larger context. Style is what you do with the

words."[31] Toni Morrison in *Sula* gives the character Hannah potent stylistic elocutions. These account for Hannah's position of supremacy in sexual wooing:

> Hannah simply refused to live without the attention of a man. . . . [She] had a steady sequence of lovers, mostly the husbands of her friends and neighbors. Her flirting was sweet, low, and guileless. Without ever a pat of the hair, a rush to change clothes or a quick application of paint, with no gesture whatsoever, she rippled with sex. . . . The smile-eyes, the turn of a head—all so welcoming, light and playful. Her voice trailed, dipped and bowed, she gave a chord to the simplest words. Nobody, but nobody could say "hey sugar" like Hannah.[32]

Jane Phillips' work "Untitled," featured in an *Ebony* article by Michele Burgen entitled "What I Love About My Beautiful Black Man," imbues the black male with the same position of supremacy in his "talkin"—sexual style. She writes:

> Miss Universe has nothing on me when you whisper that you love my brown, soft skin, when you tuck my tightly curled hair, when you call me "Baby." Honey, nobody can say "Baby" like a Black man![33]

The next chapter considers the language and speech of the black community with greater depth and precision. Suffice it here to assert that the speaking style sustaining "the sacred-secular oral tradition" of the black community may be viewed, as Smitherman purports, in terms of the "rhetorical qualities of smaller individual units of expression." Smitherman cited these qualities as exaggerated language (unusual words, High Talk); mimicry; proverbial statement and aphoristic phrasing; punning and plays on words; spontaneity and improvisation; image-making and metaphor; braggadocio; indirection (circumlocution, suggestiveness); and tonal semantics.[34] Thus, the seductive speaking style of the black community is highly characteristic, be it in the form of rap, sermon, informative speech, or jive talk. It is a style loaded with emotional qualities that richly stimulate the senses of listening audiences, increasing their attentive powers. Attention is a pertinent factor in learning.

With regard to the psychomotor domain of expression, we can speak also of a black style of locomotion, or physical movement through "walkin," gesture, dance, drama, and athletic maneuvering, all of which embody grace.

"The way a black man bops into a room, especially when he is clean (that is dressed sharply), that's style," contends Johnetta B. Cole.[35] It is easy movement. A rhythmically coordinated bobbling, as if swivel-jointed, characterizes the walk. Benjamin Cooke is a bit more descriptive:

> The basic soul walk consists of placing one foot directly in front of the other, the heel hits first and the leg drops loosely which results in a bended leg effect. The shoulders sway very slightly and naturally, with a slight dropping of the shoulder which moves forward. The overall motion is a gentle swing; the stride is rhythmic and graceful.[36]

Gestural expressions are common in the black folk community, representing a communal communicative style. Few are more popular, as Cooke pointed out, than "givin and gettin skin."[37] A celebrative greeting, it immensely enriches the formal handshake of the West. It is the physical embellishment of a sterile vocal "Hello." Giving and getting skin is also victoriously celebrative. Frequently, it is observed in team sports following the display of individual or collective excellence.

Gestural expressions have long been an acknowledged dimension of the black/African expressive style. Frobenius insisted that the gestures of all the people of Africa, in children and adults alike, were completely natural and full of "dignity and grace."[38]

Grace, a derivative of a cultivated style of physical movement, cannot be more graphically depicted than in dance and drama. Further, no one has depicted it better than Paul Lawrence Dunbar has in "Angelina":

. . . Don't you know Miss Angelina? She's de da'lin' of de place.
W'y, dey ain't no high-toned lady wif sich mannahs an' sich
    grace.
She kin move across de cabin, wif its planks all rough an' wo';
Jes' de same's ef she was dancin' on ol' mistus' ball-room flo'.
Fact is, you do' see no cabin—evaht'ing you see look grand,
An' dat one ol' squeaky fiddle soun' to you jes' lak a ban';
Cotton britches look lak broadclof an' a linsey dress look fine,
When Angelina Johnson comes a-swingin' down de line.

. . . Angelina steps so gently, Angelina bows so low,
An' she lif' huh sku't so dainty dat huh shoetop skacely show:
An' dem teef o' huh' n a-shinin', ez she tek you by de han'—
Go 'way, people, d' ain't anothah sich a lady in de lan'!
When she's movin' thoo de figgers er a-dancin' by huhse'f,
Folks jes' stan' stock-still a-sta'in', an' dey mos' nigh hol's dey
    bref; . . .[39]

Note the attention Angelina, because of her graceful style, is able
to command.

    Maya Deren encourages us to think of dance as an accumu-
lation of grace. She insists that

> If a visitor to Haiti were to spend most of his time on a
> country roadside, he would have the sense of being a
> spectator at some theater-in-the-round, where a lyric
> dance-drama of prodigious grace and infinite variety is
> in continuous performance.
>
> Dawn, like stage lights being slowly raised, reveals a
> spectacle of diverse elegance. The bodies of the market-
> bound women are like fine dark stalks, at once supple
> and steady, bearing tremendous blooms of egg-plant
> purple, tomato red, carrot orange, greens of all shades,
> on their heads. Along the side of the road sways a long
> file of donkeys. The percussion of their hooves is trans-
> mitted to the women riders and flow up their straight
> backs like a rhythmic wave, spending itself finally in the

gentle undulation of the large brims of the straw hats. Whether here, or in the men walking toward the fields, the grace of the bodies' bearing is so manifest that it imparts elegance to even the most poorly cut dress and the most patched and baggy overalls. In the backyard, the women cooking, tending the children, carrying water, forever doing laundry or braiding each other's hair possess, also, this same grace of the body.[40]

A participant in a group session we jointly conducted was able to say a great deal about herself through style involving grace of the body. Tall, with a dazzling smile, Deborah was thirty-nine years of age. Feeling that time moved much too fast for her, she put together her steps to form the basis of a walk unforgettable to any eye beholding it. Her strides combined the free hip-swirling characteristic of suggestive ladies, with the refinement of those having the status of society celebrities; she walked so as to make the clothing she wore dance on her body. As if on shimmering clouds she walked, styling, but in her case covering the yearnings of her soul.

Deborah projected an unusually exuberant feeling, one of untouchable loftiness. Those in the group who knew her closely claimed she had highfalutin' ways. Yet she was lonely. She lacked intimacy in her personal contacts. A two-time divorcee, she was determined to convince others that she was happy. It was a believable facade.

In the group sessions she had discussed, without regrets, the dissolution of both her marriages. And though she was displeased about her children's school progress, she took it pleasantly, and more, all heaped on top of a frightening financial situation.

Deborah was gracious and graceful. In this manner she side-stepped male advances. On such an occasion, after her elegant side-steps, she meandered steadily, and swiftly, as if to avoid the repeated forward advance of an on-rushing bull. Sometimes, when the bull rush had waned to a pitiful plea, she consented to satisfy the sexual longing of a suitor, delighting in the sense of control and power she wielded. "No man will ever hurt me again," she emphasized in one of the sessions, "I live for me and

me alone." For when the appetizer had been enjoyed, heightening the appetite, she withheld the dessert. "You discharged,
didn't you?" she would say, coldly. Enjoying the pain she sensed
they felt, Deborah sent them on their way. So as not to feel the
emptiness of her life when they had gone, and even while she
slept, she focused her mind on the fascination she inspired with
her style of movement.

It appeared that she was contemptuous toward others, but really she was jealous and envious, which combined to form the
basis of the cynical anger that she expressed rather beautifully,
more in her walk than in her talk. She was without insight into
her behavior prior to the particular group session in which she
made her self-presentation.

Group members had been asked in the session before to bring
something to depict how they saw themselves. They were encouraged to highlight their depictions with black expressiveness.

Deborah had waited until all other members had completed
their presentations and had absorbed the clinical discussion and
feedback which followed each presentation. It was now her turn,
a calculated turn. Guided by the saying "Saving the best for
last," she was ready to fascinate, to elicit awe.

She had chosen to model some clothes as a way of expressing
something significant about herself to the group. Sitting in a circle, the group was at her disposal. Deborah used the entire space
inside the circle the group formed. She was on top of the world
looking down, glowingly, and then up, with overtones of piety.
She walked to music that had no words. Around and across the
floor she roved, changing items of clothing in stride. In an instant
she changed from a lady taking a casual stroll to one of splendid
elegance fit for a genteel occasion. Before one's eyes could adjust
to the elegance transported by her walk, she was temptingly at-
tired in lingerie generously revealed beneath a robe which was
accented by a striking little belt tied in a most stylish knot. The
music stopped. Her steps quietened. Her arms extended upward,
receiving the group's applause. Deborah, now seated, breathed
heavily with a satisfied look on her face, not unlike the relieved
expression that follows an orgasmic pinnacle.

The clinical discussion that followed was stirring. Initially the group praised her for what was nothing less than an enlivening display of modeling talent, and astonishing garments. She enjoyed every moment but was obviously uneasy, sensing that the group saw deeper, beyond the stylistic cover that hid her from herself far more effectively than from others. Someone in the group said, "Deborah, I can't believe you're that happy and carefree." Someone else agreed. "It's almost as if," another member said, "you're off into a world of your own, closed off from other people." "True, I let others in sparingly," Deborah admitted. But not long enough for genuine intimacy, leaving her with an inner void which went neglected. Denial of its existence was Deborah's way of avoiding an unpleasant reality. She reacted to it by putting on a happy face, which was powerfully reinforced by her dashing apparel and her mobile limbs. Under the press of the group, she examined the vacuous space in her life, and was able to express much of what she had long denied as an adjustment to an unhappy situation. She seized upon her greatest attribute, her style. It had long been her trademark. And in a very real way it had kept her up in spirit against the forces of depression. She was stronger now, however, and able to face the truth of her existence. Facing the hurt helped her understand it and would help her get over it, freeing her to make genuine contact with other people. During the remaining sessions she was less animated and more reflective, reaching out to others with a sincerity that had not been apparent before. Her walk remained sensualized by her attire but without the trimmings of inner conflict.

Costume, vocal deliverance, and graceful movement—all combine in the style of black festivity and worship. Parades predominate in black festival behavior, and the styles are incomprehensible, i.e., they can oversaturate the senses as they record the unending display of individual and collective creativity.

"Those parades were really tremendous things," Alan Lomax wrote:

> The drums would start off, the trumpets and trombones rolling into something like "Stars and Stripes" or the National Anthem and everybody would strut off

down the street, the bass-drum player twirling his baton
in the air, the snare drummer throwing his sticks up and
bouncing them off the ground, the kids jumping and
hollering.[41]

New Orleans, festival city, startlingly reflects Lomax's memories. Kids jumping and hollering. "By the time they had made the
turn," Buerkle and Barker comment, "you could see them—the
second line [a New Orleans street march dance]—those young
black kids with their umbrellas, cavorting, jiving, prancing, and
strutting."[42] Behind the band, "down Royal, across Canal and
onto St. Charles," black style dominates the streets to the delight
of onlookers.

Mardi Gras is the highlight of parades. Raymond J. Martinez
writes of the "Indians," the small black carnival groups. They call
themselves "tribes." "Their main purpose is to dress up in elabo-
rate costumes resembling that of American Indians and to perform various forms of dancing, marching, and music on Mardi
Gras Day."[43] Seeing the Indians on the day of carnival is to witness the explosion of style. Their musical form is in the African
responsive style (call and response). Here, one person sings lead
and the others, to each sung statement from the lead singer, sing
a response. The response line remains the same. The beat of tambourines accompanies the singing. The beats are extremely complex in rhythmical patterns and are said to be quite similar to certain forms of West African music.

The practice sessions, in preparation for Mardi Gras Day, are
communal affairs. People are jam-packed in the bars where the
practice sessions occur. The audience participates by second line
dancing, singing with the response line, and beating out the
rhythm of songs on empty bottles. Obviously what one witnesses
is the exact replication of African communal festivity transposed
hundreds and hundreds of miles and years to the West, away
from the point of origin. Truly an African style.

They meet fully dressed on the day of carnival, and around
them large crowds gather to view, with fascination, the inviting
costumes. In the course of their marching, dancing, singing, "stylin and profilin," they meet other "tribes." Here "a wild display

of chanting and dancing" occurs. They "display themselves and
their costumes to the other 'tribe,' claiming that 'my tribe is the
best in town and I am the best dressed Indian of the whole
creation.' "[44] Note the element of braggadocio in the language, or
self-glorification, feeding the mind with the feeling of "I Am
Somebody," which is a requisite for healthy self-concept formation.

The sacred style is not too unlike the style seen in secular parades and other festival occasions. In fact the dynamics are identical: rich emotional expression, stylized through dance, singing,
and drama invoke spiritual realities to cleanse, heal, and uplift, as
in the ways of traditional Africa.

Whereas whites just sit and worship with words, blacks tradi-
tionally throw their souls, minds, and bodies wholly into the ceremony. To talk of the traditional sacred style, "an important force
in black culture," writes Smitherman, "is to speak of the holy
rolling, bench-walking, spirit-getting, tongue-speaking, vision-
receiving, intuitive-directing, amen-saying, sing-song preaching,
holy dancing, and God-sending Church! Put another way, this
church may be defined as that in which the content and religious
substance has been borrowed from Western Judaeo-Christian tradition, but the communication of that content—the process—has
remained essentially African."[45]

In the religious ceremonies of Haitian peasants, both the process and content reflect an African style. The religious leaders of
these ceremonies "develop a degree of social grace and personal
charm," identifiable even in the projection of their powers of persuasion and appeal. Under their direction, choirs "will answer
with more meticulous timing," drummers function at levels
"higher than adequacy, and altogether [these ceremonies] move
with dispatch and intensity," perhaps even with elements of
"personal style."[46]

The field of sports and athletics flourishes with black style. Style
is a prominent factor in the position of dominance that blacks
enjoy in the sports world. In a 1977 *Time* magazine article,
"Black Dominance," some notable statistics were cited.

Of the professional basketball players, close to 65 percent are black; 42 percent of the players in the National Football League are black; 19 percent of the baseball players are black (sixteen times in the past twenty-eight years the MVP award has been won by blacks); twenty-four of the thirty medals won by American track and field athletes in the Montreal Olympic Games were won by black athletes (all gold medals in boxing were won by blacks).[47] A clear dominance is evident.

Both white and black fans, players, coaches, and intellectual behavioral scientists have marveled at the black dominance and offered a wide range of theories to explain black athletic superiority. The most glaringly omitted factor in these explanations is that of the artistic style that black athletes possess, inherited from their African genesis by way of the black folk community in America. Accompanying their unusual skill and talent, the black style of movement, gesture, and dress enchants fans to the level of cathartic excitement, inciting fans to healthy, stylistic exhibitionism.

At the Muhammad Ali–Joe Frazier championship fight held in Madison Square Garden, the crowd was described as stylistically competitive with the two "ex-champs." The "People" section of *Time* magazine described it: "Muhammad Ali glowed in a white satin robe while Joe Frazier menaced in crushed velvet with 'Smokin Joe' across the back." The crowd, equally dazzling, was said to be "funk-furred and metallic threaded." Combinations of "jeans and mink" and "loud pin stripes," went along with "New York Knick Star Walt Frazier in a bold red and white blazer."[48] What a background for the Ali shuffle.

The ballet moves of wide receiver Lynn Swann, the springing, swiveling ascendance of Julius Erving, the smooth, crafty deceptiveness of quarterback Joe Gilliam, all reflect black style as the basis of the popular appeal of these athletes and their achievement of the status of folk heroes.

As in the fields of sports and athletics, style as a dimension of the black performing arts is omnipresent. Whether at the folk level or professional level, it is the performer's style, perhaps more than his talent or artistic medium, that nourishes his popularity. The manner of expression is the differentiating element. Given the same work, the same medium, and equal talent, the performer who will enjoy the greatest artistic and/or commercial success is the one with the most alluring style. The musical medium is replete with examples.

Dunbar's folk articulations are representative:

> "G'way an' quit dat noise, Miss Lucy
> Put dat music book away;
> What's de use to keep on tryin'?
> Ef you practice twell you're gray,
> You cain't stat no notes a-flyin'
> Lak de ones dat rants and rings
> F'om de kitchen to de big woods
> When Malindy sings."[49]

It is the way Malindy sings that puts Miss Lucy to shame, and establishes the indomitability of the black style.

Helene Johnson captures the element of seduction in the style of a youth performing his art:

> Little brown boy, Slim dark, big-eyed,
> Crooning love songs to your banjo
> Down at the Lafayette—Gee, boy, I love the way
> you hold your head,
> High sort of and a bit to one side, Like a prince,
> a jazz prince.
> And I love your eyes flashing and your hands,
> And your patent-leathered feet,
> And your shoulders jerking the jig'wa'.
> And I love your teeth flashing, And the way
> your hair shines in the spotlight
> Like it was the real stuff.[50]

John Broven describes the style of a drummer called Hungry in the book *Rhythm and Blues in New Orleans*. "He was the funkiest thing out. He was crazy, Hungry he'd be on drums clowning, just clowning, and the shit he'd do. He could clown and play better than the average guy could concentrating."[51] Clowning, then, represented the trademark of the drummer. The stylistic challenge here is to clown and at the same time achieve perfection. What appeal!

Will Dixon, the "dancing conductor," had a unique style. James Weldon Johnson described it in *Black Manhattan:*

> all through a number he would keep his men together by dancing out the rhythm, generally in graceful, sometimes in grotesque, steps. Often an easy shuffle would take him across the whole front of the band. This style of directing not only got the fullest possible response from the men, but kept them in just the right humor for the sort of music they were playing.[52]

Eileen Southern, citing Robert Waln, writes of Old Frank Johnson's Negro String Band, who "furnished the music" at the leading public and private balls during the antebellum period. Waln indicated that Johnson, the "remarkably gifted" fiddler, was "known to lose consciousness and go to sleep, yet go on calling figures and never make a mistake." Johnson was described as the "inventor-general" with "a remarkable taste in distorting or 'jazzing' a sentimental, simple, and beautiful song, into a reel, jig or country dance."[53] Johnson's taste in distorting the music— although the word "jazz" had not yet been invented—embodied his style and accounted for his great popularity.

A contemporary artist of gospel genius, Andre Crouch possesses a style that is not too unlike the "jazzing" ability of Old Frank Johnson. With his ability to "jazz" gospel, Crouch effectively fuses all forms of black music. What emerges is a gospel style with worldwide appeal. His popular tune "Soon and Very Soon (We are going to see the King)" is typical of his "jazzing" style. Crouch's vocal leads are answered by a choral mellowness, and are balanced by the powerfully sensuous female lead voice of Danniebelle Hall. Just when you think the tune is finished, it swells with a repetitive choral-chanting of leads and answers (calls and responses): "Oh we're go goinnnnnnng, going to see the King, yes we're goinnnnnnng going to see the King." This choral-chant is accompanied only by mouth basses, toe taps, and hand claps, leaping suddenly back through time to authentic African influences, "jazzing" the music.

Robert Hayden mirrors the style of Bessie Smith in "Homage to the Empress of the Blues":

> Because there was a man somewhere in a candystripe
> silk shirt, gracile and dangerous as a jaguar and because
> a woman moaned for him in sixty-watt gloom and
> mourned him Faithless Love Twotiming Love, Oh
> Love, Oh Careless Aggravating Love,
>
> > She came out on the stage in yards of pearls,
> > emerging like a favorite scenic view, flashed her
> > golden smile and sang.
>
> > . . . she came out on stage in ostrich feathers,
> > beaded satin, and shone that smile and sang.[54]

Zack Gilbert poetically tributes the style of Ella Fitzgerald:

> How many harps do you
> Have in your throat
> How many horns,
> Lady of the instrument
> Voice,
> Reading a lyric
> With your usual
> Non-chalance
> And cool grace?
>
> Queen of riff,
> Skipping octaves
> At will
> Without missing the beat.
> Without losing that
> Rhythmic flow . . .[55]

The interpretation performing artists give a work is style. For instance, different musicians will visually scan the same piece of music and interpret it differently, or arrange it differently. Billie Holiday could give a special uniqueness to the songs of others, as can Aretha Franklin, and George Benson, and many more. Interpretation then is a stylistic feature and allows each performer the reward of imposing a personal touch. "It's difficult," Max Roach says, "for a critic to hear Carmen McRae sing 'Jitterbug Waltz' or 'Sophisticated Lady' and say it's good, bad or indifferent, because Carmen (or Aretha Franklin, Lena Horne, or Lady Day) gives it her own special interpretation [style]."[56] Herein lies the beauty of black expressiveness. Whether in music, dance, writing, oratory, or graphics, performances or exhibitions reflect individuality or personal style, supplying audiences with an infinitude of creative self-expression. A few more musical profiles should suffice.

"The band breaks into a frantic, up-tempo tune," writes David Ritz, "and Ray [Charles] is escorted out by his assistant." The audience rises to its feet when Ray is in sight. "He does a strange skip and dance to the stage, nodding his head to the music and slapping his thighs." And then the grand stylistic finale. "On stage he stops when he reaches the piano bench still slapping his thighs, bends forward and after a few seconds opens his arms and then passionately hugs himself."[57] The self-embrace is a potent feature of Ray Charles' total style, which no doubt is exemplified in the guttural tonal qualities of his inimitable voice.

The "Queen of Raunch" she is called. Millie Jackson frequently has audiences on their feet. "Teasin', tauntin', she prowls the stage," writes Alan Ebert, "and struts her stuff in a skin-tight, ice blue pantsuit. Hand on hip, with deadly accuracy she pins an evil eye on the men in the audience."[58] It is a vengeful style that soothes the "hurt in love" females, and mobilizes their assertive-aggressive-assaultive impulses that can appropriately convert to tenderness.

With Teddy Pendergrass, it is a style that uses costume to accentuate physical male robustness destined to explode with raw energy. Christian Wormley has captured the style:

The man makes his stage entrance dressed white on white . . . premier flash in a sequined cape! . . . The

man removes his sweat soaked outwear. There nakedly
revealed are strong gleaming shoulders and a torso
sheathed in a body hugging tank top.[59]

Blacks bring an obvious style even to the classical arts, which
are far less open to freedom in expression than are the popular
arts. Leontyne Price, in a television interview on the popular
New York City based show "Like It Is," hosted by Gil Noble,
made some significant revelations. Without restraining modesty,
she accepted the host's characterization of her as one among the
best of the "best" opera singers, and indicated that she was the
best because of her blackness. When Noble appeared perplexed,
Miss Price told him of many who insisted that she had to
ferret out the black tonal qualities in her voice if she was to
realize success in the opera. Miss Price did not heed the teachers
in this regard, and she credits the blackness in her voice for her
superiority. It spun for her a style all her own, making her appeal-
ingly different from, and better than, most opera singers, whose
voices appear nearly standardized.

The point of nobility here is that one only attains moments of
perfection, or achieves one's best, when being authentically and
uniquely oneself, which is to be, through one's style, in rhythm
with one's nature and therefore with the nature of the universe.
An astonishing black achievement, this is, and an established requisite for the attainment of self-fulfillment or optimal mental
health.

Who, for America and the world, set popular fashion trends, invent popular dance forms, monopolize the vogue in popular
music, add stylistic terminology to Webster's dictionary, and in-
disputably make "magic" a reality in popular sports? Blacks do.
Collectively, the possessors of the "billion dollar style."

Should blacks be accorded legal protective rights to their individual styles? Should whites, who depend upon blacks for suit-
able and pleasing styles, be required to share the royalties on
wealth they earn by replicating and marketing the styles of their
benefactors in popular culture? Yes. Artist-lawyer Brenda J.
Saunders is unequivocally of this opinion. In her copyrighted

work "Style Is . . . the Fruit of Labor," she is brilliant and judicially wise in her arguments, pointing out that the aesthetic labor of blacks, as well as their physical labor, has gone wanting for reparation.

Miss Saunders writes that "style is not only an expression, but a separate, distinct, independent, creative element which should be avidly afforded protection by State and Federal laws." She correctly insists that artists, like the black masses, "labor to create an expression which gives self-satisfaction and public approbation." Their stylistic "qualities have been labored through massive periods of trial and error, through the venerable concept of 'practice makes perfect,' through self-induced dedication. Style comes as a direct result of these endeavors; it is its own creative energy."[60]

From the inception of patent laws up until the present, in creative endeavors "Federal protection has been restricted to 'writing.'" To create a style of movement, talking, singing, and many other expressive forms, is therefore to have a style not protected by law. This allows a kind of gainful copying that violates the concepts of fairness and decency which ought to be accorded the creator of a unique style.

Naturally, under the government of such specious laws, copying steeply escalates with each creative era. Saunders quotes Millar, who, in the book *The Drifters: The Rise and Fall of the Black Vocal Group*, notes:

> By the mid-50's the practice of covering the record of a black group by stealing the arrangement and placing it in the hands of various established homely white performers was yielding fabulous rewards. A study of the Top Ten nationwide best-selling records on March 12, 1955 shows no less than six eviscerated R(hythm) and B(lues) tunes performed by white artists.[61]

Not only is the arrangement appropriated but "the technique of movement, vocal inflection, gestures, mannerisms, improvisation and communication with the audience," even dress, or, in total, the styles of black performers who personify the stylistic fervor of the black masses.

The same is true of nonperforming artists. The work of Pablo Picasso is credited for opening the minds of Westerners to the movement and instability of the Western-perceived material world. Picasso's work convinces us that the world is only deceptively solid or fixed in form. Early in 1980, through the Museum of Modern Art's retrospective, his work enjoyed worldwide attention. Little did the world know that the honor was paid to the genius of the African mind, because much of Picasso's famous work replicates, by imitation, the African style.[62] The African style recognizes spiritual or vital forces acting upon what appear to the senses to be fixed forms. The apparent distortions of reality that African art presents, then, depict the conjoint realities of spirit and material. The world, however, marked by the West's dominance, can only laud Europe's imitation of Africa's style.

In a very real way it is the black mind that is being pirated. Isn't style the very essence of one's self, of one's personality, of one's intelligence? It presents the conscious choice of an individual as to the expressive manner of the mind's ideas. Where art is concerned, style must be viewed as creative-intellectual property, worthy of protection. And as Brenda Saunders aptly argues, "If one performer blatantly copies the style of another established performer, the former should be obliged to reimburse the latter a fixed amount based on the appropriation, for . . . the potential defendant must see something of value, worthy of imitation, when he embarks on a road of reproduction of that element."[63]

"Who'll pay reparations on my soul?"[64] Gil Scott-Heron asked the question on behalf of blacks who are masters of style. Perhaps lawyer-artists like Brenda Saunders will compel white America and the West to live up to its creeds of equity, admit their cultural transgressions against Africa's spirit, and repentantly answer, WE WILL! "Style is," indeed, "the fruit of labor."

8

JIVE TALKIN

Poetic and Prosaic Vernacular

Leopold Sedar Senghor insists on the primacy of rhythm:

One distinguishes between figures of language and figures of thought. Certainly both of these are found among Negro-Africans [languages]. Yet, since it is a question of stylistics, of the art of language and of people for whom imagery and rhythm are predominant, their originality will obviously be revealed primarily by figure of language. . . . Since rhythm . . . is the very pulsation that animates . . . Negro-African languages, the figure of vocabulary most often encountered in these languages is repetition pure and simple; . . .[1]

I might say that at the base of our languages and our songs and dances, there are the rhythms of the drum, of the tom-tom that underlie and sustain them.[2]

It can scarcely be denied that there is a language usage peculiar
to unacculturated blacks in the Western hemisphere, whether the
language be Spanish, French, Portuguese, or English. Hence,
here in America, where black slaves were forced upon arrival to
abandon their native African languages and adopt English as the
primary mode of communication, we speak of black English or
black speech. Structurally, this suggests, as succinctly stated by
Geneva Smitherman:

> The pronunciation system of black English employs the
> same number of sounds as white English (ranging from
> 45–48 sounds counting stress and intonation patterns)
> but these sounds exist in a few different patterns of
> distribution. Of course, the real distinctiveness—and
> beauty—in the black sound system lies in those features
> which do not so readily lend themselves to concrete
> documentation—its speech rhythms, voice, inflections,
> and tonal patterns.[3]

However, in addition to the structural differences between
black English and public (rather than standard) English as enu-
merated by Smitherman, there are other distinctions deserving of
equal recognition. Ernest Bornenian, in an interview with Nat
Hentoff, the expert on jazz, says:

> While the whole European tradition strives for regu-
> larity—of pitch, of time, of timbre and of vibrato—the
> African tradition strives precisely for the negation of
> these elements. In language, the African tradition aims
> at circumlocution rather than at exact definition. The
> direct statement is considered crude and unimaginative;
> the veiling of all contents in ever-changing para-
> phrases is considered the criterion of intelligence and
> personality. In music, the same tendency towards obliq-
> uity and ellipsis is noticeable: no note is attacked
> straight; the voice or instrument always approaches it
> from above or below, plays around the implied pitch
> without ever remaining any length of time, and departs

from it without ever having committed itself to a single meaning. The timbre is veiled and paraphrased by constantly changing vibrato, tremolo and overtone effects. The timing and accentuation, finally, are not *stated*, but *implied* or *suggested*. The denying or withholding of all signposts.[4]

Unlike the quotes from Smitherman and Bornenian, whose selections have underscored several technical differences between black and public language, Albert C. Barnes speaks of the aesthetics of black language:

The most important element to be considered is the psychological complexion of the Negro as he inherited it from his primitive ancestors and which he maintains to this day. The outstanding characteristics are his tremendous emotional endowment, his luxuriant and free imagination and a truly great power of individual expression. He has in superlative measure that fire and light which, coming from within, bathes his whole world, colors his images and impels him to expression. The Negro is a poet by birth. In the masses, that poetry expresses itself in religion which acquires a distinction by extraordinary fervor, by simple and picturesque rituals and by a surrender to emotion so complete that ecstasy, amounting to automatism, is the rule when he worships in groups. The outburst may be started by an unlettered person provided with the average Negro's normal endowment of eloquence and vivid imagery. It begins with a song or a wail which spreads like fire and soon becomes a spectacle of a harmony or rhythmic movement and rhythmic sound unequalled in the ceremonies of any other race. Poetry is religion brought down to earth and it is of the essence of the Negro soul. He carries it with him always and everywhere; he lives it in the field, the shop, the factory. His daily habits of thought, speech and movement are flavored with the picturesque, the rhythmic, the euphonious.[5]

Sarah Webster Fabio floods the imagination with the following direct description of the language of black people:

> Black language is direct, creative, intelligent communication between black people based on a shared reality, awareness, understanding which generates interaction; it . . . places premium on imagistic renderings and concretizations of abstractions, poetic usages . . . idiosyncrasies—those individualized stylistic nuances (such as violation of structured syntax)— which nevertheless hit "home" and evoke truth; it is an idiom of integrated insight, a knowledge emanating from a juxtaposition of feeling and fact. . . .[6]

Fabio's account of black language, like those which preceded, is well thought out and carefully recorded. Many linguistic scholars agree that black language shows great spontaneity and creativity in the naming of experience. Experience appears to be central to black language and reflects the feeling from which the language develops. The language is full of flavors and energy: an experience can be felt in the vibrations of words like "baaad," "coool," "oooh, weee." Honesty flows in the language, except, perhaps, when survival or self-worth is threatened.

Observe that often black children stammer and hesitate in the classroom, but on the street corner their speech is fluid; it bumps and moves the listener. The language conjures up images for the listener, as in the following dialogue:

FIRST SPEAKER: "Do you love me?"
SECOND SPEAKER: "Do birds fly?"

FIRST SPEAKER: "Yes."
SECOND SPEAKER: "Is coal black?"

FIRST SPEAKER: "Yes."
SECOND SPEAKER: "Are you satisfied?"

FIRST SPEAKER: "Yes."

Black language cements abstractions; it collapses or condenses varying ramifications into a minute whole, as in a nickname (a phenomenon in the black community that will be discussed at length later).

Additionally, black language is full of poetic usages, and there is a tendency to make endings rhyme. There are deliberate violations of structured syntax, as in "Unass my chair," but these violations cut right through to the point. They express insight or knowledge stemming from an abutting of feeling and fact. Irony, humor, and signifying are all characteristics of black language.

Accordingly, there can be little argument that black language usage is indeed a highly cultivated art form. The question for the mental health specialist, however, might well be: How come? The responses offered by most enlightened linguists on the subject appear to suggest two major explanations:

1. Black language usage is the manifestation of black spirit, representative of the African view of the universe.

2. Black language usage, at least in the West, represents an effort to survive and move on against the constitutions of a rare isolation within oppression.

Earlier in this work the African worldview was thoroughly explained and does not bear reopening here. However, we would do well to recall that the communication system in Africa, in both east and west, as reported by John S. Mbiti and Fela Sowande, is oral.[7] The belief sets, ways of looking at the world, and values are all transmitted through the oral tradition—by word of mouth from one generation to the next. Given the vocal manifestation in African society, oral language plays a large role, and appears on very different levels, in social and religious life. Religious ceremonies accord considerable place to chants, to the recitation of devices—some recitations last through entire nights. Marriages, funerals, and other institutionalized rituals have their own particular oral language, consisting of special chants and declamations. Various labors are accompanied by chants, sometimes peculiar to each trade: chants of the farmers, chants of the weavers, of the fisherman, etc. Apprenticeships in certain ordinary activities may go hand-in-hand with the accompanying oral language.

The most favorable moment for the transmission of the oral language tradition is without doubt the evening gathering, which brings together, on the village square or in the homes, women, children, and young people. There the favorite pattern is the exchange of riddles and proverbs, and the recitations of the storytellers. A distinction is usually made between tales, in which the protagonists are human beings, and the fables, which are concerned with animals endowed with speech and human actions. The themes are numerous, but are to be found with widespread permanence throughout many societies. In particular, the principal animal heroes are found in a large area corresponding roughly to the geographical area where the actual animal prototypes are to be found. In addition to illustrating the relatively simple lessons in social ethics, the symbolic value attributed to these animal characters serves to give also a kind of instruction in rapport with the deeper knowledge of the culture.

The riddles and proverbs stand generally halfway between prose and poetry. The exchange of riddles often inaugurates an evening of pleasure and amusement. Proverbs, which are innumerable, are the vehicle of traditional wisdom and of an elementary social morality. Proverbs are often used as a means of comment on the lessons to be drawn from stories.

The oral tradition also includes the famous "griots," of whom several varieties are known. Some are attached to the families of chiefs, for whom they serve as keepers of tradition or, so to speak, their historiographers. Others are strolling poets and musicians who sing the praises of some famous person who has engaged them to perform at celebrations. There once were griots attached to particular social categories; for instance, the "hunter's griots" exalted the courage of the hunters before an expedition, by singing epic poems to the glory of ancient heroes.

In numerous African societies there appeared professional storytellers who would go from village to village to amuse the inhabitants by retelling their inexhaustible repertoire of stories, legends, and comic tales.

The audiences differed according to circumstance, but who-

ever they were, they always reacted with enthusiastic participation. Chants were taken up in chorus, stories were punctuated
by assorted exclamations or by corrections, if necessary, for the
listeners often knew the repertoire too, and their pleasure came
more from the form that the recitation took than from the novelty
of the material. These experiences played a social and psychological role as aesthetic pleasure and personality exaltation was
enjoyed.

This same tradition is readily observed among black people in
the West. Geneva Smitherman puts this interesting phenomenon
in this context:

> Naturally, Black Americans, having had to contend with
> slavery and Euro-American ways, have not been able to
> practice or manifest the traditional African world view
> in its totality. But . . . the African world view persists,
> and serves to unify such seemingly disparate Black
> groups as preachers and poets, bluesmen and Gos-
> pelettes, testifiers and toast-tellers, reverends and revo-
> lutionaries. Can I get a witness?[8]

The African brought to America with him the oral tradition.
Now, how can we use it? Black language, a surviving relic of our
African heritage, has been the motor energizer of American culture. It is the breath or spirit infused into alien, near-at-hand materials (pick-up English, Methodist hymns, old Scottish ballads).
Black language and the oral tradition have been a mainstay in
our struggle to survive an oppression beyond mention. Black language usage records the history of the black experience and black
exceptional creativity. It rolls steadily to a momentum that is
about equal to the will to live; signifying, parodying the gestures
of the jailers, commenting, searching out regrets, and turning, always, to the new and inventive, leaving strange, marvelous bits
of genius for others to borrow: "the real McCoy," "O.K.," "jive,"
"jass," "right-on," etc. What can be the ultimate value of language creativity so certain of its movement that it is neglectful
even of its own old successes—spirituals, animal tales, field

hollers, work songs, blues, gospel music, the "dozens"—all of them world-stunners.

Black language usage has been forced by the overbearing presence of race, slavery, and aggression into a language of awareness. Black folk language springs from different levels of pain, different age groups of creativity, and altered historical circumstances. Always, though, stands an awareness of the situation, a kind of cultural self-consciousness. A part of this self-consciousness is the sharp clarity of a people whose identity has been honed against continued world oppression. So there is little innocence in black language, not much decorativeness, and no cuteness at all. Which means, of course, that not everyone feels comfortable with black expression. In fact, black speech frightens many who are guided by the American ethos, which, as suggested by Stanley Edgar Hyman, "denys death, resists the tragic experience, represses sexuality, over uses pieties, frantically emphasizes the rationalistic, the inconsequential, and the optimistic."[9]

Living only on the edge of the American dream, particularly materially, the rejected black has had little need to nourish the American dreams and myths and has been able through the use of the language to express some of life's stark realities and to allow for an exercise of many emotions that are suppressed by others. Bessie Smith perhaps expressed the feeling best when she recorded the following:

> *If I go to church on Sunday*
> *Then just shimmy down on Monday*
> *Taint nobody's business if I do.*
> *If I do . . .*

> *I swear I won't call no copper*
> *If I'm beat up by my papa.*
> *Taint nobody's business if I do.*
> *If I do.*[10]

Through this process of refusing to allow others to dictate how we see life, our reality has included what blacks say, and how they say it. The preacher, the hustler, the black mothering figure, the black scholar, the wild young blood, all have contributed to the broad, varied black language portrait.

One of the great pieces of American literature issues from the lips of a preacher who renders his concept of the creation in a poem by James Weldon Johnson, a noted black poet. Following is a portion of Johnson's version of the biblical story of the creation. His models were the sermons of rural black ministers he had heard throughout the nation, but mainly in the South.

The Creation

And God stepped out on space,
And he looked around and said:
I'm lonely—
I'll make me a world.

And far as the eye of God could see
Darkness covered everything
Blacker than a hundred midnights
Down in a cypress swamp.

Then God smiled,
And the light broke,
And the darkness rolled up on one side,
And the light stood shining on the other,
And God said: That's good![11]

On the other hand, the hustlers have their reality too, as expressed in "Bill and Lil," a toast devoted entirely to abuse, a highly developed verbal skill, especially among the young "in the life" (pimps). The joke that follows is especially popular among young people and is representative of a fond myth of "the life": that a pimp can depend upon his women to remain faithful while he is in prison. It is recited with animation.

Bill and Lil

Dear Lil:

I'm sitting here in this man-made hell,
Thinking of nature's beauty from my prison cell.

Wondering how life is treating you
And why your letters are so short and few.

Girl, you swore you'd write me each day
And fix it so I'd give the commissary a steady play.

But ten long years of bitter regret
Won't stop me busting your ass when I get back on the set.[12]

A major black poet, Mari Evans, asks: "Who Can Be Born Black?"

> Who
> can be born black
> and not
> sing
> the wonder of it
> the joy
> the
> challenge
>
> Who
> can be born
> black
> and not exult?[13]

While the black scholar W. E. B. DuBois describes, in one paragraph, the essence of the black dilemma in this moving excerpt from *The Souls of Black Folk.*

> After the Egyptian and Indian, the Greek and Roman,
> Teuton and Mongolian, the Negro is a sort of seventh
> son born with a veil, and gifted with second sight in this
> American world, a world which yields him no true self-
> consciousness, but only lets him see himself through the
> revelation of the other world. It is a peculiar sensation,
> this double consciousness, sense of always looking at
> one's self through the eyes of others, of measuring one's

soul by the tape of a world that looks on in amused contempt and pity. One ever feels his twoness—an American, a Negro, two souls, two thoughts, two unreconciled strivings; two warring ideals in one dark body, whose dogged strength alone keeps it from being torn asunder.[14]

Another towering black writer, Gwendolyn Brooks, chides the young in their "coolness" in twenty-four very short words:

We Real Cool
The Pool Players
Seven at the Golden Shovel

We real cool. We
Left school. We

Lurk late. We
Strike straight. We

Sing sin. We
Think gin. We

Jazz June. We
Die Soon.[15]

When black speech is observed closely with a knowing ear, it represents a massive anthology—from the sublime to what might seem ridiculous, or to put it as John Bernard did: "It [black speech] diminished the most dignified subject into ludicrous laughs and elevated the most trivial into importance."[16] Yet it all fits into a composition of many motifs and images, populated by millions of characters who foreshadow the black multitudes. This language, born of an African heritage, bondage, and oppression of unrelenting force and cruelty, shines through to offer ethical principles; stratagems and guides to political behavior; a hierarchy of values; a concept of life; an understanding of human urges; an appreciation of nature free of Western narrowness, and a sense of humor and style, personal and national, and a sense of purpose and identity. Black language, then, is an art form of survival for black people.

It needs to be reiterated here that Africans view life holistically and in all our endeavors this point is never lost. Amiri Baraka (LeRoi Jones) in his *Blues People* underscores this characteristic when he says: "It was, and is, inconceivable in the African culture to make a separation between music, dancing, song [speech], the artifact, and a man's life or his worship of his gods, expression issued from life, and was beauty."[17] Hence, in the section which follows we will include all lyrics, be they spoken, sung, or shouted, as black language. For further classification, it may be well to include another excerpt from *Blues People*. Baraka continues:

> And just as the lyrics of the African songs were usually as important or more important than the music, the lyrics of the work songs and the later blues were equally important to the Negro's concept of music. In fact the "shouts" and "field hollers" were little more than highly rhythmical lyrics. Even the purely instrumental music of the American Negro contains constant reference to vocal music. Blues playing is the closest imitation of the human voice of any music I've heard; the vocal effects that jazz musicians have delighted in from Bunk Johnson to Ornette Coleman are evidence of this. (And it seems right to conclude that the African and blues scales proceed from this concept of vocal music). . . .[18]

Jones further makes it abundantly clear that all art, including language, is a purely functional entity for the African. It differs decidedly in this regard from Western "art," which is most often decorative or commercial.

> If we think of African music as regards its intent, we must see that it differed from Western music in that it was a purely *functional* music. Borneman lists some basic types of songs common to West African cultures:

songs used by young men to influence young women
(courtship, challenge, scorn); songs used by older men
to prepare the adolescent boys for manhood, and so on.
"Serious" Western music, except for early religious
music, has been strictly an "art" music. . . . In the
West, the "triumph of the economic mind over the
imaginative," as Brooks Adams said, made possible this
dreadful split between life and art. Hence, a music that
is an "art" music as distinguished from something someone would whistle while tilling a field.[19]

More interesting and amazing than all of the above have been
the devices used by black people in the West to communicate in
a society completely dedicated to destroying every vestige of the
African past, and even ready to punish blacks for speaking the
forbidden languages of the continent. But we have already seen
that the nefarious plot failed. Because of the creative spirit of
these new Americans, blacks were able to invent semantic devices where the African ethos and the tone of the West African
languages would survive both bondage and severe oppression.

This propensity was observed very early, even during slavery.
Frederick Douglass recorded the following slave saying:

> We raise de wheat
> Dey gib us de corn;
> We bake de bread,
> Dey gib us de crust;
> We sif da meal,
> Dey gib us de Luses;
> We peel de meat,
> Dey gib us de skin;
> And dats de way
> Dey take us in;
> We skim de pot,
> Dey gib us de liquor,
> And say dats good enough for nigger.[20]

Black language, as illustrated above, creates the opportunity to make dialogue possible. The language takes words and projects a man's image onto himself and onto other men by transforming the monologue of inner feeling into almost concrete impressions, by using everyday occurrences and language to express complex emotions.

Another brilliant example of this usage of language is found in the traditional Negro spiritual. Clarence Cameron White in his background study of the spiritual "Nobody Knows the Trouble I've Seen" gives an interesting observation which suggests that the song sprang from the heart of a slave whose trials were almost more than he could bear. After his wife and children had been sold away, he withdrew to his cabin and poured out his sorrow in this song,

> *Nobody knows the trouble I've seen,*
> *Nobody knows my sorrow,*
> *Nobody knows the trouble I've seen,*
> *Glory Hallelujah.*
>
> *Sometimes I'm up, sometimes I'm down.*
> *Oh, yes Lord.*
> *Sometimes I'm almost to the ground.*
> *Oh, yes Lord.*
>
> *Although you see me going 'long so*
> *Oh, yes Lord.*
>
> *I've got my troubles here below.*
> *Oh, yes Lord.*

The lyrics of blues which flow from the black community is another example of use of the device of taking words and rendering the feelings more concrete. Listen to a portion of Bessie Smith's song "Put It Right Here or Keep It Out There," written by Porter Grainger:

> *I've had a man for fifteen years, give him his room*
> *and board;*

Once he was like a Cadillac, now he's like an old,
  worn-out Ford;
He never brought me a lousy dime and put it in my
  hand;
So there'll be some changes from now on, according
  to my plan:

  He's got to get it, bring it, and put it right here,
  Or else he's goin' to keep it out there;
  If he must steal it, beg it, or borrow it somewhere,
  Long as he gets it, I don't care.[21]

For another modern-day review of the ability of black English
to take experience and render that experience into a reflection of
great feeling, look at Melvin Van Peebles' expression from a
young black male ghetto dweller:

Just dont make no sense
The way my corns are hurting me
When the man runs his game
Lord know he sure runs it mean

Four buses gone by for them
And not one gone by for me

Cruise on in your bad rado brother
Let the world know we is somebody

No just dont make no sense
The way my corns are hurting me
When you black even waiting aint easy
Stand here I'm loitering
If I walk I'm prowling
And if I run I'm escaping
No just dont make no sense
The way my corns are hurting me

If I sit I'm shiftless
But lord knows there'd be hell to pay
If I look like I was even getting ready
To get on my feet someday
Everybody be getting in the race to keep me in my place

My brothers be rushing in there to fat mouth me down
And the man to shoot me down.

And it just dont make no sense
The way these corns are hurting me

Frown—you hostile
Smile—you a tom
Look tired you on junk
Stumble—you drunk
If I wash I'm a pimp
If I dont—I'm a bum
And these feet
Well these feet wont let me be

Naw just dont make no sense
The way my corns are hurting me

Yeah I wanna get on
Why you think I'm standing here huh
Damn right I been waiting long
Aint you never heard of rapid urban transportation

All you folks think black folks is for is waiting
Waiting for the supreme courts latest jive decision
Waiting
Waiting for the man to pick who is qualified
Waiting in the emergency ward to die
Naw just dont make no sense
The way these corns are hurting me

I dont get me a seat the revolution is here
You step on these feet and the revolution is right now.[22]

Oral language, among African descendants, takes on the aspect, too, of an order, an invitation to action, often without the direct suggestion for action. Again the spiritual is an excellent example. Read "Go Down Moses," a traditional spiritual:

When Israel was in Egypt's Land
Let my people go!
Oppressed so hard they could not stand
Let my people go!

REFRAIN:
Go down Moses, 'Way down in Egypt's Land
Tell old Pharaoh, Let my people go!

"Thus said the Lord," Good Moses said,
Let my people go!
"If not I'll smite your first-born dead,"
Let my people go!

No more in bondage shall they toil,
Let my people go!
Let them come out of Egypt's Land
Let my people go!

REFRAIN:
Go down Moses, 'Way down in Egypt's Land
Tell old Pharaoh, Let my people go!

Note that this song for action is a coin with two sides: the condemnation of the slaveholder and the insistence upon immediate action—freedom. In this case, only a very obtuse listener can miss the point. It says flatly that Moses freed the Egyptian slaves boldly and justly because slavery is wrong. It clearly projects the principles of this experience to all the world. It wastes no words and moves relentlessly toward its goal of filling every listener with a pervasive contempt for oppression and a resounding enthusiasm for freedom.

A modern-day call to action is "Wake Up Everybody" as sung

by Harold Melvin and the Bluenotes. It is a song of action, and it teaches as well:

Wake up ev'rybody, no more sleeping in bed
No more backward thinkin', time for thinkin' ahead
The world has changed so very much from what it used to be
There is so much hatred, war an' poverty
Wake up all the teachers, time to teach a new way
Maybe then they'll listen to watcha have to say
'Cause they're the ones who's coming up an' the world is in their
*   han'*
So when you teach the child, teach them the very best ya can
The world won't get no better if we just let it be
The world won't get no better
We gotta change it for you an' me.[23]

The word or language of the black community often takes on the aspect of an order, an invitation to a precise line of conduct, as we have seen in "Wake Up Everybody." The spoken word does not only aim at the ears of those who make up the listening audience, but also, and above all, at the wills.

Black language, or the word, is not without humor, either. Often the black man, wherever he is, lives intensely, and he enjoys a little "partying." He loves life; he longs to live happily in abundant health and enjoy the good things fortune brings. He wants to live forever. This boundless and touching thirst for life brings him to deal frankly with the crucial problems that life and people from foreign cultural traditions set upon him. Thus, one of the means of relaxation is humor.

There is no wonder then that people of African extraction are often extremely talented with the art of humor in their language. Richard Pryor, LaWanda Page, Redd Foxx, Flip Wilson, Maria Gibbs, Bill Cosby, and many more continue to help the nation relax while giving only a glimpse at this rich propensity of black/ African people. Humor comes out of the language through exaggerations about size, strengths, power, etc. These exaggerations may not be taken seriously, but they make one laugh. Observe the exaggeration heard in a scene from Zora Neale Hurston's work *Their Eyes Were Watching God.* Here are several men in a skin game (a game of cards), and the conversation that ensues during the game. In this Florida Everglade setting, the speech is referred to as "woofing" and "boogerbooing." Hear them speak:

Ed Dockery was dealing one night and he looked over at Sop-de-Bottom's card and he could tell Sop thought he was going to win. He hollered, "Ah'll break up dat settin' uh eggs."

Sop looked and said, "Root de peg." Bootyny asked, "What are you goin' tuh do? Do do!" Everybody was watching that next card fall. Ed got ready to turn. "Ah'm gointuh sweep out hell and burn up de broom." He slammed down another dollar. "Don't overspot yourself, Ed," Bootyny challenged. "You gittin' too yaller." Ed caught hold of the corner of the card. Sop dropped a dollar. "Ah'm gointuh shoot in de hearse, don't keer how sad de funeral be." Ed said, "You see how this man is teasin' hell?" Tea Cake nudged Sop not to bet. "You gointuh git caught in uh bullet storm if you don't watch out." Sop said, "Aw 'tain't nothin' tuh dat bear but his curly hair. Ah can look through muddy water and see dry land." Ed turned off the card and hollered, "Zachariah, Ah says come down out dat syca-more tree. You can't do no business." Nobody fell on that card. Everybody was scared of the next one. Ed looked around and saw Gabe standing behind his chair and hollered, "Move, from over me, Gabe! You too black. You draw heat! Sop, you wanta pick up dat bet whilst you got uh chance?" "Naw, man, Ah wish Ah had uh thousand-leg tuh put on it." "So yuh won't lissen, huh? Dumb niggers and free schools. Ah'm gointuh take and teach yuh. Ah'll main-line but Ah won't side-tract." Ed flipped the next card and Sop fell and lost. Every-body hollered and laughed.[24]

Humor also comes from satire, and another common device is

the use of circumlocution (indirection). Much of the humor, though, comes not from an event as it actually occurs, but in the manner in which the language and body are used. There is dramatization through the use of facial expression, voice inflection, altered rhythm of speech, mimicry, and enlivenment by various actions with the body to enhance the meaning of the message intended. Observe this example of tonal semantics to make the words sound good and important to the listener. This is an excerpt from a performance of the late Moms Mabley, a noted comedian. She said of the man her father forced her to marry when she was a teenager:

> This O-L-D . . . . puny . . . . moanin' man. I mean an O-L-D man. Santa Claus looked like his son. He was older than his mother. . . . The nearest thing to death you've ever seen in your life. His shadow weighed more than he did. He got out of breath threading a needle. And U-G-L-Y! He was so ugly he hurt my feelings.[25]

Nor is humor confined to any special place. One finds humor any place where there are people. The church is no exception. Some of the more humorous moments can be experienced in a church service, often from the minister himself, who uses the device as a method of motivating his congregation to be attentive and receptive to the more serious moments during the service. An illustrative example can be found in a recent sermon heard on the radio in a southern city. The minister was speaking:

CONGREGATION: Talk Reverand!
PREACHER: Yea, last week I heard that one of my members, one of your sisters, a leader in this church . . .
CONGREGATION: Lord, Jesus.
PREACHER: Yea, this silly woman done told hur husband, a good man, that she wanted to be liberated.
CONGREGATION: Lord no!
PREACHER: Now, hear dis, that silly woman went out and

bought some mo wigs, new dress and all kind o mess to look good in.

CONGREGATION: Do Jesus.

PREACHER: Talkin bout she wants a open marriage. —That white folks mess.

CONGREGATION: Have mercy Lord.

PREACHER: But lemme tell yall somethin—

CONGREGATION: Talk Rev.

PREACHER: That woman cain't take care one man, how she go add another?

CONGREGATION: Preach.

PREACHER: Huh, them A-rabs aint got a nough oil to heat up her cold tail—and she talkin bout another man.

CONGREGATION: (Hearty laughter)

This exchange between the minister and his congregation illustrates another example of black language usage. In addition to humor, he has also engaged in what is known as signification (signifyin), a way of saying what one wants to say about another without insulting the individual. The ritual is always carried out in humor, and is generally accepted. It is doubtful that any parishioner in the minister's charge had made such an overt suggestion as the Reverend described in his sermon, but he probably had picked up hints that some of the members had expressed such notions. The Rev. was letting them know that he had heard about "their nonsense" and he did not appreciate it. Yet he never confronted any one directly. However, this ritual can be more direct and still acceptable to the participants.

The "Dozens" is another example of signification that has its own rules and rituals. Besides, the dozens is played by non-church people and most often among the younger people in the community, though not always. In the dozens, you ridicule the relatives of the individual with whom you speak. Any family member can be discussed; however, the mother, since she is considered the closest relative, is the prime target for jest.

One of the familiar recitals of the dozens was recorded by Lee Rainwater. It goes:

Your mama don't wear no drawers
She wash'm in alcohol
She put'em on a clothesline
The sun refused to shine
She put'em in a garbage can
They scared old garbage man
She put'em on the railroad track
The train went back and back.
She put'em in the midnight train
They scared old Jesse James.[26]

The "put-down" in the black community can be, and often is, done with great elegance. Read Ntozake Shange's poem from *For Colored Girls*, "lady in red," as a young lady speaks to her errant boyfriend:

without any assistance or guidance from you
i have loved you assiduously for 8 months 2 wks & a day
i have been stood up four times
i've left 7 packages on yr doorstep
forty poems 2 plants & 3 handmade notecards i left
town so i cd send to you have been no help to me
on my job
you call at 3:00 in the mornin on weekdays
so i cd drive 27½ miles cross the bay before i go to work
charmin charmin
but you are of no assistance
i want you to know
this waz an experiment
to see how selfish i cd be
if i wd really carry on to snare a possible lover
if i waz capable of debasin my self for the love of another
if i cd stand not being wanted
when i wanted to be wanted
& i cannot

so

with no further assistance & no guidance from you
i am endin this affair

this note is attached to a plant
i've been waterin since the day i met you

you may water it

yr damn self[27]

The use of the nickname is another interesting means of communicating found among common black people. Nicknames are
almost always a condensed reflection of some aspect of our personalities. They are a means of direct feedback with regard to how
others see or experience us. The nickname is a means of telling
the individual how he is "coming down"—a reflection of his personal demeanor, appearance, strengths, weaknesses. It can be
flattering or devastating, at least initially. In this regard, we recall
a clinical situation where an eight-year-old black boy was referred for assistance due to his acting-out behavior in school. His
appearance was normal, except that he had almost no neck. Upon
arrival the youngster announced that he knew why he had been
sent to see "the head doctors." We asked, why? He said immediately: "These teachers think I'm bad, but these ole children tease
me and I don't like it." We asked, "What don't you like?" However, before he could answer, another black boy about his age
saw him with us and shouted: "Hey, Head and Shoulders!" Our
client became alarmed and yelled, "That what they call me!"
while motioning to chase the fleeing boy.

We, psychologists, recognized that this "nicknaming" was a
common practice in the community and that it would continue
until our client became used to the idea that he looked different.
Of course it appears cruel, but, knowing the community, we had
to accept the fact that the practice had its benefits. It was used to
enable the inhabitants to accept themselves as they were and to
learn to ignore the taunts that usually accompany one's being
different.

Discussion of this case triggered the memory of one of the
most prosperous businessmen in a similar community where one
of the co-authors had lived as a boy. This gentleman had sus-
tained an injury when he was a young boy, and the injury left

one of his arms severely crippled. He was known by all as
"Crook-arm Joe." Crook-arm Joe was not only a successful busi-
nessman but also a ladies' man with no inferior feelings about his
arm or the nickname. A nickname, as most people in the community appreciate, does not always denote negative images. One of
Crook-arm Joe's wives was nicknamed "Pearly" because of her
rare beauty and lovely teeth.

Again, the nickname is no doubt a derivation of the practice
everywhere in Africa of considering the name a distinct part of
the individual. Since here in the West we use Christian names
that have no meanings, as far as we understand, the nickname
helps us, and the recipient, to formulate an identity, accept an
unfortunate disability, or maintain, alter, or change a behavior
characteristic. A short list of common nicknames follows:

CHARACTERISTIC	NICKNAME
Short	"Shorty," "Stump"
Tall	"Tree," "Sky"
Fat	"Fatso," "Piggy," "Fats," "Chunky"
Thin	"Slim," "Reed"
Ruddy complexion	"Red"
Dark	"Smokey," "Night," "Shade"
Light	"Pinky"
Pretty girl	"Peaches," "Foxy"
Fast Mover	"Speedy," "Train"
Dull-witted	"Lame-brain"
Popular male	"Sport," "Sportin-life," "Pimp," "Player," "Stud"
Cruel person	"Stone"
Sloven	"Greasy," "Grease"
Foolish person	"Jive," "Shortstop"
Backward	"Lame"
Clever operator	"Mack"
Pretty woman	"Queenie," "Foxy"
One-armed	"Wing"
One-legged	"Peg"
Clever with deceit- ful intent	"Slick"

Leisurely hailing a cab on a warm summer night, we soon were taxiing from the airport to our downtown hotel in Bridgeport, Barbados. Our driver was a congenial Barbadian fellow, who commented, with a British-flavored West Indian accent, on our observation of sparse vehicular traffic on the paradise island. "You should see the cars on weekends Mahn! They be going ZOOM ZOOM!!!" He simulated racing engine sounds with remarkable exactness.

His language reflects the African practice of using natural sounds of objects in the environment to enhance one's vocabulary.

Phillip A. Noss refers to terms which mimic nature's speech as ideophones, also known as onomatopoeia. He explains this language technique as a part of speech that weds verbs and adjectives. The union gives birth to words which not only state actions, or describe items, but express them both concurrently while inducing emotion or feeling. Noss is persuasive and graphic.

> It creates a picture; it is sensual, enabling the listener to identify a feeling, a sound, color, texture, expression, movement, or silence through his own senses. The ideophone is poetic; it is in the purest sense imagery.[28]

An excerpt from an African tale will illustrate the ideophone in speech:

> Rabbit customarily wanders about the country looking for food. . . . He determines to challenge Lion. He takes some eggs, fashions himself a great bell, and goes to hide in the reeds *Mek Mek Mek Mek Mek Mek* [the sound made by Rabbit's movement through thick weeds], where Lion sends his underlings for water. Soon Fox comes along *Kirik Kirik* [leaping bounding run of a fox] and begins to wash out his water pot *hokoro hokoro* [a rattling sound, scraping against a clay pot]. At that, *Abévévévévévévé!* [sound of a loud ringing bell]. Rabbit rings his great bell and sings a hunting song sicking his great imaginary dog onto the game. Fox

tries to run away and rolls *Kiliwili* [rolling sound of a large object or person on the ground].[29]

The tale goes on with repeated episodes of Rabbit's trickster pranks. The language is animated by the use of ideophones.

A dialogue between bluesman Howling Wolf and Eric Clapton during a rehearsal of a Howling Wolf classic, "Little Red Rooster," is another example. Eric Clapton fails to persuade Wolf to play chords on his guitar that he (Clapton) is having trouble grasping. Wolf prefers to teach him otherwise. Follow:

CLAPTON (playing electric guitar): Right.

WOLF: Now you play it that way.

CLAPTON: You sure you wouldn't like . . . Why don't you play acoustic on it?

PEOPLE IN STUDIO: Yeah . . . Come on, man.

WOLF: Naa . . .

CLAPTON: . . . With us, man . . . If you play . . . See if you played with us, Wolf, then we'd be able to follow you better.

PEOPLE IN STUDIO: Yeah, come on.

WOLF: Naa . . .

CLAPTON: Like . . . Like . . . You were doing it right then, man.

WYMAN: You're there!

CLAPTON: That's how we should record it.

WOLF: You see . . . I . . .

CLAPTON: If I can follow you, I can see what you're doing . . .

WYMAN: You're there, man!

DAYRON: Really, man . . . You . . . You just sit there and do it! So cool it.

WOLF: Well let's . . . all right . . . Let everyone get together here and we'll try and make it.

CLAPTON: Ok, let's try it.

WOLF: Ah, ha . . .

CLAPTON: I doubt if I can do it without you playing.

WOLF: Oh man, come on! He . . . He ain't got nothing to do but count it off, an uh . . . An uh change on a . . . You know

. . . When you say . . . One . . . Two . . . Three . . . Four
. . . You change! See he . . . See he . . . Drops in when . . .
He says . . . He says Boom![30]

So it is experience of the universe's voice that regulates the African's tongue. (He uses words that render him one with nature.)

Not all blacks express themselves in these modes. There are assimilated blacks, who use "public" language exclusively and would not allow themselves or their children to use such utterances as we have described. But, on the other hand, there is a huge segment of unacculturated blacks who do indeed express themselves as we have explained. These are the blacks who have taken their African heritage, often without understanding the process, and sensualized their sufferings, joys, and hopes into expressions of rare beauty. It is a beauty devoid of self-consciousness and therefore natural. These aesthetic behaviors are, however, often lost or used sparingly once the black person is acculturated or assimilated into the general culture.

What we say here is that black people in the West have been rooted up from their past. A past steeped in the oral tradition. A tradition, not for the lack of initiative in inventing a written script, but a tradition that understood the meaning and significance of the "word" passing from mouth to ear. A human endeavor that recognizes the intricate relationship of man communicating with man. Africans have long known the secret of dispelling pain, expressing joy, conveying unpleasant thoughts, and holding their history through the use of the most effective medium—word of mouth.

It is little wonder, then, that the same tradition is maintained by many of the children of Africa wherever they are, even without the knowledge of why, or the notion of the continuance of the race through the use of language. But, be that as it may, the tradition is alive and well. Black speech is still used to convey one's honest feelings as concisely, humorously, and humanely as possible. It is not a language of deceit and scheming, although if life and existence are threatened, the language can be convoluted. However, it is always done to raise horizons, rarely to diminish the life chances of others. For ordinary black people, the party or church is still attended in order to enjoy other people and oneself. It is most unlike language usage in many Western institutions, where the intent is to scheme and deceive, "with dignity," for the enhancement of the marketplace.

9

ROCK STEADY BABY

Expressive Movement

If the dance is pleasing, even the lame will crawl to it.

African saying

The importance of physical exertion in traditional African society, simply for survival, makes physical expression a natural outgrowth of experience. As an instrument of expression, the body is a distinctive medium. Its movements can convey joy, fear, hate, anguish, every nuance of emotion.

Lee Warren[1]

The place was the New Orleans Superdome. The occasion, the annual Southern University–Grambling State University football game. Long after the gun had sounded signaling the end of the 1979 Bayou Classic, the crowd, approaching 70,000, stood still, murmuring, moaning, gasping, gesturing, some few with vehemence, boasting, and lamenting at the outcome of the game. Emotionally suspended, the crowd, held at the peak of cataclysm, hardly noticed the Southern University team member who victoriously wallowed on the playing field, furiously, and violently, unreservedly expressing joy. Nineteen hundred and sixty-nine (1969) had been the last opportunity to rejoice, unless you were a "Gramblingite."

An extended moment of emotional exaltation had begun fermenting some three hours before, when the 70,000 or so gracefully converged on the artistically designed dome and brought it to life with laughter and cheer. There was glitter as the crowd approached the dome; "high steppin" and "low walkin" held sway. The finest clothing uniquely cut was the way of dress, and spicy jabbering and cool braggadocio was the way of "talkin."

There was a pause as the invocator offered, on behalf of all, a prayer of considerable length, which increased in power with duration, putting a strangle-hold on the excitement that buzzed within the dome. The invocator's "Amen" was quickly dashed, its ending disallowed, by a roar that strained the ceiling hovering over the exuberance below.

By half time, tension in the air was even greater as the crowd roared in response to, and in concert with, the Southern University Marching Band (note the African dynamics of the performer-audience relationship). With the installation of dance, drama, singing, and other aesthetic movements that seem to work tricks on the eyes, the band rid the "military march" of its conventional "robotism." Their dancing, singing, and playing was not unlike the way of African tribal life. An African choral group we observed in Lagos, Nigeria, at the Second World Festival of Black and African Arts and Culture, was in the shadow cast by the band, a shadow vibrating with and overlapped by the correspondent marching, arching, dancing, prancing, singing rhythms of the crowd, all belonging to the same African source. Like the

African choral group, the band's emotionally inspired aesthetic demonstrations and the teams' dashing motions became the embodiment of rhythmic beauty, alluring the crowd to a point of surrender, of voluntary submission, to the several hours of perfect black motion.

The tradition of the school band playing a major role at athletic events is not peculiar to Southern University or Grambling. Most of the southern black colleges and universities (Florida A&M, Tennessee State, North Carolina A&T, Bethune Cookman, etc.) have historically utilized high-stepping bands to enliven the games.

With their expressiveness, it is in this manner that blacks color life, a colorfulness propelled by a deep and rich feeling capacity that vividly shades every phase, every manifestation, every thought, every endeavor of life, with movement.

In earlier chapters we referred to three major aspects of personality: (1) cognitive or intellectual aspects, (2) affective or emotional aspects, (3) psychomotor or action aspects (movements). We also suggested that the healthy personality is able to fuse the three and respond to the environment as a total organism or whole being, and thereby relate to his surroundings with spontaneity and integrity. The example cited from our experience in the New Orleans Superdome exemplifies the latter two of the three aspects of personality with precise clarity.

When one studies closely the psychomotor (movement) domain, one is impressed that movement is incorporated in all life and is without a doubt a prerequisite for life. All behaviors require either internal or external movement. Among them is one offered by Abernathy and Waltz which contends that human movement has purpose which is initiated by the individual when he desires to achieve a certain objective, to communicate a concept or idea, to express a feeling or emotion, and to respond to his environment.[2] Human movement, however, is product-oriented and therefore restricted by levels of physical ability and by restraints imposed by physical laws. The modifiers of human movement listed by Abernathy and Waltz are: movement experiences, personality structure, personal perceptions, social-cultural environment, and physical environment.

Hans Kraus defines man as motion,[3] and Amita Harrow suggests that "most people interpret psychomotor as dealing with observable human motion. When the term is separated into its two component parts, psycho and motor, it connotes mind movement or voluntary motion."[4]

Both Kraus's and Abernathy and Waltz's discussion of movement help us to understand the characteristics of black people, who respond to affective stimuli with movement. For the African, there is a total relationship between body and mind. Movement, then, is a part of the life-style, not something added to it.

The African seems to know that the first reality is the reality of the body. The first testing of reality takes place through motor activity: what can be altered in the external world by motor activity is real. The views one has of reality are, indeed, influenced to some extent by the images one has of one's bodily self. The body is the model according to which, through movement, we construct the world as a whole. It is the model to which we continually return and refer during the course of development. It serves as a general outline for understanding the world as a whole. The very first learning concerns itself with things that relate to our own bodies. As the child's knowledge of the outside world expands, it relates itself automatically to that which has already been experienced in his bodily world. He seeks to find in outside objects images reflecting his own bodily images. Each new unit of the outside world comes to have special significance with relation to various parts of the body.[5]

Since the African seems to understand this principle, it is therefore understandable that the African appears to have extreme bodily sensitivity. Perhaps he retains his sense perceptions and sensuous responses from childhood and works with them in sharpening an awareness based on a delicate sense of bodily rhythm. Alfons Daver writes:

> European rhythm . . . is mainly an element of time, which is extremely important to our culture. The African is not bound to a temporal conception. His rhythm consists of a physical-sensual perception of accent impulses and their transformations into movements. Afri-

can rhythm . . . is a physical experience, a power with a
definite regulated effect, a "modal" power which is able
to increase human vitality.[6]

It appears that the Africans feel music with the body and carry
the appreciation into motion, as though they and the music were
one. The question becomes, where does the music end and the
movement begin?

The African transforms the sound of music into kinetic energy,
that is, music to motion. John Lovell says of this tendency:
"When this metronome sense is turned on, nothing in the world
can disturb it."[7] There is the tendency to keep to the beat of the
sound of music.

Daver speaks of African dance and African music when he
reminds us "of the European habit of treating the body in the
dance as a stiff linear unit in space." Daver continues:

> The African, on the other hand, does not seek the move-
> ment of his body in space, but rather just the experience
> of moving the body itself. In contrast to the monocen-
> tric dance-body of the European, is the polycentrics and
> polyrhythms of African music. It realizes different simul-
> taneous, rhythmic courses of movement through kinetic
> transformations of movement which are released ac-
> tively by various body centers or intensified system-
> atically to frenzies of ecstasies. All over Africa are areas
> of agreement in dance style and in movement models,
> stretching throughout all cultural zones, demonstrating
> dance forms of the same function and natural tend-
> ency.[8]

Pierre Erny believes that the African child enjoys an especially
favorable affective climate in the first few years of life and, therefore, in quite a few regions he attains a legacy of psychomotor
development which noticeably surpasses that of the European
child.[9] The African body is particularly lively and alert. Could it
be, then, that the reflexes of the African are therefore more spon-

taneous, which means that he reacts more easily to affective stimuli or responds naturally to the rhythm of the environment?

There is evidence that the African's experienced use of the motor system may be of unusual significance. R. W. Sperry has stated that it is readily apparent that the sole product of brain function is muscular coordination. Of course, he includes neurohumora (nerve fluids) and glandular components under motor functions, yet assigns them a relatively minor role in his discussion of the mid-brain problem. Sperry is saying that from his studies of the brain, it appears to him that the entire output of our thinking process goes into the motor system. In the past, however, attempts to describe the higher functions of the brain have been made in terms of how sensory inputs are processed from the receptor on up to the higher cortical centers. Sperry makes a strong case for another approach; that is, he thinks it possible to understand the human nervous system, even its most complex intellectual functions, if the operation of the brain is analyzed in terms of its motor output rather than in terms of its sensory input.[10]

It is especially significant that Sperry singled out thought in placing stress on the unique importance of the motor system, because this places thought and movement in closer proximity. His principle states that any directed, organized behavior sequence (including thought) involves the motor system. The muscles are the terminals (ends) of this system and, of course, are required for activities like walking, running, and speaking, but the principle does not require that muscles actually have to contract in order for thinking to occur. However, when electromyography (sensitive machines measuring muscle activity) has been used, muscular activity has almost invariably been recorded during thinking. Electromyography (EMG) shows that the motor system is involved in the "silent acts" because the EMGs reflect what is going on upstream in the brain.

Sperry also has the following to say with regard to the motor system and visual perception:

> If there be any objectively demonstrable fact about perception that indicates the nature of the neural proc-

ess involved it is the following: In so far as an organism perceives a given object, it is prepared to respond with reference to it. This preparation to respond is absent in an organism that has failed to perceive. . . . The presence or absence of adaptive reaction potentialities of this sort, ready to discharge into motor patterns, makes the difference between perceiving and not perceiving.[11]

Sperry tells us that thinking improves when patterned sensory stimulation is increased.

Apparently the Africans were remaining in tune with nature when movement to the beat of the drum was infused into the total of their lives. This predisposition toward bodily movement of black people everywhere is readily seen in full display in every endeavor. But perhaps most often it is observed here in the West through the dance and athletics. In fact, the entire culture of African people is highly action-oriented, with much physical participation in the environment—life. Physical involvement and emotional fervor appear to be connected with black people's ability to trust and accept their human drives as human attributes. The fear of human instincts shows in attempts to suppress or control them excessively, which leads to stiff, tight, rigid posturing. Unassimilated black people are in touch with their bodies and use them to communicate with others, indeed, to express who they are and what they feel.

One sees this interesting phenomenon in the rhythmic, cooperative dancelike togetherness of black people in almost any communal setting or gathering. The movement or physical involvement is accentuated through repetition, referred to earlier as the call-and-response concept, particularly when repetitive stimuli are verbal. The repetitive stimuli are proportionately increased and continue to the point of explosion, as in the Black Litany of Reverend Jesse Jackson, the famous founder of Operation PUSH.

SPEAKER: "I am"
AUDIENCE: "I am"

SPEAKER:	"Somebody"
AUDIENCE:	"Somebody"
SPEAKER:	"I may be poor"
AUDIENCE:	"I may be poor"
SPEAKER:	"But I am"
AUDIENCE:	"But I am"
SPEAKER:	"Somebody."
AUDIENCE:	"Somebody."

The church is a place where bodily movement is often seen. Malcolm X in his autobiography writes:

> I would sit goggle-eyed at my father, a minister jumping and shouting as he preached, with the congregation jumping and shouting behind him, their songs and bodies devoted to singing. . . .[12]

Maya Angelou also describes a church scene replete with movement in her autobiography. She says of Sister Monroe, a member of her church congregation:

> Once when she hadn't been to church for a few months, she got the spirit and started shouting, throwing her arms around and jerking her body, so that the ushers went over to hold her down, but she tore herself away from them and ran up to the pulpit. She stood in front of the altar, shaking like a freshly caught trout. She screamed at Reverend Taylor, "Preach it. I say, preach it." . . . Then she screamed an extreme fierce "I said, preach it" and stepped up on the altar. The Reverend kept on throwing out phrases like home-run balls and Sister Monroe made a quick break and grasped for him. . . . She caught the minister by the sleeve of his jacket and his coattail, then she rocked him from side to side. . . . The pandemonium spread. The spirit infused

Deacon Jackson and Sister Wilson. . . . At the same time Deacon Jackson . . . gave a scream like a falling tree leaned back on thin air and punched Reverend Taylor on the arm. . . . In the same second Sister Wilson caught his [the preacher's] tie, looped it over her fist a few times, and pressed down on him. . . . All three of them were down on the floor behind the altar. Their legs spiked out like kindling wood. Sister Monroe, who had been the cause of all the excitement, walked off the dais, cool and spent, and raised her flinty voice in the hymn, "I came to Jesus, as I was, worried, wound, and sad, I found in Him a resting place and He has made me glad."[13]

Today, the scene described above is repeated every Sunday throughout much of the black community. However, it is not an expression started during Sister Monroe's generation. As early as 1867, H. E. Krebiel described the black-Christian Church service:

> . . . old and young, men and women, sprucely dressed
> young men, grotesque half-clad field hands—the women
> generally with gay handkerchiefs twisted about their
> heads and with short skirts, . . . young girls bare-
> footed, all stand up in the middle of the floor, and when
> the "sperichil" [spiritual] is struck up begin first walk-
> ing and by and by shuffling around, one after the other,
> in a ring. . . . More frequent a band, composed of some
> of the best singers and tired shouters, stand at the side
> to "base" the others, singing the body of the song and
> clapping their hands together or on the knees. . . .
> When the shout last into the middle of the night, . . .
> thud of feet prevents sleep within half a mile of the
> praise house.[14]

Amiri Baraka says that this continuing presence of movement in black religious life is a carryover from Africa incorporated into Afro-Christian worship. "The Negro Church, whether Christian

or 'heathen' has always been a 'church of emotion.' In Africa, ritual dances and songs were integral parts of African religious ob-
servances, and the emotional frenzies that were usually con-
comitant with any African religious practice have been pretty
well documented, though I suppose, rarely understood."[15]

Further, the tendency for blacks to allow naturalistic body
movement can be seen often in the way blacks walk. Many
blacks under observation can be seen using bodily motion as a
gesture of revelation or testimony. The body holds many nuances
and expressive movements and is therefore capable of delivering
many messages to onlookers.

Hurston writes of a fictional character, Daisy Blunt:

> Daisy is walking a drum tune. You can almost hear it by
> looking at the way she walks. . . . She is parading and
> blushing at the same time.[16]

This characteristic of gesturing with body motion is not restricted to black females. Black males often portray their manliness through their walk. On a recent trip from Philadelphia to
New York City, one of the co-authors observed a young black
male use the body gesture to indicate his high regard for himself
on a commuter train coach. The young man approached the
coach, rather shabbily dressed and walking quite normally to find
himself a seat. However, upon observing that the others in the
coach, including a pretty black girl, were all well dressed, he
stopped, placed one arm behind his back, bent over ever so
slightly, and proceeded to shuffle up the aisle in a style often seen
in the black ghetto when one is "profiling" (showing off).

In all the examples cited above, including the seductive scenes,
each individual's movement suggested that the individual had a
basic concept of himself/herself, an attitude, and a willingness to
express it. The awareness of the rhythms and postures of one's
own body and its way of moving gives one direct, immediate
experience of oneself from within. Further, recognizing these
movement patterns in others may be one basis for a quick, intuitive, empathic understanding of others, and probably plays a
great part in many black interpersonal relationships.

Theater people are well aware how much bodily movement can contribute to warming up an audience and quickening the response to the presentation, especially when the movement is presented at the optimum moment. These facts appear to come naturally to common black folks. Rarely among black audiences are there mere spectators; we are an audience of participants. The audience participates with the preacher, musician, singer, dancer, actor, or poet in a shared experience. This best expresses the urge, from the African heritage, to unite physically with an affective stimulator, which is ultimately nature, the universe.

One of the more common and enjoyable means of physical exertion and expression among blacks everywhere is dance—most often in groups. Dance in Africa is part of the life-style, not something appended. In Africa the human body is used to bring rhythm and movement to everyday tasks, to re-create situations by exaggerating and abstracting these very movements in a mime. Many African dances are mime versions of actual experiences. Harvest dances express thankfulness for the fruits of the earth. The welcome of a child into the adult community in the puberty dance, or the farewell to the chief in the royal funeral dance—whatever occasion, the particular dance that is used for it is an appropriate one. It is suited in both mood and style to the people who dance it.

While the dance lasts, dancers and musician become so completely absorbed that a dance may continue for hours or days without loss of the performers' interest. These dances always reflect the community's traditional way of life. It is a reflection of specific aspects of their lives. Africans dance for joy, and they dance for grief; they dance for hate; they dance to bring prosperity, and they dance to avert calamity; they dance for religion and they dance to pass the time.

How much do the recitals above resemble the popular dance in America? But, of course, this is no wonder, since it is common knowledge that popular dance in the West is dependent upon blacks for its foundation and vitality.

Melville Herskovits was prompted to say that "The dance itself has . . . carried over into the New World to a greater degree than almost any other trait of African culture."[17] What happened to African dances when they reached the United States? We know that the slaves from Africa, when they were allowed, continued to use the steps and movements as they had done at home, and there is evidence that some dances were brought to the New World almost in their entirety. For example, an old dance in the South, the Buzzard Lope, originated in West Africa as the buzzard dance, a dance that closely imitated the movements of the buzzard. In Africa the members of the group "went around in a circle," according to Herskovits, "moving with bodies bent forward from their waists and with arms thrown back in imitation of the bird from which their spirit took its name."[18]

However, in the United States, the Buzzard Lope became a part of a dance-story in which a turkey buzzard goes around eating a dead cow. It was danced on Sapelo Island, Georgia, where it had been repeated for years. When it was seen by Lydia Parrish it was performed by a family, the Johnsons. Parrish writes: "Of the twins, Naomi did the patting while Isaac did the dancing; an older brother rhythmically called out the cues in a sharp staccato and another one lay on the floor of the wide veranda representing a dead cow."

> March aron!
> Jump across!
> Get the eye!
> Go Glad!
> Get the guts!
> Go to eatin!
> All right—cow mos' gone!
> Dog comin!
> Scare the dog!
> Look aron for more meat!
> All right!—Belly full!
> Goin to tell the rest![19]

The records of this scene suggested that she saw a combination of the old African buzzard dance from Africa and more modern steps added at this recital. Later, the Buzzard Lope was reported to have been seen in the town of Sunbury, Georgia, and even later, sixty years, the Buzzard Lope was seen in Birmingham, Alabama. The Buzzard Lope apparently is not danced today; however, movements similar to those in the Buzzard Lope popped up as part of the Big Apple dance popular as late as the 1950s.

Another African dance, the Giouba, was changed radically in the United States by adding new movements, some of which survived in popular dance. The Giouba was probably the famous Juba of Georgia and the Carolinas.[20] Among the black folks of the South, "'Juba' was a kind of dance step," says Thomas Talley. There were "two dancers in a circle of men . . . while the following lines are being patted:

> Juba circle, raise de latch
> Juba dance dat Long Dog Scratch
>   —Juba! Juba![21]

The dancers in the circle, with raised foot, ended during a step called "Dog Scratch." "Then when the supplement 'Juba! Juba!' was said, the whole circle of men joined in the dance step 'Juba' for a few moments."

The Juba dance participants go around in a circle with one foot raised—aeratic shuffle—and it is danced by the surrounding circle of men before and after each performance of two men in the center. It is interesting that both the words and steps are in a call-and-response form, and the words must sound out as rhythmically as a drum solo. The two men in the center start the performance with the Juba step while the surrounding men clap, and then change to whatever new step is suggested in the call, just before the response "Juba! Juba!" sounds and the circle moves again. In the verse above, the lead dancers in the center switch to "Long Dog Scratch," which has been called out. Some of the other steps introduced later are: "Pigeon Wing," "Blow Dat Candle Out," "Yaller Cat," and "Jubal Jew."

Marshall and Jean Stearns write that "the result is a completely choreographed, continuous group dance, combining the call-and-response pattern, dancing in a circle (generally counterclockwise), the Shuffle, improvisations, and the rhythms of call and clapping. These characteristics are a fair list of the major Afro-American traits in the blend of vernacular dance."[22]

During the days of the Minstrel, the period when the African presence was infused into the popular culture of America, the name Juba was used for the dancers as well as the dance. However, the Juba dance was also spoken of as a jig and numbers of performers got started in show business featuring the Juba dance steps.

Pattery Juba, a clapping of hands to encourage another dancer, started the routine of clapping hands, thighs, knees, and body in order to keep a rhythmic beat. This seems to have been a substitute for the drum, which was banned in the United States for fear of slave revolt. By the 1890s white performers in blackface were using this technique regularly in their productions.

The Stearnses write:

> A minor detail attached itself to Pattery Juba in the course of its evolution into a display piece and then became a part of the more pretentious style of Charleston: crossing and uncrossing the hands on the knees as they fan back and forth. Encouraged by Joan Crawford's example as a Charleston-dancing flapper in "Our Dancing Daughters," most teen-agers of the twenties mastered this trick. Thirty years later the same thing turned up in a rock-and-roll dance named the Charley-Bop, a revival of the Charleston.[23]

The directions toward African rhythms and dance styles have long been utilized in the West, but the explosion came during the 1950s when white teenagers in large numbers began to dance to music that blacks had danced to for centuries. Rock-and-roll was popularized by record companies and disc jockeys nationwide. In 1955, "Rock Around the Clock" by Bill Haley and his Comets sold three million copies. The black sound and dance were big business. And with the coming of Elvis Presley, who utilized the motions and rhythms made popular long before by black performers like Bo Diddley and a Harlem dancer of the 1920s, Earl Tucker, America for the first time accepted almost completely black vernacular music and dance movements. In less than ten years Elvis Presley sold 100 million records.

Popular dances emerged during this period that strongly resembled old dances that blacks had long abandoned. Something strongly reminiscent of the Charleston emerged as the Mashed Potato and the Charley-Bop; bits of the old Eagle Rock returned in the Fly; an unintentional parody of the Lindy became known as the Chicken. . . . Elvis Presley's initial popularity was among white youth who began to dance in the black vernacular. However, in 1960 Chubby Checker, a black singer, made the Twist a popular dance among white adults. The Twist was followed by the Monkey, the Bug, the Pony, the Frog, the Watusi, the Jerk, the Boogaloo, etc.

During the 1970s and early 1980s, discothèques were popular. However, the disco was not a new concept of the period. The Stearnses write: "When dancing at discothèques became popular—for years it was known in the South [among blacks] as jukin and you inserted your own nickel in the juke box—yet, because of the advancement of sound technology, discothèques offer an atmosphere more conducive to dancing."

The brief history outlined above simply indicates that the African style of dance movement—with its freedom of body; respect for nature, particularly other animals; freedom in individual expression and improvisation; natural concentration of movement in the pelvic region; and propulsive rhythm, which give a swinging quality—has found its way to the West and added a humanistic dimension which allows one, at least for a short time, to form a full deep involvement in life.

This can be seen on such popular black television productions as "Soul Train," a dance show. There are moments, if one observes carefully with an understanding eye, when it is difficult to distinguish where the music ends and the dancing begins, while the dancers are executing exacting steps that complement those of their partners. You know, as an observer, that thought is in process, yet you wonder how, when the body appears to flow with the music, oblivious of technique.

Also, the flow of emotions and energy through dance can be quite useful in therapy. A case will illustrate.

Short in stature, with skin shaded in color between light brown and dark tan, he had a dim smile that romanticized his appearance. Ray, called "Ray Baby" by his peers, was a handsome youngster of eighteen. Too shy. He was hardly able to speak above a whisper. He was not restricted by vocal abnormalities; raging self-doubt subdued him.

Ray had been a member of a therapy group conducted by one of the co-authors for six sessions, over a period of six weeks, when he wholly and totally asserted himself.

Each member of the group had been asked to make an autobiographical presentation, placing in context the problem or problems of greatest concern to them. As is usual in therapy groups we conduct, they were encouraged to utilize black expressive forms, to include music of any variety, poetry (folk or literary), drama, stories, dance, and such illustrations as pictures, slides, paintings, drawings, sculpture, or other expressive forms to vitalize their depictions.

By group consensus, Ray was nominated to make his presentation first. A long silence ensued as he readied himself. He smiled. His smile was well known to the group. Except in this instance, it hovered about his face rather weakly, giving notice of strain and tension. Rising slowly, he looked toward the floor. Glancing quickly at eyes that focused kindly upon him, he moved toward the record player that was available for the group's use. Without an introduction, Ray finally proceeded with a presentation that did not stop short of a personal transformation.

Suddenly, he was positioned in a crouch, profiled against the group. His arms were extended, though, with the appearance of being weighted down. He seemed to have been holding up the heaviness of the world. Ray bowed suddenly. With equal suddenness his arms extended. He dropped the world! Downward came his arms and there before us was dance motion that perfectly matched the accompanying song, "Shoe Shine Boy," popularized by Eddie Kendricks, former lead singer of the famous Temptations. "Trying to make a living to go somewhere," Kendricks' voice soothed attentive ears, while Ray's movements widened attentive eyes. He motioned with a carefully paced swing of the right arm to suggest searching, then with passion, and in marvelous rhythm, he jerked with shoe shining motion to suggest striving. Searching, striving, searching, striving, he danced.

We were to learn that his searching and striving was to overcome conditions of poverty, the heritage of his family. It was a heritage that he had not understood, developing a massive inferiority complex as an adjustment to it. His shortness of stature combined with his state of poverty to make him feel little, crushed by a world overcrowded with superior people, he thought.

The tempo changed, reflectively. "Though it's a long way up, you'll reach the top." The stanza ended instructively. "Now when you finally get there, don't forget from where you came." Ray's dance motions echoed the song's instructions. He reached high, tip-toeing for a closer view of the top. He gracefully whirled, accelerating to a spin. Out of the spin, he shined shoes reverently, expressing devotion to the "Roots of his soul," the heritage of suffering, of joy, of the universe's rhythm, that, in the moment, twisted his muscles into beautiful turns.

He ached to be known, to be somebody, to come out of hiding, to dismiss the anger lurking beneath the smile that was often uneasy. "So many things in life to learn"—the song spread this kind of wisdom with each note. Now Ray moved with wonder, adventure, exploration, opening himself to receive from a world that appeared less severe.

Ray was later to talk about his family, school, and the way he saw the world. From a family of six children, he was the oldest child. He had few happy memories. Predominantly, they dwelled upon the lack of material adequacy, though he credited his father for diligence and steadfastness in support of the family. He remembered assuming responsibility early in life, recalling his father's favorite imperative, "You got to learn to do for yourself, boy, that's the only way to make it in this world."

Ray was soon to be overtaken in height by his brother, the second child. It was about that time he remembered having decisive feelings of inferiority. Something was wrong with him, he thought. It was a feeling from which he had not since known relief.

His school record had been only fair, curbed by his lack of assertiveness. He remembered feeling physically vulnerable, incapable of defending himself against all the little giants around him. So he learned to smile, softly. It calmed violent impulses in others. But he was never secure, always expecting wrath, feeling that his small but sturdy frame was too obvious an invitation to punitive impulses in others. Ignorant of the power his smile held, he now approached the borders of manhood feeling on the whole rather unmanly. His moment had come.

"Shoe shine boy," the song called to him. "Don't you know that you're a star, just the way you are?" Ending with repetitions of the call, the song incited Ray's movements. They were not unlike the holy dances of sacred places, and he was obviously filled with emotion. He burst. Tears flowed, first sorrowfully, then happily and happily and happily. The song was started again. The group joined him. They copied each movement in response to him. Call-and-response. African practices, alive in the New World, transforming existences.

It was a powerful experience for all of us, but especially for Ray. Through the dance of his life, a dance loaded with the fervor of his soul, he discovered self-worth and self-respect. Renewed with the power of his being, now freely engaging the group, he maintained his smile more comfortably.

Another astonishing exhibition of control of body movement by blacks is to be seen in sports or athletics. And again, one is reminded of the African heritage. Achebe writes in *Things Fall Apart* about a wrestling match in Nigeria:

> At last the two teams danced and the crowd roared and clapped. The drums rose to a frenzy. The people surged forward. The young men who kept order flew around, waving their palm fans. Old men nodded to the beat of the drums and remembered the days when they wrestled to its intoxicating rhythm.[24]

Participation in sports is an old pastime in West African culture and a pastime cherished by all. The winners, particularly the creative ones, are most highly regarded. Achebe attests to this in this passage:

The crowd burst into a thunderous roar. Okafo was swept off his feet by his supporters and carried home shoulder high. They sang his praise and the women clapped their hands:

> "Who will wrestle for our village?
> Okafo will wrestle for our village.
> Has he thrown a hundred men?
> He has thrown four hundred men.
> Has he thrown a hundred cats?
> He has thrown four hundred cats.
> Then send him word to fight for us."[25]

Note that the crowd burst into a roar. This signaled the end of the match, for Okafo had clearly won over his opponent Ikezue. Yet the roar of approval was made mostly to applaud the means by which Okafo rendered his opponent defenseless. He had performed a most creative act with his body by raising his right leg and swinging it over his rival's head. An artful feat that the crowd enjoyed as much as the fact that he won the match.

Clayton Riley, a noted black literary critic, has characterized this behavior among blacks who enjoy victory in contest less than the style in which a victory is won. Note the following succinct statement:

> White boys only want to know what the final score was; they're only interested in the results. Brothers want to know what happened in the game, like, "did O.J. (Simpson) dance?"[26]

In the black community, interest in making the body dance while winning is not uncommon. In other words, to enjoy the game. Now, for a look at a few popular athletes to see if they danced.

Earl Monroe—Basketball. He is called "Earl the Pearl." Driving for a lay-up, Earl would suddenly pass the ball quickly behind his back. And what started out as a right-handed shot often became a left-handed one. It all happened so fast people weren't sure how it happened. He played with a flair—the behind-the-back dribble, the Globetrotters' pass, and body control that makes lies of the laws of natural science.

Gayle Sayers—Football. Gayle was known as the fastest back in the league, fastest at getting to the sideline, fastest at turning the corner, fastest always. On a foggy December day, Gayle was passed a screen pass. It was a play in which the receiver was surrounded not only by blockers but by defenders as well. Sayers caught the ball in the crowd, spotted a narrow alley through the wall of unfriendly faces closing in on him, and instinctively dashed through. A wiggle, a squirm, a feint, then nothing but sheer speed, and he was gone for eighty yards.

"Buddy" Young—Football. Buddy was 5 feet 4½ inches, weighed 166 pounds in his prime, and seemed to merit the nickname "Buddy." During his freshman year at Illinois he scored thirteen touchdowns, matching the school record set by Harold (Red) Grange. He averaged 9.2 yards carrying the ball, and he scored on runs of 92, 82, 74, 63, 40, 31, and 24 yards.

There are gripping tales about unheralded black athletes who dominated playground games without landing scholarships or professional contracts. The two stories that follow are told by Pete Axthelm.

> For a few minutes Earl seemed to move slowly, feeling his way, getting himself ready. Then he got the ball on a fast break. Harper, who was six-feet-six, and Val Reed, who was six-feet-eight, got back quickly to defend. You wouldn't have given Earl a chance to score. Then he accelerated, changing his step suddenly. And at the foul line he went into the air. Harper and Reed went up too, and between them, the two big men completely surrounded the rim. But Earl just kept going higher, and finally he two-hand dunked the ball over both of them. For a split second there was complete silence, and then the crowd exploded. They were cheering so loud that they stopped the game for five minutes. Five minutes. That was Earl Manigault.[27]

"Well . . . I went out there one-on-one with Helicopter. Well, it was a disastrous thing. I tried lay-ups, jump shots, hooks. And everything I threw up, he blocked. The word had gone out that Helicopter [Joy "Helicopter" Vaughn] was there, and a crowd was gathering and I said to myself, 'You got to do something. You're getting humiliated.' But the harder I tried, the more he shoved the ball down into my face. I went home and thought about that game for a long time. Like a lot of other young athletes, I had been put in my place."[28]

Who would deny that the list of black athletes who have dominated, and continue to dominate, such sports as boxing, track, basketball, and football is long and distinguished. It is a phenomenon long discussed and analyzed, with little agreement, yet it remains a fact. For us writers, it is further evidence of the children of Africa's ability to fuse all the personality components including movement into a whole. One of the results is the perfect athlete who enjoys playing the game as he relates, naturally, to his environment.

Finally, the ability to use muscular energy (rocking steady baby) is a creative product of African people, for the service of black people. And it has served us well. Its usage is to be found in everything we do, from serving God to playing games; that is, we use motor behaviors in all areas of our lives. Our experiences are enriched by movements, and we learn innovative movements through our experiences. Where we black people are, there is action. We carry it with us and mold challenging conditions through the use of it. It has been with us historically, it comforts us, it aids us in cruel times, and most often it helps us to remain sane in hostile environs. The whole of life for ordinary black people is accompanied by movement to the rhythm of the universe, which allows us to employ the entire body as a medium of expression. We are vital and free to use music with our bodies as we "rock steady" to the beat of drums.

PART III

SUGGESTIONS FOR USING BLACK EXPRESSIVENESS

APPENDIX
EXPRESS YOUR WAY TO GOOD HEALTH AND HAPPINESS

---

*Guides for
Positive Living
and Learning*

Defining the Blues, a Bluesman recalls:

I've heard my grandmother say it was a boat they called the Choctaw. She says she used to roll a whole barrel of syrup or molasses, she used to roll them barrels right alongside of her husband and she used to cut sprouts with him when they was cleaning up. Those blues come from way back when they had to study something to try to give them some consolation. The man was doing them so bad, taking all they had and working them to death. They just had to do something, so they sang about what they felt.

Jasper Love[1]

"Why the King of Love Is Dead?" Nina Simone mournfully asks this question in a song expunging our hearts of sorrow and grief, after the death of Dr. Martin Luther King, Jr. It is in this manner that black expressions, a rich source of aesthetic-spiritual emotion, in church pews, concert halls, and family living rooms, strengthen the cohesion of social groups offering security and support for their individual members. Black expressions uplift the downhearted and express the joys and sorrows of the black situation.

Explaining the history of "Precious Lord," Thomas Dorsey explained (in an interview told by Alfred Duckett):

> That's a sad story. "Precious Lord" came twisting out of my very heart because of the death of a dear one. A songwriter named E. C. Davis and I were scheduled to go out of town to sing at a revival meeting. My wife— my first wife, Nettie (Harper)—was in the late days of a pregnancy. I told her goodbye, got in my car with Davis and drove about 30 miles, headed from Chicago to St. Louis. Suddenly, I reached down to feel for the briefcase in which I carried all my music and—lo and behold —I had forgotten to bring it. I turned around and drove the 30 miles back home, went back into my house and got my briefcase. My wife was asleep and I didn't want to disturb her. As I got back into the car, Davis got out the other side. "I don't think I'll go," he told me. "What's the matter with you, man?" I objected. "I can't run this revival by myself." He repeated, "I don't think I'll go," and walked away. Sometimes when I think back on it, I believe Providence was working on me—the forgotten briefcase, E. C.'s abrupt departure—to tell me to stay home. But I travelled on all alone. The next night at the revival meeting, they brought me a telegram. The baby was doing fine. But my wife had been lost down in the valley and the shadow of death. I was a mess. Rev. Jesse Adams, a friend, volunteered to drive me home. I'd have never made it at the wheel. When I got home, they hadn't even moved the body. But they wouldn't let

me see her. I did see the baby (who died shortly thereafter).

All the heart for writing gospel music went out of me
during those hours of grief. I thought: "There ain't no
sense in my trying to write songs of hope any more. I
ought to just go back into the blues business." But I
didn't. For, out of that awful trauma came the greatest
song in my catalog. It happened like this: The late
Professor Theodore Frye had a lovely music room here
on what is now known as Dr. Martin Luther King
Drive. You could go there and rehearse. He and I went
up there one night not long after Nettie's death. We just
planned to go over some stuff. I began fooling around
on the piano and a tune came to me. It was an old tune,
but I found myself stumbling up on some new words
which suited my mood of dejection and despair: *"Precious Lord—take my hand. Lead me on. Let me stand, I
am tired."* True, I was so tired. *"I am weak. I am worn.
Through the storm."* Plenty storm in my life now.
"Through the night." Hard night. *"Lead me on to the
light."* There had to be a light somewhere. There must
be some happiness left somewhere. There must be success somewhere. *"Precious Lord. Take my hand. Lead
me on."*

The words were so simple. It was a simple song, but it
came right out of me almost as if God had personally
dictated every syllable.[2]

It is this tendency, exampled by Simone and Dorsey, that restores the rhythm response to its normal pulsation when it is interrupted by painful emotions such as depression from grief, sorrow, rejection, anger, etc. It is evident that the body has
automatic healing potential that can be maximized curatively if
we utilize the expressive outlets at our disposal.

Note the great depth of feeling that the examples of Simone
and Dorsey conjure within. Simone's and Dorsey's submissions
summoned the automatic pilots from within to steer them
through the winds of depression. It is closely akin to the concept

of "letting be," or becoming barely attentive to perceptive sensations. It is from such a state that creative expression emerges, formed in song, dance, drama, oratory, poetry-prose-narrative (automatic writing), and other expressive devices.

What seems obvious is that the first step toward becoming more expressive is to open up to, perhaps even surrender to one's feelings rather than suppress, deny, intellectualize, or deploy other defenses to ward off the sensations of the "right mind." Defenses offer ready-made or concocted answers to explain away signals from inside of us. Ready-made answers fall far short of the truth of our existence.

One of the intentions of this compendium is to give advice with regard to ways individuals can become more expressive, more soulful. It offers guidance to those seeking ways to live a more enriched life, that is, one with reduced stress and anxiety, and increased joy and happiness—contentment. We have established that expressive behavior is fundamental to optimal mental health, and that black expressive behavior, because it is more soulful, represents the best style of self-expression for maximum effectiveness. Because black expressiveness is woven into the fabric of much of popular Western culture, it has become socially useful to all people who share in the culture, without regard for their racial origin. And though the expressive advice here is founded on premises which underlie black/African reality, its use by races other than blacks is expected and encouraged. In other words, American popular culture is an American commodity that significantly overlays the folk culture of African Americans. It is thereby already used by many different racial and ethnic groups to satisfy their social appetites for entertainment. To the same extent that it is used socially, it is used therapeutically, in the quest for joy, relaxation, or other satisfying experiences. The therapeutic value is achieved quite naturally, without conscious intent.

It is conscious intent that the expressive guidance emphasized here brings, attempting to systematically increase the utilization of black expressive forms as a way of achieving more optimal mental health. The advisory suggestions are listed in the order of the aspects of black expressiveness presented in Part II of this work: Depth of Feeling; Naturalistic Attitudes; Stylistic Rendering; Poetic and Prosaic Vernacular; and Expressive Movement. Together these make up the fabric of black expressive behavior.

A fuller utilization of the feeling capacity by blacks is most readily evident in the aesthetic form of song (music). Song is a common and popular medium of black expression. When depression visits the soul stemming from the unkindness of life, song has the power to put down depression, not by suppression, but by complete and full expression of the troubling matter. Alain Locke, who was both catalyst and interpreter of African American culture, perhaps best known for his work *The New Negro,* has spoken to this point. He suggests that blacks should "become musical by nurture and not rest content with being musical by nature."[3] He urges that blacks should re-establish themselves as musicians. More fundamentally the suggestion calls for greater cultivation of man's feeling capacity through musical, expressive forms.

Some concrete suggestions follow for liberating the artist in yourself and/or in those with whom you work. These were derived, as were all the suggestions in the section, from the different ways blacks in the folk culture have used them to increase their survival chances. With reference to all of the advisory suggestions, there is no order or sequence in their use. Frequency and variety are the important factors for maximum effectiveness. Do as many different ones, singularly or together, as often as you can, and be guided mostly by the way you feel.

1. Whistling, yodeling, moaning, and humming are ways of making contact with feelings and expressing them. You may do this with a known tune or you may allow the process to chart its own creative course. It is particularly useful when you are alone performing routine chores or work tasks; these practices offer wholesome diversions of distractions from the burden of uninspiring work.

2. Sing along with sincerity and intensity, with emotionally relevant recordings, or at live occasions in churches, clubs, concert halls, street corner symphonies, etc. Too often in these sit-

uations, we refrain from participating or our voices are barely audible. Fling the whole self more into it. You'll get more out of it.

3. Cultivate your interest in and skills at playing a musical instrument. More importantly, it is particularly useful to create simple instruments of your own initially, to finger the edges of your feelings.

4. When you are troubled, have someone you know who is skilled in instrumental or vocal music perform selections for you which will both heighten the intensity of your feelings and also calm the storm within you.

5. When emotionally relevant tunes are being played, position yourself in your most relaxed manner, and self-induce trance-like states, as in fantasies, and allow a musical-drama to suspend your mind on the edges of another reality. When you return to ordinary consciousness, you'll feel lighter, freer of much of the heaviness that before the fantasy weighed you down. Much psychic ventilation occurs vicariously.

6. It is useful quite often to write down one's fantasies and make up a song from the fantasy material, giving it your own arrangement.

7. Make up songs about troubling matters through recordings of your own spontaneous utterances. Just let the words and arrangement come, and carry you through the bondage of depression.

Note that the emphasis in the preceding suggestions has centered on troubling or painful emotions, but the same procedures can be used, as in the black folk community, to heighten joyous states.

A naturalistic attitude is captured in this line: "Don't push it, don't force it (Let it happen naturally)." Popular recording artist Leon Haywood issues this request in a song by the same title. "Don't push the river, it flows by itself," the late and famed psychotherapist Frederick Perls used to say, presenting patients with the formula for living happily—being natural.

Being natural, then, is fundamental to optimal mental health and is a mark of the black/African heritage. It begins with an attitude of comfort regarding one's body; its shape, its drives, its odors, and its acquired scars or mangled parts. Self-acceptance is based upon acceptance of nature. This attitude is achieved by a prideful surrender to truth; nature is truth; and the body is of nature; and therefore natural.

Being one with nature, then, is a prerequisite to healthy living. This means that you must become one with your own inner nature by tuning in to your rhythmic pulse or beat, or developing an increased awareness of your body's voice, a voice that derives momentum from the right side of the brain. The following is advised:

1. "Is it natural?" Let this be the question by which you are guided in much of your conduct, particularly with regards to your personal appearance and general attitudes about your bodily drives and impulses. Giving in to that which is natural reduces stress and tension, and softens the repressive structure in the mind. Just let your own wave of rhythm propel you through life with ease and comfort.

2. Cultivate relationships with some few elements of the natural world. Inject something of your own character into objects, items, and substances of the physical universe, and take from them something of their eternal character. Heavenly bodies, waters, airy and earthy elements, plants, animals, rocks, mountains, etc., all can be targets of your affection.

3. Do not underestimate the power of holistic medicine. Scientific medicine has yet to cure all ills, and quite often are only extractions of the same herbs, roots, and other curative plants, that make up naturalistic medicine.

4. Resist formalizing and standardizing your existence. Remain more casual in your approach to life. It gives you greater flexibility and range, opening you more to the experience of the universe's rhythm and your own inner fancies.

5. Guard against doing the same thing over and over again the same way, which is usually an associate of "time addiction." Take a different route home, eat lunch earlier or later, rest when you feel like it, or, in other words, strive to inject as much newness and refreshment into your life as possible.

6. Do some things only when you feel like doing them, and negotiate for as much freedom from time compulsion as you can in your daily pattern. Differently stated, whenever possible, be less concerned with being "on time," and become more concerned with being "in time," more particularly in those life areas that are not fraught with consequences for violations of punctuality. For example, don't overplan your after-work or after-school hours with activities having exact time designations, requiring you to be "on time." Many of these things you can do when you feel like it, or "in time." That is, viewing time as one continuance, rather than as mathematical units on a continuum which is involved in being "on time."

7. Tact and diplomacy are useful interpersonal mechanisms, but they, by their own meanings, hide or subvert the truth. As much as you can, with care, be frank, honest, and to the point. Avoid the outright lies that are often advanced in the name of tact and diplomacy, effectively hiding the inner being.

8. Move as naturally, as relaxed, and as rhythmically as your body allows. It is not necessary to put forth effort, simply "let be," and grace will subsume you.

9. Love life, love the making of life, love yourself, and wish to see yourself multiply—many times—and problems of sexual limitations will diminish.

How does one develop style? Recall that style is the peculiar manner of self-expression unique to each individual. It is subdued by the conformity imperative that characterizes mainstream America. Such conformity is agreeable to the technological ends of a society such as ours; it is believed that these ends are more efficiently achieved if human beings are controllable, regulated, predictable, or in short, robotlike, which divests humans of their essence and style. No doubt it has been in part due to the systematic exclusion of African Americans from the mainstream of the nation that style proliferates in the communities of common black folk.

It appears essential, then, that the first step in achieving style is to free oneself of the conformity addiction that is the heritage of Middle America. "Feelin' Free" is the benefit of recovery from conformity addiction, and is the song title of an applicable tune by Jermaine Jackson. It goes:

> *Feelin' Free*
> *. . . like a drifter*
> *I'm flying high on the wind*
> *If my heart beats too loud*
> *it's the sound of the world at my feet*
> *my condition is too contagious to treat*
>
> *It makes you want to shout*
> *Throw your hands up*
> *say hey!*
> *Live your life out*
> *each day . . .*[4]

Such an achieved free state is consistent with one of Maslow's elements of healthy people: "A high degree of autonomy." Healthy people seem to be able to remain true to their feelings or themselves, without regard for their popularity or acceptability quotients. They are indeed themselves with or against the mainstream of things. In autonomy, there is the freedom to express oneself in keeping with one's inner dictates. It is the freedom that ushers forth a style that is grand to the individual. A few suggestions follow:

1. Get to know and appreciate who you are. You start this process by listening to the voice inside, and little by little, act in accordance with the yearning of your inner reality.

2. Begin doing some things the way *you* want to do them, par-

ticularly when consequences are not threatening. Wear the flashy apparel, sport the different hairstyle, walk the different walk, talk the different talk, if the need for expression comes from within. In other words, be guided by your emotions sometimes, not always your thoughts, social pressures, or conventionality.

3. Let the achievement of relaxation, a sense of easiness within yourself, be a quest for you. Such a state lifts the ordinary constraints we place on our own natural rhythm, which manifests most conspicuously in our bodies. When an easiness within oneself is achieved, a natural grace infuses the body's movements and will reveal for you your own style of rhythmic movement.

4. Once having developed a skill in keeping with the rules of an art, be it in athletics, education, performing arts, or any other field of endeavor, be persuaded by the impulses to "jazz" the skill. Improvise around the standard beat of the method so as to put yourself into it. This then gives it your style. It makes the act you, not a procedure.

5. Refuse to ferret out tonal qualities or other characteristics that represent birthmarks of your ethnicity. It gives your voice and being a special distinctiveness. If cultivated, you will develop a speaking style and way of behaving consistent with who you are, in terms of your ethno-cultural heritage.

To recognize the special gifts of blacks for "gab" is only to edge the inherent tremendous therapeutic and educational possibilities. Their language is indeed their password and the pathway into their souls. To enter and follow the path leads to the attendant embrace of Africa as the best source for vital, verbal self-expression. What colorful words escape from their lips, words that do wonders for both speaker and listener. The suggestions which follow are intended to enjoin you to develop the potency of the black language style.

1. In the tradition of Africa, make personal use of story-telling. Take your yearnings, longings, hurts, joys, or whatever, and ex-

press them through story form. It is necessary to be both dramatic and graphic. Make use of ideophones, music, and dance as necessary to give your story the proper emotional affect. It is further useful to tell stories already in existence that parallel your own emotional situation. The suggestion is adaptable to educational situations also.

2. Take your emotional experiences and convert them into riddles. This can give others a deeper rapport with your life situation, while allowing you, the creator of the riddle, to take what are often confusing and disturbing thoughts and feelings and convert them into cummunicable and explainable truths, freeing you from the confused state.

3. Secure or create proverbs that speak to your inner reality, and offer guidance and direction for your future behavior.

4. Construct some hopeful declarative statements about your life situation and convert them into chants. Chanting can heighten feelings and also induce fantasy and other trancelike states which may bring confidence and determination to situations of doubt and despair.

5. Find black language already constructed in speeches, songs, or narratives that advise wisely, and render them into guidance statements for the troubled soul or unmotivated and uninspired individual.

6. Don't forget to laugh, even at your own misfortunes. Take a troubling matter and try making a "joke" out of it, or at least weave elements of humor into it. This can serve as a cushion to soften the pang of lacerating emotions.

7. "Signifyin" is particularly useful in expressing feelings of anger and disgust. This can be a monologue or a written attack. Competitive "signifyin" can be a substitute for physical sparring if the two participants are of equal verbal agility and the competition is appropriately officiated.

8. Braggart "rappin" is useful in bolstering feelings of self-esteem. During the 1970s and '80s, popular examples could be

seen in the recordings of the Sugar Hill Gang, Kurtis Blow, and in Nikki Giovanni's poem "Ego Tripping."

9. Coin your own nickname to crystallize your experience of yourself in an emotionally straining situation. The nickname helps you reduce the strain to a manageable size and enhances the process of working through, even though it may initially appear derogatory, downing, or just plain uncomplimentary. Nicknames are useful, too, in interpersonal situations where personal feedback is desirable. In educational situations, particularly in literature involving stories, dramas, or poems with prominent characters, have children give nicknames to characters as a way of communicating understanding of the characters' personalities, motives, interests, etc.

As you have seen, the motor system is a powerfully expressive one. Its power is derived from the mind, as movement is the end product of the mind's labor. African man is like the universe: in perpetual motion. It is motion, graced by rhythm and sensuality, that puts African man synchronously in the currents of the earth's orbital and axial motion—polyrhythmic action. To move, then, is to bring balance to one's mental system by increasing congruence between one and nature. Oneness with nature, with all things, is the platform on which optimal health sets, and it can be enhanced, even optimally attained, through movement. Some suggestions follow:

1. Pluck, clap, pat, shoulder rock, etc., to stimulating sounds, such as music. It is particularly useful when driving your automobile, or during other situations where a necessary level of body control has to be maintained.

2. Take your pressing life situations and, utilizing mime, as in African dance, put in rhythmic motion (with the help of music or your own self-paced beat) the troubling items, objects, people, etc., in your life. Flavor the movement with the emotions you feel.

3. Relax your efforts to control your body while walking. This

gives your strides a rhythmic buoyancy, allowing you to feel a lift-off sensation, close to the feeling of floating in space.

4. Do physical exercises to the rhythm of music. The interface of sensual rhythm with the repetitiveness of exercise movements wards off boredom and the physical discomfort often associated with the sterility of exercise. A beat gives your movements a sharper time, and makes the exercise more enjoyable.

5. Permit the body to vigorously move in response to music, in drama, or dramatic oratory, discothèques, theaters, parties, or concert halls.

6. Dance along to popular recordings, moving not necessarily to vogue patterned steps, but as your own rhythms steer you. Let your body sway as loosely as possible to the music, without effort to guide the movement.

7. Choreograph your story of emotional troubles. This can be solo movement or you may direct the movement of others to fashion a musical-drama of your being.

8. Become involved in action-oriented sports. Action is the opposite or reverse of depression and gloom. Moreover, physical action dismisses anxiety, tension, and stress. Wherever possible, enrich the action with the sound of a beat.

We have offered all of the above suggestions for those individuals who may be seeking to overcome personal unhappiness or to live life more richly. We have further specified the advisory elements in our clinical practices that have come to us from the ways of common folk of black/African heritage. Professional people, such as teachers, counselors, social workers, psychiatrists, psychologists, ministers and other helpers, certainly can adapt the suggestions to their own professional roles.

We have more to share with the helper, however. It is our conviction that black expression can increase the skill capacities of helping practitioners. Its relevancy for the teaching-learning-living process cannot be denied. We have found through our work, mostly with groups (children, adolescents, and adults), that the use of black expression vitalizes methodology and therefore motivates and inspires group members in educational or therapeutic settings just as it does in popular culture. We therefore share some examples of the cathartic, curative, and educational aids we have formulated using music, drama, poetry, folklore, expressive movement, and graphic expression.

I. FOSTERING SELF-ESTEEM AND ACHIEVEMENT MOTIVATION

A. *General Purpose or Rationale*

To help young people understand that with a clear sense of their past achievements, they will come to appreciate who they are and will view more realistically their own possibilities.

B. *Method(s) of Facilitation*

Tell orally and dramatically the story of the "Eagle," as told in a recording of a speech by historian and curator of black culture Dr. Edward Robinson.[5] The story emphasizes the strength, courage, durability, achievements, historical rooting, and beauty associated with black ethnicity.

a. Have group members reflect on aspects of their own lives about which the story makes them feel better, or about insights they may have gained.

b. Have group members discuss their individual reflections on aspects of their lives touched by the story, and create art forms with them, i.e., turn the reflections into stories, poems, songs, short plays, paintings, picture stories, movement, etc., and share these with the group.

C. *Intended Learning Experiences*

1. To help group members gain confidence in challenging and developing meaningfully perceived weaknesses in themselves.

2. To help group members make use of their own creative, expressive style as they endeavor to exhume potential buried within themselves.

3. To help group members develop a pattern of inquiry relative to knowledge about themselves, so as to better enable them to realize their true potential and sustain high levels of intrinsic motivation, which will increase the likelihood of excellence as they pursue their chosen careers and life goals.

II. PROMOTING EDUCATIONAL EXCELLENCE AND SCHOOL RETENTION

A. *General Purpose or Rationale*
To help school-age youth more fully appreciate the liberating value of a good education and realize that ultimate human freedom lies in knowledge.

B. *Method(s) of Facilitation*
1. Select a list of proverbs that speak of the value of knowledge and understanding and use it to have group members create a group poem. Each member will orally recite one of the proverbs and the group will repeat in unison (chant) the lines recited by each member. This brief list of African proverbs from G. K. Osei's pamphlet *The African Philosophy of Life* will serve to illustrate:

MEMBER: The lack of knowledge is darker than night.

GROUP: *The lack of knowledge is darker than night.*

MEMBER: An ignorant man without force can be made a slave.

GROUP: *An ignorant man without force can be made a slave.*

MEMBER: Whoever works without knowledge, works uselessly.

GROUP: *Whoever works without knowledge, works uselessly.*

MEMBER: Not to know is bad; not to wish to know is worse.

GROUP: *Not to know is bad; not to wish to know is worse.*

MEMBER: A man with wisdom is better off than a stupid man with any amount of charm.

GROUP: *A man with wisdom is better off than a stupid man with any amount of charm.*

MEMBER: If you can only find it out, there is a reason for everything.

GROUP: *If you can only find it out, there is a reason for everything.*[6]

"Let's talk about the message for you in this proverbial poem," is a sample question to facilitate interaction, and could be followed by dialogue regarding the feelings of group members when they find themselves "not knowing" in interpersonal situations.

2. Adapt, in story form, the short narrative on the desire of slaves for an education from John Lovell's book *Black Song*.[7] The narrative shows the courage, persistence, and artistry employed in slaves overcoming immoral but legal barriers to their right to learn—their right to be free. The lives of Nat Turner, Frederick Douglass, Denmark Vesey, and others who used education in their pursuit of freedom are mentioned.

   Have group members reflect on the quest and struggles of their enslaved kinsmen for an education and relate their quest and struggles to our current-day educational achievements and privileges, and our continuing struggles.

3. Show group members the attitude of the black folk community toward the liberating powers of education as it is reflected in numerous spirituals by having them listen to recordings or sing in unison. The often thinly veiled but profound and deep educational desire and determination for satisfaction thereof is expressed in many of the spirituals. Some are listed in Lovell's *Black Song*.[8] "I Have a Right to the Tree of Life," "I Know I Would Like to Read," "This Little Light Is Mine," "Oh My Little Soul Goin' Shine Like a Stahr," and others.

Play recordings, if possible, while the group follows written words of the song. Then have group members share their reflections on resolves that they might make with respect to their own lives as related to attaining the benefits of a good education.

C. *Intended Learning Experiences*

1. To help group members realize that when education is defined as enlightened training for a place in society and for individual personal development, it was a thing highly respected in Africa.

2. To have group members come to a realization that for thousands of slaves the desire for education was intense and that this desire continues in the black community today.

3. To help group members feel a sense of personal duty, obligation, and responsibility to fulfill the wishes and dreams of their ancestors, not only by remaining in school but also by making excellence the only acceptable quality of performance for themselves as they move up the educational ladder.

III. DEVELOPING DETERMINATION AND PERSIST-
ENCE IN WORTHY ENDEAVORS

A. *General Purpose or Rationale*
   To help the young and the emotionally troubled, who
   lack constant and firm courage, to appreciate the necessity for developing fortitude and endurance in the
   face of misfortune, pain, and calamity.

B. *Method(s) of Facilitation*
   1. Dramatically read the lyrics of some work songs
      and/or spirituals to show that praise and admiration
      were commanded by those who prevailed under un-
      bearable circumstances. Langston Hughes and Arna
      Bontemps, in the *Book of Negro Folklore*, provide
      examples of work songs, "Can't You Line It," and
      "Chilly Win' Don' Blow," respectively:

      "A nickel's worth of bacon and a dime's worth of
         lard,
      I would buy more but time's too hard . . .
      Wonder what's the matter with the walking boss,
      It's done five-thirty and he won't knock-off . . .

      I ast' my Cap'n what's the time of day.
      He got so mad he thowed his watch away . . .

      Cap'n got a pistol and he try to play bad,
      But I'm gonna take it if he makes me mad . . ."

      The "hanh!" in "Chilly Win' Don' Blow" represents
      an explosion of breath, as at the end of a blow with
      an ax or pick.

      "Captain, Captain, *hanh!* don' be so hard, *hanh!*
         on long-time man, *hanh!*
      Says, you worked me, *hanh!* in de rain, *hanh!*

An' you worked me, *hanh!* in de snow, *hanh!*
So I, Captain, *hanh!* cain' hard-, *hanh!* -ly go,
hanh!

An' its' oh, howdy me
An' its' oh, howdy my
Says, I make it where de chilly win' don' blow."[9]

Lovell in *Black Song* shows blacks, harnessed by oppressive conditions, depicting fortitude and courage in the spirituals:

"We want no cowards in our band,
We call for valiant-hearted men,
You shall gain the victory, you shall gain the day."

And, too, while living amidst discouraging circumstances, they sing, "Don't ever feel discouraged, Neighbor, you bear your load!" and best said in:

"O stand the storm, it won't be long,
We'll anchor bye and bye . . ."[10]

2. Recite orally or play the recording of "Just Don't Make No Sense," from Van Peebles.[11] The song shows a black man, standing up, though bent over under the weight of his problems and the problems others cast upon him.

  a. Have group members, after reflecting on facilitative stimuli, talk about difficult circumstances in their own lives where they must mobilize inner reserves of strength to help them prevail, and help group members assess their own values and behavior as they serve to hinder or facilitate their ability to prevail.

  b. Have group members dramatize their revelations in short plays, stories, songs, poems, dance, or other forms reflecting changes that they must make in their own lives so that they may avail themselves of more of their inner strength, and share these artistically transformed revelations with the group.

C. *Intended Learning Experiences*
   1. To help group members understand that their ancestors prevailed under one of the most horrendous experiences known to the human family and that they have inherited this incontestable endurance.

   2. To help group members understand that with consistent and persistent struggle, coupled with knowledge, they cannot only match but go beyond the achievements of their foreparents.

   3. To create in group members an awareness of the need to continue to search within themselves and their past experiences, particularly those who are members of oppressed groups, for the best options for dealing with troublesome encounters in their personal lives.

IV. HELPING TROUBLED YOUTH GAIN DEEPER INSIGHTS INTO THEIR BEHAVIOR

A. *General Purpose or Rationale*
To help troubled youth gain insight into the tensions and confusion in their lives. They must be sensitized to who they are, what they are doing, where they are going, and where they could go with a higher sense of self. Members of the target group are deeply troubled with obvious emotional conflicts. These are youth who are victims of early arrest, gang abuse, and commitment to correctional facilities, and they are prime candidates for drug use and imprisonment.

B. *Method(s) of Facilitation*
   1. Because these youngsters are often active and ex-

pressive, ask them to present dramatic portrayals
of troubling incidents among youth who live as they
do. To complement their depiction and heighten
the depth of feeling, ask them to select works from
black recording artists that parallel their dramatic
portrayals.

2. Following the playing of each complementary record, with written words to follow, the group should
be guided into a discussion in an attempt to eluci-
date the sources or environmental forces underlying the troublesome incidents portrayed.

3. Portray alternative remedies for the troublesome
occurrences.

C. *Intended Learning Experiences*
1. To enable the youths to gain a vantage point far
enough removed from the confused and explosive
pattern of their day-to-day lives to give them a more
objective and lucid glimpse into their existence.

2. To enable the youths to realize that there are alternative reactions to troublesome incidents, and
some are more beneficial than others.

3. To create in the group members an awareness of
the need to continue to search for the best alternative for dealing with troublesome incidents, particularly as an oppressed people seeking liberation.

V. UNDERSTANDING AND OVERCOMING PROB-
LEMS OF COLOR

A. *General Purpose or Rationale*
To help adolescents understand and overcome their
ambivalent feelings with respect to the color black.
The target group comprises young blacks and other
races of adolescent age level and up.

B. *Method(s) of Facilitation*

1. Have group members listen to the Supremes' rendition of "Living In Shame."

2. Have the group read together the following three passages taken from *How Do "Negroes" Feel About Whites and How Do Whites Feel About "Negroes"?*

   a. "I could clearly see that my father strongly disliked whites but he made a few statements about 'Negroes' which led me to believe that he didn't care too much for them, either. Even though whites were evil and untrustworthy, my father thought that 'Negroes' were morally and intellectually inferior to whites. He would make statements such as 'a nigger ain't worth a hill of beans,' and 'if I were white I wouldn't want "Negroes" to sit beside me either.' My father's attitudes toward 'Negroes' and whites served only to confuse me. . . ."

   b. "My mother's admiration for white or light skin was very obvious. But she would have been deeply hurt and indignant if I had accused her of favoring white skin over black skin. . . . One could become two shades darker after an hour in the sun. My mother has a remedy for this— bleaching cream. Her attitude toward light skin gave me the impression that dark skin was something to be ashamed of."

   c. "When does a 'Negro' first feel his societal status? When did I first feel it? Who knows, for all of a sudden I knew that wherever I wandered the railroad tracks would be there."[12]

3. Have group members extract those lines in the record and passages that show feelings of ambivalence, and have them discuss how this ambivalence has affected the lives of people and their relationships to one another.

4. Have group members look at the use of such statements as "a nigger ain't worth a hill of beans," and
help them trace such statements to their origins.
Discuss their intended purposes and the effects such
statements have had on the development of their
identities and beliefs.

5. Creatively acquaint students with the role of melanin in the determination of color, and help them
understand the role of physical features in surviving environmental harshness. Then have them write
poems, songs, stories, dramatic skits, etc., using the
concepts derived from their understanding of melanin and its physiological associates.

C. *Intended Learning Experiences*
1. To have all people begin talking about the color
sickness that has been perpetrated on us by a world
afflicted with color mania.

2. To have people understand they must rid their consciousness of the illness, as it is one that hinders us
from uniting in the struggle for liberation and other
life-enhancement goals.

3. To have blacks understand that a solid, strong, mentally healthy state begins with an appreciation of
and reverence for blackness—color, culture, and
consciousness—more particularly color because of
the importance to physical health, longevity, and
aesthetic qualities.

VI. MODELING POSITIVE IMAGES FROM THE BLACK COMMUNITY

A. *General Purpose or Rationale*
To provide all youths with positive black images
with which to interact within their consciousness that

will inspire vigilance, pursuit of excellence, and self-confidence. The makers of positive images for young people in the general populace are numerous and permeate every institution, but for the black youngster, exposure to black image-makers is a rarity. Therefore, the effort to create positive images must be vigorously stimulated. This activity will help them use the lives of popular black figures as behavior models.

B. *Method(s) of Facilitation*

1. Allow students to choose names of black people known in various areas of black expression. Some examples are listed:

> Music
> Dance
> Poetry
> Song Writing
> Short Stories
> Novels
> Theater
> Playwrighting
> Fashion
> Oratory
> Comedy
> Painting

2. Each member of the group is to research the person whose name he or she draws. Students present to the group something of interest that they have found out about that person. Records, drawings, tapes, books, poems, stories, dramatic readings, dance, or pictures may be used in the presentations, utilizing particularly mime as in African portrayal through movement.

3. The group members should enter into interaction with respect to message(s) inherent in each presentation, and glean meanings for their own lives.

C. *Intended Learning Experiences*
   1. To stimulate young minds with positive black images with which to build strong black identities where black youths are concerned.

   2. To make the students aware that it is highly possible, with struggle, to achieve excellence or greatness.

   3. To make black youth understand that it is the responsibility of the talented to achieve maximally and to share the rewards of achievement with the total black community.

VII. HELPING UNDERACHIEVERS

A. *General Purpose or Rationale*
   To help potential dropouts enhance their chances for academic success. Potential dropouts usually can be detected during the early elementary years. They are generally boys who are from broken homes, large families, and impoverished circumstances. Their informal learning and expressive styles have been their tools of survival, yet teachers, counselors, and psychologists ignore the valuable assets that the youngsters bring with them and attempt to formalize the learning experience in a cultural context foreign to the one from which the children come. Hence, the schools promote their early dropping out.

B. *Method(s) of Facilitation*
   1. Give dramatic readings from some selected black oral folklore (e.g., Langston Hughes and Arna Bontemps' *Book of Negro Folklore*).

   2. After the reading, allow the youngsters to portray characters from the works through mime.

   3. Allow them to deduce and discuss the moral impli-

cations of the reading. This is of particular importance, and moves the school or helper toward the
role of proper moral guidance, but from an ethno-
cultural perspective.

4. If done for teaching purposes, extract a list of words
that they appear to be ready and anxious to learn
and define them in words from their existing vocabulary. These same words can be used for spell-
ing lists, stimulus for story telling, and work with
synonyms and antonyms to increase their facility
with "public language."

C. *Intended Learning Experiences*
1. To help the youngsters recognize that they have
acquired learning that is valued and appreciated.

2. To help them understand that blacks have used the
language creatively to express their thoughts, values, and ideas, and that very often it is unlike the
language used in schools.

3. To provide an opportunity for the youngsters to
exercise their expressive propensities in an acceptable framework.

4. To help youngsters to understand that blacks have
always had a strong moral code supporting a value
system by which they too should live, but that oppressive conditions often subvert one's sense of
morality.

VIII. VALUE ORIENTATION: COMMITMENT AND RACE PRIDE

A. *General Purpose or Rationale*
To engender prideful feelings about oneself and kind,
and commitment to values emanating from black culture. It is our contention that a sense of black identity

is imperative for optimal mental health for blacks. When counseling for value orientations of the nature specified, the counselor, as we see it, must deliberately structure the group process to effect dignity, pride, identity, and commitment to the black struggle. With the proper value set blacks can live more abundantly, and this set is available to them in their own expressive forms.

B. *Method(s) of Facilitation*
Black popular music can be used to instill values such as dignity, pride, identity, and commitment to struggle. The counselor may play a message-oriented song, then lead, and have group members share feelings, thoughts, images, etc., regarding the inherent message. The counselor involves himself with the meaning in the song and serves as a live, immediate model and catalyst for appropriate group behavior.

Songs that we see as being appropriate include:

"To Be Young, Gifted, and Black" (Nina Simone)
"I Wish I Knew How It Would Feel to Be Free" (Nina Simone)
"Message from a Black Man" (The Temptations)
"Say It Loud—I'm Black and I'm Proud" (James Brown)
"Black Is Beautiful" (Nancy Wilson)
"Black Woman" (Don Covay)
"Black Pearl" (Sonny Charles)
"Together We're Truly Black Power" (Curtis Mayfield)
"Keep On Going On" (Curtis Mayfield)
Ghettos of the Mind (Bama and the Village Poets)
"Who'll Pay Reparation on My Soul" (Gil Scott-Heron)
"Buffalo Soldier" (The Persuasions)
Truth Is on Its Way (Nikki Giovanni)

C. *Intended Learning Experiences*

1. To present popular models who espouse healthy ideas about self-acceptance, and the importance of blackness.

2. To show youngsters that prideful feelings about self and kind are important to one's personal happiness and fulfillment, and essential for unity in the race.

3. To advance an attitude of commitment to acquiring all that is legally and constitutionally necessary to safeguard the rights and privileges that allow for the wholesome pursuit of happiness.

Even in conventional forms of group counseling, black expression can be useful in vitalizing the methodology. Note the examples of counselor techniques that follow:

1. *Self-Disclosure.* "Present and talk about a song, poem, literary passage, dramatic excerpt, piece of sculpture, etc., that says something about you." Group members should take turns talking about themselves through expressive mediums. Members should be encouraged to react to each other and give additional meanings they get from black expressions presented by others, to show their understanding of and interest in what a member is saying about himself.

2. *Feedback.* "Talk about a song or another expressive device that says something about a particular group member or each group member."

3. *Interpersonal Communication.* "Talk to group members about an emotionally relevant expressive theme that communicates some special feeling you have toward a member or members of the group."

As in group work, black expressions in popular culture are useful in the individual counseling relationship. Note the conventional relationship techniques that follow:

1. *Reflection of Feelings*

EXCERPT 1. The client had been in counseling with one of the authors and the problem was tangentially related to marital discord. After many intense sessions the client learned some things about herself and about her relationship with her husband.

CLIENT: [Joyfully] I really can't believe how much better things are with us. I really can't believe it. [Pause] You know [concentratedly], I thought I had lost him and thought he didn't give a damn about me and the kids, and now I'm so glad I didn't do the foolish thing I almost did. We really seem to be tuned in together, you know what I mean?

COUNSELOR: Ain't understanding mellow? [Song title of a rhythm-and-blues tune about the resolution of conflict in a relationship between a man and a woman]

CLIENT: [Shaking her head as if in disbelief] Oh! That song is so true for me. [Slight pause] And that part that says something about "thank God above for showing us just how wrong we were," that's so true for me . . . because it got to the point where I just didn't know what to do. . . .

The counselor, using a reflective technique with a song title that deals with her experience, helps the client to further explore her state of joyfulness and to heighten her experience. It is important to note here that the counselor is using a medium that jives with the client's accepted cultural outlet for expressing emotions.

EXCERPT 2.

CLIENT: [At the point of tears] One of my boys got killed by the police. They said he was a robbery suspect. My oldest daughter got pregnant at fourteen and now has three children. My youngest boy, they've sent him off to the boys' school. I don't know . . . I tried my best . . . Just don't seem like I can do it by myself. My husband got hurt years ago on a construction job and ain't been able to work since. I've got to be everything to everybody.

COUNSELOR: [In distress] You have really paid some dues, haven't you? [Recurring line from the song "Why I Sing the Blues," recorded by B. B. King]

CLIENT: [Sobbing] The Lord knows I just can't give anymore.

2. *Reassurance or Sharing to Counselor Experience*
EXCERPT 3.

CLIENT: I feel so alone sometimes. You see, I'm up here all by myself, and there is just no one to turn to. I don't want to go back home. . . . I mean I'm a grown woman now, and I got to be able to make it on my own. But I'm having to go through so many changes at one time, and I need somebody to turn to, somebody just to talk to or something, you know?

COUNSELOR: You said that so pleadingly. I'm moved by your plight, but I feel a sort of helplessness, too, to help you deal with that in your life. I feel something else, too. I want you to know that it's all right in this moment of your despair to "Lean on Me" [Song title]. As Bill Withers puts it, "We all need somebody to lean on."

CLIENT: Thank you . . . I play that record over and over and over. . . .

3. *Acceptance through Structured Silence*
EXCERPT 4. The student was sent to the counselor because from the beginning of the day the student had been sporadically crying.

COUNSELOR: Can you tell me what's bothering you?

CLIENT: [Sullen, avoiding eye contact with counselor] No. I don't want to talk about it. I just wish people would stop bugging me about what's bothering me and just leave me alone.

COUNSELOR: I'm a lot like you in that respect. I'd rather not have people questioning me about what's wrong when I'm low. I'd rather have some time and some peace of mind to work it out for myself, and that seems to be what you're saying.

CLIENT: You're right, that's what I want—some peace of mind.

COUNSELOR: [Turns up the very low-toned, recorded soul music] Why don't you try to express that desire through a song, poem, story, picture, or something else like that? Think and feel, or just do what you want to do in your own head. If you want to write about it or draw about it, you can.

The counselor in the foregoing excerpt has done several things to the client's benefit. The client's natural way of dealing with his problems has been honored and facilitated with the use of his culture's expressive outlets. He is not forced into a talking-out process. Additionally, the counselor has provided some optional ways of using the silence. The attempt here is to communicate to the client that he has ultimate choice about his situation.

Confrontation, counselor leads, and other traditional relationship techniques can be handled similarly in individual counseling using black expressions.

Creative expression, in work and play, is now fully accepted as a sign of good mental health. To be expressive in a creative way takes us spontaneously to the depths of our personalities, and renders what we find there fully observable to a peering world. It is little wonder, then, that the artist is often "taken to be the model of the wholesome and sane" while "the rest of us have to" frequent "meditation and encounter group,"[13] in search of the elusive peace of mind. What this work stresses, taking cues from the ways of the common folk of black/African heritage, is that all human beings have the capacity for creative expression and therefore creative existence. Recall, however, that to be creative one must strive to subdue, if not abandon, the straight-line, analytical mode of thinking that smacks of clean, unscrambled information processing, predicting the forms of one's regurgitations. While creative existence often involves dabbling with neurotic characteristics such as regression, or affinity for primitive or infantile impulses, fantasies, etc., the wholesome person is able to re-emerge from regressive functioning with something new and beautiful for the continuous enrichment of life, while gaining release from conflict that may have initially given rise to the expressive impulse. In other words, the wholesome are unafraid of the human capacity for madness and are thereby able to inventively express themselves as a hedge against madness, though often giving the appearance of flirting with lunacy. Such acts represent those of the fully functioning, integrated person who has fused all aspects of the personality into a wonderful and marvelous whole.

For optimal functioning, then, retain in the psyche the mystery and wonder that the child knows. Use these, as do common black folk, in the shaping of the universe, and in the expressions of the soul. Let it color life in all of its manifestations and be guided by the intelligence of J. A. Rogers, who said, "Those who laugh and dance and sing are better off even in their vices than those who do not."[14]

REFERENCES

CHAPTER 1

1. Al Young, "Miz Chapman Tell Us the Score: A Memoir, 1947," *Parabola* 5, no. 3 (August 1980): 6.

CHAPTER 2

1. Alfred Pasteur and Ivory Toldson, "Joseph Walker Exhorts Black People to Deal with Themselves," *Journal of Non-White Concerns in Personnel and Guidance* 4, no. 3 (1976): 103-4.
2. Edwin Kiester, Jr., and David W. Cudhea, "Robert Ornstein: A Mind for Metaphor," *Human Behavior*, June 1976, pp. 16-24.
3. Robert Ornstein, *The Psychology of Consciousness* (New York: Viking Press, 1972).
4. Lilyan Kesteloot, *Black Writers in French*, trans. Ellen Conroy Kennedy (Philadelphia: Temple University Press, 1974), p. 106.
5. A. Ehrenzweig, *The Psychoanalysis of Artistic Vision and Hearing* (New York: Julian Press, 1953), p. 14.
6. Gilbert J. Rose, *The Power of Form* (New York: International Universities Press, Inc., 1980), pp. 125-27.
7. Ibid., p. 127.
8. Ibid., p. 128.
9. Ibid., p. 130.
10. Leopold Sedar Senghor, *The Foundations of "Africanite,"* trans. Mercer Cook, (Published in Paris: Présence Africaine, 1971) p. 44.
11. Maurice Nadeau, *Histoire In Surréalisme* (Paris: Editions du Seuliel, 1964), p. 19; quoted in Vere W. Knight, "Negritude and the Isms," *Black Images* 3, no. 1 (Spring 1974): 5.
12. Rose, op. cit., p. 138.
13. Geneva Smitherman, *Talkin and Testifyin* (Boston: Houghton Mifflin, 1977), p. 92.

14. Ortiz M. Walton, "A Comparative Analysis of the African and the Western Aesthetics," in Addison Gayle, Jr., *The Black Aesthetic* (Garden City: Doubleday, 1972), p. 157.
15. Ibid.
16. Francis Beby, *African Music*, trans. Josephine Bennett (New York: Lawrence Hill, 1969), p. 122.
17. Janheinz Jahn, *Muntu, The New African Culture*, trans. Margorie Grene (New York: Grove Press, 1961), p. 85.
18. Ibid., p. 67.
19. Ibid., from Fernando Ortiz, *La Africanía de la Música Folklorica de Cuba*, La Habana, 1950, p. 251.
20. John Lovell, Jr., *Black Song* (New York: Macmillan, 1972), p. 40.
21. Allan Paivio, *Imagery and Verbal Processes* (New York: Holt, Rinehart and Winston, 1971).
22. M. C. Wittrock, "The Generative Processes of Memory," in M. C. Wittrock et al., *The Human Brain* (Englewood Cliffs: Prentice-Hall, 1977), pp. 170–71.
23. Ibid., pp. 171–72.
24. Cedric X. (Clark), D. Phillip McGhee, Wade Nobles, & Luther X. (Weems), "Voodoo or I.Q.: An Introduction to African Psychology" *The Journal of Black Psychology*, no. 2, (1975), p. 17.
25. F. Daniels, Jr., P. W. Post, and B. E. Johnson, "Theories of the Role of Pigment in the Evolution of Human Races," in Vernon Riley, ed., *Pigmentation: Its Genesis and Biologic Control* (New York: Meredith Corporation, 1972), p. 14.
26. Ibid., p. 14.
27. Legrand H. Clegg II, "Why Blacks Run Faster," *Sepia*, July 1980, pp. 18–22.
28. Daniels et al., op. cit., p. 15.
29. "Measuring Melanin in the Brain," *Science News* 112 (July 2, 1977): 6–7.
30. Richard F. Brando and John W. Eaton, "Skin Color and Photolysis: An Evolutionary Hypothesis," *Science* 201 (August 1978): 625.
31. "Vitamin D and the Races of Man," *Time*, August 18, 1967, p. 52.
32. Brando and Eaton, loc. cit.
33. Ibid.
34. Ibid.
35. "Scorecard (Ochi Chorney)," *Sports Illustrated*, May 15, 1978, p. 16.
36. Clegg, op. cit., p. 21.
37. Ibid., pp. 21–22.
38. "Can Blackness Prolong Life?" *Ebony*, June 1977, pp. 124–27.
39. J. A. Rogers, "100 Amazing Facts About the Negro with Complete Proof" (Helga M. Rogers, 1957), pp. 15 and 42.
40. Cedric X. (Clark), op. cit., p. 16.

41. "Pigment Hormone May Color Behavior," *Science News* 101 (January 29, 1972): 78.

42. Ibid.

43. Ibid.

44. Abba Kastin and Andrew V. Schally, "MSH Release in Mammals," in Riley, op. cit., p. 221.

45. Mark Miles Fisher, *Negro Slave Songs in the United States* (New York: Citadel Press, 1953).

CHAPTER 3

1. From program notes of the "Haverly Mastodow Minstrels," May 31, 1880.

2. "Interview with Ben Calton," *New York Mirror*, July 3, 1897.

3. Calton, ibid.

4. Carolyn Wane, ed., *The Cultural Approach in History* (New York: 1940), pp. 228–42.

5. William Bascom, "Four Functions of Folklore," *Journal of American Folklore* 66 (1953): 283–90. See also Alan Dundes, ed., "The Function of Folklore," *The Study of Folklore* (Englewood Cliffs: Prentice-Hall, 1965), pp. 277–337.

6. Richard Moody, *America Takes the Stage: Romanticism in American Drama* (Bloomington, 1955); also, Richard M. Dorson, "The Yankee on Stage," *New England Quarterly* 13 (1940): 467–93.

7. Robert Rourke, *American Humor* (New York: Excelsior Publications, 1880), pp. 45–47.

8. Daniel Boorstin, *The American: The National Experience* (New York: Vintage, 1965), parts six and seven; Benjamin T. Spencer, *The Quest for Nationality: An American Literary Campaign* (Syracuse, 1957).

9. J. P. Sartre, *"Black Orpheus,"* trans. John MacCombie, *Massachusetts Review* 6 (1964–65): 13.

10. Robert Ornstein, *The Psychology of Consciousness* (New York: Viking Press, 1972).

11. Carl Rogers, *Client-Centered Therapy* (Boston: Houghton Mifflin, 1951).

12. Sidney M. Jourard, *The Healthy Personality* (New York: Macmillan, 1974), pp. 1–26.

13. Ibid., pp. 266–83.

14. Ibid., pp. 24–26.

15. Robert Armstrong, *The Affecting Presence* (Urbana: University of Illinois Press, 1971), pp. 3–5.

16. Leopold Sedar Senghor, "The Psychology of the African Negro," in *Negritude: Essays and Studies*, Albert H. Berrian and Richard A.

Long, eds., (Hampton: proceedings from conference held at Hampton Institute, summer 1967), p. 49.

17. Harold Cruse, *The Crisis of the Negro Intellectual* (New York: William Morrow, 1967), p. 109.

18. Albert Barnes, "Negro Art and America," in Alain Locke, ed., *The New Negro* (New York: Atheneum, 1977), p. 24.

19. Agnes de Mille, *The Book of Dance* (New York: Galkin Press, 1963), p. 65.

20. Jean and Marshall Stearns, *Jazz Dance* (New York: Macmillan, 1968), p. xiv.

CHAPTER 4

1. Larry Neal, "Some Reflection on the Black Aesthetic," in Addison Gayle, Jr., ed., *The Black Aesthetic* (New York: Anchor Books, 1972), pp. 23–30.

2. E. A. Hurley, "Guy Tirolier: In search of an attitude," *Black Images* 3, no. 1 (Spring 1974): 61.

3. Eugene Redmond, quoted in Ortiz M. Walton, *Music: Black, White and Blue* (New York: William Morrow, 1972), p. 92.

4. Harold S. Burr, cited in Edward Mann, *Orgone, Reich, and Eros*, (New York: Simon and Schuster, 1973), pp. 117–30.

5. J. A. Rogers, "Jazz at Home," in Addison Gayle, Jr., op. cit., p. 108.

6. Melville J. Herskovits, *The Myths of the Negro Past* (New York: Harper and Brothers, 1941), p. 147.

7. Wilfred Cartey, *Whispers from a Continent* (New York: Vintage Books, 1969), p. 282.

8. Aimé Cesaire, *Cahier d'un Rétour au Pays Natal* (Paris: Présence Africaine, 1956), pp. 44–45.

9. Pierre Erny, *Childhood and the Cosmos*, trans. Alexandre Mboukou (Rockville, Maryland: Media Intellectics Corporation, 1973), p. 15.

10. P. Chike Onwuachi, "African Identity and Ideology," *Festac '77* (Lagos, Nigeria: Africa Journal Ltd. and The International Festival Committee, 1977), p. 16.

11. Chinua Achebe, *Things Fall Apart* (Greenwich, Conn.: Fawcett Publications, 1959), pp. 164–65.

12. John Mbiti, *African Religions and Philosophy* (Garden City: Anchor Books, 1969), p. 20.

13. Erny, loc. cit.

14. Jean Paul Lebeuf, "Traditional African Architecture," in *Colloquium on Negro Art*, organized by the Society on African culture (Editions Présence Africaine, 1968), p. 314.

15. Janheinz Jahn, *Muntu: The New African Culture*, trans. Margorie Grene (New York: Grove Press, 1961), p. 83.
16. Cartey, op. cit., pp. 226–27.
17. Quoted in Michael Dash, "Towards A West Indian Literary Aesthetic—The Example of Aimé Cesaire," *Black Images* 3, no. 1 (Spring 1974): 26.
18. Cartey, op. cit., p. 224.
19. John Mbiti, "African Cosmology," *Festac '77*, p. 44.
20. Zora Neale Hurston, "High John de Conquer," in Langston Hughes and Arna Bontemps, eds., *Book of Negro Folklore* (New York: Dodd, Mead, 1958), p. 93.
21. Mata Deren, *Divine Horsemen: The Voodoo Gods of Haiti* (New York: Dell Publishing, 1970), p. 25.
22. Jahn, op. cit., p. 106.
23. Erny, op. cit., p. 64.
24. Ibid., p. 59.
25. L. S. Senghor, "Black Culture," *Festac '77*, p. 13.
26. Ben Enwonwu, "African View of Art," *Festac '77*, p. 53.
27. L. S. Senghor, "Language et poésie négro-africaine," *Second Biennial of Poetry* (Knakke, Belgium, 1954), pp. 7–8. See also "Les lois de la culture négro-africaine" in the special issue of *Présence Africaine* devoted to the First Congress of Black African Writers and Artists, nos. 8, 9, 10 (Paris: Présence Africaine, June–November 1956), p. 51.
28. Ibid.
29. L. S. Senghor, "Mediterranée," in *Hosties Noires* (Paris: Seuil, 1948), p. 97.
30. Francis Beby, *African Music*, trans. Josephine Bennett (New York: Lawrence Hill, 1969), p. 128.
31. Ibid.
32. Ibid., p. 17.
33. L. S. Senghor, "Trois poètes négro-americaine," in *Poésie et Language* (Brussels: Maison du Poète, 1954), p. 45.
34. Gwendolyn Bennett, "To a Dark Girl," in Arnold Adoff, ed., *The Poetry of Black America* (New York: Harper and Row, 1973), p. 81.
35. Larry Neal, "For Our Women," in Gloria M. Simmons and Helen D. Hutchinson, eds., *Black Culture* (New York: Holt, Rinehart, and Winston, 1972), p. 30.
36. David Diop, "To a Black Dancer," in Gerald Moore and Ulli Beir, eds., *Modern Poetry from Africa* (Baltimore: Penguin Books, 1963), p. 65.
37. Viriato da Cruz, "Black Mother," in Wole Soyinka, ed., *Poems of Black Africa* (New York: Hill and Wang, 1975), p. 82.
38. Roy Ayers, "Rhythm," from the album *You Send Me*, ASCAP Music Co., Polydor Incorporated, 1978.

39. Haki Madhabuti (Don L. Lee), "Black Women," from the album *Rise, Vision, Comin,* Nationhouse Positive Action Center–Institute of Positive Education, 1976.
40. Mari Evans, "Princeling," in Woodie King, ed., *Black Spirits* (New York: Vintage Books, 1972), p. 71.
41. Ntozake Shange, "Dark Phrases," *For Colored Girls Who Have Considered Suicide When the Rainbow is Enuf* (New York: Macmillan, 1977), pp. 3–5.
42. Deren, op. cit., p. 228.
43. Ibid., p. 191.
44. Ibid.
45. Cartey, op. cit., p. 106.
46. Melvin Van Peebles, *Aint Supposed to Die a Natural Death* (New York: Bantam Books, 1973), pp. 72–73.
47. Ibid., pp. 23–24.
48. Sam "Lightning" Hopkins, "New Short-Haired Women," recorded on the album *Lightning Hopkins: The Blues,* by Mainstream Records, Inc.
49. Joseph Walker, *The River Niger* (New York: Hill and Wang, 1973), pp. 36–38.
50. Ibid., p. 135.
51. Frantz Fanon, *Black Skin, White Mask* (New York: Grove Press, 1967), p. 116.
52. Leon Damas, *Pigments* (Paris: Guy Levi Mano, 1931), reprinted in *Présence Africaine,* 1962, p. 35.
53. Ibid., p. 36.
54. Randolph Hezekiah, "Bertène Juminer and the Colonial Problem," in *Black Images* 3, no. 1 (Spring 1974): 29–36.
55. Ibid., p. 30.
56. Ibid.
57. Ibid., p. 31.
58. Cesaire, op. cit., p. 90.
59. Ivory L. Toldson and Alfred B. Pasteur, "Developmental Stages of Black Self Discovery. Implications for Using Black Art Forms in Group Interaction," *Journal of Negro Education* 44, no. 2 (Spring 1975): 130–37.

CHAPTER 5

1. John Lovell, Jr., *Black Song* (New York: Macmillan, 1972), p. 45.
2. Robert Hayden, *Selected Poems* (New York: October House, 1966), p. 65.
3. Elouise Loftin, "Weeksville Women," in Arnold Adoff, ed., *The Poetry of Black America* (New York: Harper and Row, 1973), p. 515.

4. Askia Muhammad Toure, "Floodtide for the Black Tennant Farmers of the South," ibid., p. 338.
5. St. Clair Drake, "Social and Economic Status," in Talcott Parsons and Kenneth B. Clark, eds., *The Negro American* (Boston: Beacon Press, 1969), pp. 9–10.
6. Geneva Smitherman, *Talkin and Testifyin* (Boston: Houghton Mifflin, 1977), p. 73.
7. Bob Marley, "Survival," Bob Marley Music LTD, all rights administered by Almo Music Corp., ASCAP, 1979.
8. Lerone Bennett, *The Negro Mood* (New York: Ballantine Books, 1965), p. 89.
9. St. Clair Drake, loc. cit.
10. H. G. Osgood, "Sperichils," *Musical Courier* 93 (August 12, 1926): 14.
11. Eileen Southern, *The Music of Black Americans* (New York: W. W. Norton, 1971), p. 231.
12. Craig Mott, "Folk Song for Langston Hughes," in *Black World* 22, no. 11 (September 1973): 46.
13. Claude McKay, *Banjo,* Harvest edition (New York: Harcourt Brace Jovanovich, 1957), pp. 57–58.
14. Richard Jobson, *The Golden Trade or a Discovery of the River Gambra and the Golden Trade of the Aethiopians* (London, 1623; reprint, New York, 1968).
15. Paul Guillaume, *Primitive Negro Sculpture* (New York: Harcourt Brace and Company, 1926), p. 19.
16. Francis Beby, *African Music,* trans. Josephine Bennett (New York: Lawrence Hill, 1969), p. 132.
17. Robert Plant Armstrong, *The Affecting Presence* (Urbana: University of Illinois Press, 1971), p. 55.
18. Birago Diop, Senegalese poet, "Souffles" in Beby, op. cit., p. 126.
19. Beby, op. cit., p. 134.
20. J. H. Kwabena Nketia, "Music in African Culture," in *Festac '77* (Lagos, Nigeria: Africa Journal Limited and the International Festival Committee, 1977), p. 28.
21. Ibid.
22. Ibid.
23. Lovell, op. cit., p. 38.
24. Alex Haley, *Roots* (New York: Doubleday, 1976), p. 21.
25. Southern, op. cit., p. 153.
26. Ortiz Walton, *Music: Black, White, and Blue* (New York: William Morrow, 1972), p. 3.
27. Ibid.
28. Janheinz Jahn, *Muntu, the New African Culture,* trans. Margorie Grene (New York: Grove Press, 1961), p. 221.

29. Lovell, op. cit., p. 66.
30. Ibid., p. 65.
31. Melville Herskovits, "Patterns of Negro Music," Springfield, Illinois, Illinois State Academy of Sciences, 1941, p. 33.
32. Lucy McKim Garrison, quoted in William Frances Allen et al., *Slave Songs of the United States* (New York: Peter Smith, 1951), p. vi.
33. Walton, op. cit., p. 9.
34. James Baldwin, *If Beale Street Could Talk* (New York: Dial Press, 1975), p. 31.
35. G. E. Lambert, *Duke Ellington* (New York: A. S. Barnes and Company, 1959), p. 22.
36. Southern, op. cit., p. 147.
37. Quoted in Maude Cuney-Hare, *Negro Musicians and their Music* (Washington, D.C.: Associated Publishers Inc., 1936), p. 88.
38. Solomon Northup from *Twelve Years a Slave* cited in Southern, op. cit., p. 156.
39. Frederick Douglass, *Narrative of the Life of Frederick Douglass* (Boston: Harvard University Press, 1960).
40. Smitherman, op. cit., p. 56.
41. Cedric X. (Clark) et al., "Voodoo or IQ: An Introduction to African Psychology," *Journal of Black Psychology* 1, no. 2 (February 1975): 9–29.
42. Jahn, op. cit., p. 219.
43. James Baldwin, *Go Tell It on the Mountain* (New York: Dell Publishing, 1954), p. 15.
44. Ibid., p. 113.
45. Lovell, op. cit., p. 29.
46. Paul Carter Harrison, "Black Theatre and the African Continuum," *Black World* 21, no. 10 (August 1972): 43.
47. Pierre Erny, *Childhood and Cosmos*, trans. Alexandre Mboukou (Rockville, Maryland: Media Intellectics Corporation, 1973), p. 24.
48. Danniebelle Hall, "Like a Child," Lexicon Music, Inc., 1975.
49. Lovell, op. cit., p. 198.
50. Frederick Douglass, *The Life and Times of Frederick Douglass* (New York: Pathway, 1941), p. 178.
51. Walton, op. cit., p. 29.
52. J. D. Short, quoted in Leonard Goines, "The Blues as Black Therapy," *Black World* 23, no. 1 (November 1973): 31.
53. Ralph Ellison, *Shadow and Act* (New York: Random House, 1964), p. 78.
54. Gil Scott-Heron, "Bicentennial Blues," *It's Your World*, Arista Records, 1976.
55. B. B. King and Dave Clark, "Chains and Things," Pamco Music, Inc.

56. Walton, op. cit., pp. 49–50.
57. Ibid.
58. Ibid.
59. Richard Wright, *The Outsider* (New York: Harper and Row, 1953), p. 40.
60. Langston Hughes, "The Negro Artist and the Racial Mountain," in John A. Williams and Charles F. Harris, eds., *Amistad 1* (New York: Vintage Books, 1970), p. 304.
61. Lovell, op. cit., p. 50.
62. Martha Cobbs, "Africa in Latin America," *Black World* 21, no. 10 (August 1972): 6.
63. Ibid., p. 15.
64. James Weldon Johnson, *The Autobiography of an Ex-Coloured Man* (New York: Hill and Wang paperback, 1960), p. 87.
65. Harold Cruse, *The Crisis of the Negro Intellectual* (New York: William Morrow, 1967), p. 69.
66. J. Kennard, "Who Are Our National Poets?" in *Knickerbocker Magazine* 26 (1845): 9.
67. Publication on Scott Joplin, by the Toronto Ragtime Society, quoted in Walton, op. cit., p. 45.
68. Ibid.
69. Southern, op. cit., p. 337.
70. Jean and Marshall Stearns, *Jazz Dance* (New York: Macmillan, 1968), p. 123.
71. Don Heckman quoted in Eileen Southern, op. cit., p. 449.
72. "John Lennon Credited Black Music Creators With Beatles Success," *Jet*, December 25, 1980, pp. 58–59.
73. Ibid.
74. Cruse, op. cit., p. 105.
75. Ibid., p. 108.
76. Quoted in Frank Kofsky, *Black Nationalism and the Revolution in Music* (New York: Pathfinder Press, 1970), pp. 14–15.
77. "The Loneliest Monk," *Time*, June 20, 1964, p. 86.
78. Ibid.
79. Scott-Heron, op. cit.
80. Barry Ulanov, *Duke Ellington* (New York: Creative Press, 1946), p. 276.
81. Hughes, op. cit., pp. 304–5.

CHAPTER 6

1. Joel Kovel, *White Racism* (New York: Vintage Books, 1970), p. 83.

2. Terry Callier and Larry Wade, "Segue 3—The Origin of Funk," on the album *Sweet As Funk Can Be,* published by Butter Music/Chappel & Co. CRT Corporation, 1972.

3. Toni Morrison, *The Bluest Eyes* (New York: Pocket Books, 1972, 1974), p. 131.

4. Ibid., p. 68.

5. Henry Allen, "Funk Is in the Eye of the Beholder," *Washington Post,* January 11, 1973, p. 9.

6. Stephen Henderson, "Inside the Funk Shop," in *Black Books Bulletin* 1, no. 4 (Fall 1973): 10.

7. Ibid.

8. Ibid.

9. George Clinton, B. Collins, and B. Warrell, "P. Funk (Wants to Get Funked Up)" from the album *Mothership Connection,* published by Malbiz and Ricks Music, Inc., for Casablanca Records, Inc., 1975.

10. Bill Berry, "The Hottest of the Hot Groups," *Ebony,* July 1978, p. 40.

11. Quincy Jones, George Johnson, and Louis Johnson, "Get the Funk Out of My Face," published by Kidada Music Co./Goulgris Music, for A&M Records, Inc., 1976.

12. Olaudah Equiano, *The Interesting Narrative of the Life of Olaudah Equiano, or Gustavus Vassa, the African,* excerpts in Richard Barksdale and Kenneth Kinnamon, eds., *Black Writers of America* (New York: Macmillan, 1972).

13. Alice Walker, "View from Rosehill Cemetery," from the book *Revolutionary Petunias,* reviewed by Mary Helen Washington in *Black World* 22, no. 11 (September 1973): 52.

14. Pierre Erny, *Childhood and Cosmos,* trans. Alexandre Mboukou (Rockville, Maryland: Media Intellectics Corp., 1973), p. 43.

15. Frank Wilson and Pam Sawyer, "(It's the Way) Mother Nature Planned It," Jobete Music Company, Inc., 1972; quoted in Ivory L. Toldson and Alfred B. Pasteur, "Therapeutic Dimensions of the Black Aesthetic," *Journal of Non-White Concerns in Personnel and Guidance* 4, no. 4 (April 1976): 106.

16. John Lovell, Jr., *Black Song* (New York: Macmillan, 1972), p. 26.

17. MacKinley Helm, *Angel Mo and her Son Roland Hayes* (Boston: Little, Brown, 1942), p. 11.

18. Melville Herskovits, *The Myths of the Negro Past* (New York: Harper & Brothers, 1941), p. 241.

19. Mata Deren, *Divine Horsemen: The Voodoo Gods of Haiti* (New York: Dell Publishing, 1970), pp. 161–62.

20. Alfred B. Pasteur and Ivory L. Toldson, "A Black Playwright Exhorts Counselors to Deal with Themselves," *Journal of Non-White Concerns in Personnel and Guidance* 4, no. 4 (April 1976): 103.

21. Ibid., p. 104.

22. Toni Morrison, *Sula* (New York: Random House, 1973), p. 69.
23. Sam Greenlee, *The Spook Who Sat by the Door* (New York: Bantam Books, 1969), p. 124.
24. Chinua Achebe, *No Longer at Ease* (New York: Fawcett, 1960), p. 27.
25. Ralph Ellison, *Invisible Man* (New York: Signet Books, 1952), p. 232.
26. Ibid.
27. John Mbiti, *African Religions and Philosophy* (New York: Anchor Books, 1970), p. 24.
28. Ibid., p. 23.
29. Ibid., p. 21.
30. Alex Haley, *The Autobiography of Malcolm X* (New York: Grove Press, 1965), p. 145.
31. George Davis, "Coming Home," in John A. Williams and Charles F. Harris, eds., *Amistad 1* (New York: Vintage Books, 1970), pp. 97–98.
32. Lonnie Elder, *Ceremonies in Dark Old Men* (New York: Farrar, Straus and Giroux, 1965), p. 91.
33. William Melvin Kelley, *Dancers on the Shore* (Chatham, N.J.: Chatham Bookseller, 1964), p. 56.
34. Haley, op. cit., p. 366.
35. Ntozake Shange, *For Colored Girls Who Have Considered Suicide When the Rainbow is Enuf* (New York: Macmillan, 1975), pp. 32–33.
36. Ibid., p. 35.
37. Achebe, op. cit., p. 23.
38. Alan Ebert, "Millie Jackson," *Essence*, March 1979, p. 127.
39. Alex Haley, *Roots* (New York: Doubleday, 1977), p. 368.
40. Achebe, op. cit., p. 20.
41. David Ritz, "Being with Ray," *Essence*, August 1979, p. 141.
42. Frantz Fanon, *Black Skin, White Mask*, trans. Charles Lam Marksmann (New York: Grove Press, 1967), pp. 19–20.
43. Kelley, op. cit., p. 160.
44. C. Gilbert and K. Gamble, "Be for Real," recorded by Harold Melvin and the Bluenotes, published by BMI, CBS, Inc., 1972.
45. Eileen Southern, *The Music of Black America* (New York: W. W. Norton, 1971), p. 110.
46. Haley, op. cit., p. 43.
47. Kenny Gamble and Leon Huff, "Groovy People," as recorded by Lou Rawls on the album, *All Things in Time,* published by Mighty Three Music, 1976, CBS, Inc.
48. Shange, op. cit., p. 50.
49. "Ebony Minds, Black Voices," in Toni Cade, ed., *The Black Woman* (New York: Signet, New American Library, 1970), p. 181.

50. Hubert Laws, "False Faces," Hulaws Music (BMI), 1977, CBS, Inc., 1978.
51. K. Gamble, L. Huff, and C. Gamble, "False Faces," Mighty Three Music, 1979, CBS, Inc.
52. Sidney Jourard, *The Healthy Personality* (New York: Macmillan, 1974), p. 124.
53. R. D. Laing, *The Divided Self* (London: Tavistock, 1960), pp. 67–81.
54. Chinua Achebe, *Things Fall Apart* (New York: Fawcett Premier, 1969), pp. 7–8.
55. Nicholás Guillén, "Madrigal," trans. Langston Hughes, in Martha Cobbs, "Africa in Latin America," *Black World* 21, no. 10 (August 1972): 17.
56. Deren, op. cit., p. 252.
57. Ibid.
58. Jourard, op. cit., p. 140.
59. Larry Neal, "Kunta," in Stephen Henderson, *Understanding the New Black Poetry* (New York: William Morrow, 1973), pp. 294–95.
60. Ibid.
61. Edward Mann, *Orgone, Reich, and Eros* (New York: Simon and Schuster, 1973), p. 38.
62. Wilhelm Reich, quoted in Edward Mann, op. cit., p. 38.
63. Fanon, op. cit., p. 126.
64. Janheinz Jahn, *Muntu,* trans. by Margorie Grene (New York: Grove Press, Inc., 1961), p. 104.
65. Ibid., p. 109.
66. Miles Mark Fisher, *Negro Slave Songs in the United States* (New York: Citadel Press, 1969), p. 6.
67. Phyl Garland, *The Sound of Soul* (Chicago: Henry Regney Co., 1969), p. 27.
68. Fanon, op. cit., p. 185.
69. Ngugi Wa Thiong'o, *The River Between* (London: Heinemann, 1965), p. 23.
70. Tom Driver cited in Calvin C. Hernton, "Blood of the Lamb and The Fiery Baptism (Post Script)" in John William and Charles Harris, eds., *Amistad 1* (New York: Vintage Books, 1970), p. 203.

CHAPTER 7

1. Langston Hughes, "When Sue Wears Red," in Stephen Henderson, *Understanding Black Poetry* (New York: William Morrow, 1973), p. 126.
2. Harvey Scales, et al, "It Ain't What You Do (It's How You Do It)," Groovesville Music (BMI) and Conquistador Music, 1977.

3. George Frazier, "A Sense of Style," *Esquire*, November 1967, pp. 76–78.
4. Ibid.
5. Amy Gross, "What Style Is—And Isn't—All About," *Mademoiselle*, September 1974, p. 123.
6. Robert Plant Armstrong, *The Affecting Presence* (Urbana: University of Illinois Press, 1971), p. 15.
7. Maya Angelou, "Country Lover," in *And Still I Rise* (New York: Random House, 1978), p. 4.
8. Melvin Van Peebles, *Aint Supposed to Die a Natural Death* (New York: Bantam Books, 1973), p. 121.
9. Zora Neale Hurston, *Mules and Men* (Philadelphia: Lippincott, 1935), p. 125.
10. Sam Greenlee, *The Spook Who Sat by the Door* (New York: Bantam Books, 1970), pp. 37–38.
11. Helene Johnson, "Bottled: New York," in Arnold Adoff, ed., *The Poetry of Black America* (New York: Harper and Row, 1973), p. 104.
12. Miles Mark Fisher, *Negro Slave Songs in the United States* (New York: Citadal Press, 1953), p. 33.
13. Maurice Delafosse, *The Negroes of Africa*, trans. F. Fligleman (Washington, D.C., 1931), p. 155.
14. Hubert Howe Bancraff, *History of Central America* (New York [no date]), II, 389, n. 5.
15. Henry Bradshaw Fearon, *Sketches of America* (London, 1819), p. 9.
16. J. S. Buckingham, *The Eastern and Western States of America* (London, 1842), I, 11.
17. Frances Trollope, *Domestic Manners of the Americans* (New York, 1901), I, 237 f.
18. Chinua Achebe, *No Longer at Ease* (New York: Fawcett, 1960), p. 9.
19. Ibid., p. 22.
20. Ibid., p. 24.
21. Ibid., p. 35.
22. Mabel Dove-Danquah, "Anticipation," in Langston Hughes, ed., *An African Treasury* (New York: Crown Publishers, Inc., 1960), p. 164.
23. Thomas Edward Bowdich, *Mission from Cape Coast Castle to Ashantee* (London, 1819) quoted in *The Music of Black America* by Eileen Southern (New York: W. W. Norton and Co., Inc., 1971), p. 6.
24. Chinua Achebe, *Things Fall Apart* (New York: Fawcett World, 1969), p. 68.
25. Camille Yarbrough, *Cornrows* (New York: Coward, McCann and Geoghegan, Inc., 1979), [no pagination].

26. Ibid.
27. Louie Robinson, "The Blackening of White America," *Ebony*, May 1980, p. 162.
28. L. Frobenius, *Histories*, p. 16; quoted in Lilyan Kesteloot, *Black Writers in French*, trans. Ellen Conroy Kennedy (Philadelphia: Temple University Press, 1974), p. 94.
29. Hurston, op. cit., p. 33.
30. Ibid., p. 92.
31. Geneva Smitherman, *Talkin and Testifyin* (Boston: Houghton Mifflin, 1977), p. 16.
32. Toni Morrison, *Sula* (New York: Random House, 1973), pp. 42–43.
33. From Michele Burgen, "What I Love About My Beautiful Black Man," *Ebony*, February 1978, p. 144.
34. Smitherman, op. cit., p. 94.
35. Johnetta B. Cole, "Soul and Style," *Festac '77* (Lagos, Nigeria: Africa Journal Limited, 1977), p. 117.
36. Benjamin G. Cooke, "NonVerbal Communications among Afro-Americans," in Thomas Kochman, *Rappin' and Stylin' Out* (Chicago: University of Chicago Press, 1972), p. 55.
37. Ibid., p. 33.
38. Frobenius, op. cit., p. 15.
39. Paul Lawrence Dunbar, "Angelina," in *Little Brown Baby* (New York: Dodd and Mead, 1944), p. 89.
40. Maya Deren, *Divine Horsemen: The Voodoo Gods of Haiti* (New York: Dell Publishing, 1970), p. 225.
41. Alan Lomax, "Louisiana Town," *Mister Jelly Roll* (Berkeley: University of California Press, 1973), p. 12.
42. Jack Buerkle and Danny Barker, *Bourbon Street Black* (New York: Oxford University Press, 1973), p. 50.
43. Raymond J. Martinez, *Portraits of New Orleans Jazz* (New Orleans: Hope Publications, 1971), p. 50.
44. Ibid., p. 51.
45. Smitherman, op. cit., p. 90.
46. Deren, op. cit., p. 161.
47. "Black Dominance," *Time*, May 9, 1977, p. 57.
48. "Muhammad Ali," *Time*, February 11, 1974, p. 46.
49. Dunbar, "When Malindy Sings," op. cit., p. 7.
50. Johnson, op. cit., p. 103.
51. John Broven, *Rhythm and Blues in New Orleans* (New Orleans: Pelican, 1978), p. 95.
52. James Weldon Johnson, *Black Manhattan* (New York: Arno Press & The New York Times, 1968), p. 122.
53. Eileen Southern, *The Music of Black Americans* (New York: W. W. Norton, 1971), p. 113.

54. Robert Hayden, "Homage to the Empress of the Blues," in *Black Writers of America*, Richard Barksdale and Kenneth Kinnamon, eds. (New York: Macmillan, 1972), p. 678.
55. Zack Gilbert, "For Ella: Our First Lady of Song," *Black World*, September 1973, p. 69.
56. Carole A. Parks, "Self-Determination and the Black Aesthetic: An Interview with Max Roach," *Black World*, November 1973, p. 65.
57. David Ritz, "Being with Ray," *Essence*, August 1979, p. 95.
58. Alan Ebert, "Millie Jackson," *Essence*, March 1979, p. 68.
59. Christian Wormley, "The Stroke of Midnight: Teddy Pendergrass," *Essence*, February 1979, p. 22.
60. Brenda J. Saunders, "Style Is . . . the Fruit of Labor," copyright © 1976, p. 1.
61. Millar, *The Drifters: The Rise and Fall of the Black Vocal Group*, quoted in Brenda Saunders, op. cit., p. 11.
62. Roland Penrose, *Picasso: His Life and Work* (New York: Harper and Brothers, 1959), pp. 131–33.
63. Saunders, op. cit., pp. 21–22.
64. Gil Scott-Heron, "Who'll Pay Reparations on My Soul?" from the album *Small Talk at 125th and Lenox*, copyright © 1970, music published by Bob Thiele Music, Ltd.-ASCAP.

CHAPTER 8

1. Leopold Sedar Senghor, *The Foundation of Africanite*, trans. Mercer Cook, (Paris: Présence Africaine, 1971), p. 74.
2. Ibid., p. 76.
3. Geneva Smitherman, *Talkin and Testifyin* (Boston: Houghton Mifflin, 1977), pp. 16–17.
4. Nat Hentoff and Albert J. McCarthy, eds., *Jazz* (New York: Rinehart, 1959), pp. 23–24.
5. Albert C. Barnes, "Negro Art and America," in Alain Locke, ed., *The New Negro* (New York: Atheneum, 1977), pp. 19–20.
6. Sarah Webster Fabio, cited in J. A. Emanuel, "Blackness Can: A Quest for Aesthetic," in Addison Gayle, Jr., ed., *The Black Aesthetic* (New York: Anchor Books, 1972), pp. 182–211.
7. John S. Mbiti, *African Religions and Philosophy* (New York: Anchor Books), 1970.
8. Smitherman, op. cit., p. 76.
9. Stanley Edgar Hyman, "The Child Ballad in America," *Journal of American Folklore*, 70 (1957), p. 139.
10. Porter Grainger ("Taint Nobody's Business If I Do"), GP33 Bessie Smith.

11. James Weldon Johnson, *God's Trombones* (New York: Penguin Books, 1927), p. 17.
12. Dennis Wepman, *The Life* (Los Angeles, California: Holloway House, 1974), pp. 152–57.
13. Mari Evans, *I Am a Black Woman* (New York: William Morrow, 1970), p. 93.
14. W. E. B. DuBois, *The Souls of Black Folk* (New York: Fawcett Publications, 1953), p. 16.
15. Gwendolyn Brooks, *The World of Gwendolyn Brooks* (New York: Harper and Row, 1959), p. 73.
16. John Bernard, *Retrospections of America, 1779–1811* (New York: Harper, 1965), p. 126.
17. Amiri Baraka (LeRoi Jones), *Blues People* (New York: William Morrow, 1963), p. 63.
18. Ibid., p. 28.
19. Ibid.
20. Frederick Douglass, *The Life and Times of Frederick Douglass* (Revised ed., 1892, Collier reprint ed., New York, 1962), pp. 146–47.
21. Ibid., p. 228.
22. Melvin Van Peebles, *Aint Supposed to Die a Natural Death* (New York: Bantam Books, 1973), pp. 6–10.
23. J. Whitehead, G. McFadden, and V. Carstarphens, "Wake Up Everybody," recorded by Harold Melvin and the Bluenotes on the album *Wake Up Everybody,* copyrighted CBS, Inc., 1975.
24. Zora Neale Hurston, *Their Eyes Were Watching God* (New York: Lippincott Co., 1973), pp. 200–1.
25. Moms Mabley, Chess Records, LP1477.
26. Lee Rainwater, *Behind Ghetto Walls.*
27. Ntozake Shange, *For Colored Girls Who Have Considered Suicide When the Rainbow is Enuf* (New York: Macmillan, 1975), pp. 13–14.
28. Phillip A. Noss, "Description in Gbaya Literary Art," in Richard M. Dorson, ed., *African Folklore* (Garden City: Doubleday, 1972), p. 75.
29. Ibid., p. 76.
30. Live Dialogue from the album, *The London Howling Wolf Sessions,* as recorded by Chester Burnett (Howling Wolf), Chess Producing Corp., Chicago, Illinois.

CHAPTER 9

1. Lee Warren, *The Dance of Africa* (Englewood Cliffs: Prentice-Hall, Inc., 1972), pp. 23–24.

2. Ruth Abernathy and Maryann Waltz, "Art and Science of Human Movement," *Quest II: The Art and Science of Human Movement*, NAPECW and NAPWAM (April 1964), pp. 1–7.

3. Hans Kraus, *Hypokinetic Disease* (Springfield, Ill.: Thomas, 1961).

4. Amita Harrow, *A Taxonomy of the Psychomotor Domain* (New York: David McKay Co. Inc., 1972).

5. Lauretta Bender, *Child Psychiatric Techniques* (Springfield, Ill.: Thomas, 1952).

6. Alfons Daver, quoted in John Lovell, *Black Song* (New York: Macmillan, 1972), p. 44.

7. Lovell, ibid.

8. Daver, loc. cit.

9. Pierre Erny, *Childhood and Cosmos: The Social Psychology of The Black African Child* (Rockville, Maryland: Media Intellectics Corp., 1968), p. 91.

10. R. W. Sperry, "Neurology and the Mid-brain Problem," *American Scientist*, 1952, pp. 40, 291–312.

11. Ibid., p. 301.

12. Alex Haley, *The Autobiography of Malcolm X* (New York: Grove Press, 1965), p. 5.

13. Maya Angelou, *I Know Why the Caged Bird Sings* (New York: Random House, 1970), pp. 32–33.

14. H. E. Krebiel, *Afro-American Folksongs* (New York: G. Schirmer, 1914), p. 33.

15. Amiri Baraka (LeRoi Jones), *Blues People* (New York: William Morrow Co., 1963), pp. 43–44.

16. Zora Neale Hurston, *Mules and Men* (Bloomington: Indiana Univ. Press, 1935), p. 99.

17. Melville J. Herskovits, *The Myths of the Negro Past* (New York: Harper and Brothers, 1941), p. 76.

18. Melville J. Herskovits and Francis S. Herskovits, *Rebel Destiny* (New York: Whihersey House, 1938), p. 76.

19. Lydia Parrish, *Slave Songs of the Georgia Sea Islands* (New York: Creative Age Press, 1949), p. 111.

20. "Creole Slave Songs," *Century Magazine*, 31 (April, 1886): 808.

21. Thomas W. Talley, *Negro Folk Rhymes* (New York: Macmillan, 1922), pp. 296–97.

22. Marshall and Jean Stearns, *Jazz Dance* (New York: Macmillan, 1968), pp. 28–29.

23. Ibid., p. 29.

24. Chinua Achebe, *Things Fall Apart* (New York: Fawcett World, 1969), p. 47.

25. Ibid., p. 50.

26. Clayton Riley, "Did O.J. Dance?" *Ms. Magazine* Vol. 2. (March, 1974): 96.

27. Pete Axthelm, *The City Game* (New York: Harper Magazine Press, 1970), p. 103.
28. Ibid., p. 107.

APPENDIX

1. Jasper Love, quoted in William Ferris, *Blues from the Delta* (New York: Anchor Press/Doubleday, 1979), p. 26.
2. Alfred Duckett, "An Interview with Thomas A. Dorsey," *Black World*, July, 1974, pp. 13–14.
3. Alain Locke, quoted in Ronald Wellburn, "The Black Aesthetic Imperative," in Addison Gayle, Jr. (ed.), *The Black Aesthetic* (Garden City: Doubleday, 1972), p. 129.
4. Jermaine Jackson, Hazel Jackson, Maureen Baily, "Feelin' Free," recorded on the album *Let's Get Serious,* by Jermaine Jackson, copyright © 1980 by Motown Record Corporation.
5. Edward Robinson, live speech recorded on album *Black Rhapsody* by Building Foundation through Corrective History, manufactured by Human Development Associates, Philadelphia, 1970.
6. G. K. Osei, *The African Philosophy of Life* (London: The African Publication Society, 1970), p. 19.
7. John Lovell, *Black Song* (New York: Macmillan, 1972), pp. 163–69.
8. Ibid., pp. 637–56.
9. Langston Hughes and Arna Bontemps, *Book of Negro Folklore* (New York: Dodd, Mead & Co., 1958), pp. 401–3.
10. Lovell, op. cit., pp. 320–22.
11. Melvin Van Peebles, "Just Don't Make No Sense," *Aint Supposed to Die a Natural Death* (New York: Bantam Books, 1973), pp. 6–10.
12. A. Campbell, *How Do "Negroes" Feel About Whites and How Do Whites Feel About "Negroes"* (Ann Arbor: University of Michigan, Institute for Social Research, 1971), pp. 31, 35, and 40.
13. Meredith Skura, "Creativity: Transgressing the Limits of Consciousness," *Daedalus* (Spring, 1980), pp. 127–46.
14. J. A. Rogers, "Jazz at Home," in Addison Gayle, Jr. (ed.), *The Black Aesthetic* (Garden City: Doubleday, 1972), pp. 104–11.

INDEX

V